Great Characters
From Cricket's Golden Age

The Beautiful and Damned

Great Characters From Cricket's Golden Age

The Beautiful and Damned

Jeremy Malies

Robson Books

First published in Great Britain in 2000 by Robson Books, 10 Blenheim Court, Brewery Road, London N7 9NT

A member of the Chrysalis Group plc

British Library Cataloguing in Publication Data
A catalogue record for this title is available from the British Library

ISBN 1 86105 344 4

Typeset by FiSH Books, London
Printed in Great Britain by Creative Print & Design, Ebbw Vale

To Mazin Al-Khafaji

Contents

Acknowledgements

Count Basie once said that you should thank the biggest people first.

My gratitude is due to Michael Parkinson, Michael Foot, David Frith, Frank Keating, the late Jim Swanton, the late Dr Gerald Brodribb, Dr Eric Midwinter, the Earl of Verulam and David Sampson.

Russell Levinson not only commented on every chapter with intelligence and wit but undertook original research when I was unwell. Oliver Andrew spent hours polishing the manuscript and made good some spectacular deficiencies.

The writings of Alistair Cooke, Fred Inglis, Joan Didion and Clive James are a deep and pervasive influence on everything I say. Ern Toovey sent much useful information from Australia. Roger Packham and Mike Spurrier were tireless correspondents and made invaluable suggestions at various levels. David Smith was helpful, patient and consistently charming. Michael Wolton of the MCC library gave me access to the club's archives, passed on valuable contacts and assisted with photographs.

Many Test cricketers contributed recollections. They include: Cyril Washbrook, Bill Brown, Hubert Doggart, Bob Wyatt, Dave Gilbert and Tommy Mitchell. Geoff Amey's biography of Julius Caesar proved indispensable while Peter Mayne's history of Godalming CC was also of great value.

The archivists and librarians at many of the first-class counties were supportive, most notably Norman Epps and Rob Boddie at Hove who gave unflagging encouragement. I received similar help from Tony Stedall at Taunton, Roger Hancock at The Oval, Barrie Watkins, Keith Hayhurst and the Rev. Malcolm Lorimer at Old Trafford, Peter Wynne-Thomas at Trent Bridge, Neil Jenkinson and Dr David Allen at

Southampton and Chris Taylor at Canterbury.

The relatives of my subjects provided invaluable scrapbooks and letters. Sir Dudley Forwood and the late Lady Forwood (née Mary Gwendoline Foster) were supportive with the chapter on Basil Foster. Gordon Hutton opened up new angles as I researched his stepfather, Raymond Robertson-Glasgow. Walter Coningham went to immense trouble in assisting me with the chapter on Arthur Coningham while Frank and Alex Coningham gave me useful referrals. Sue Weigall, David Weigall, Rosemary Henderson (née Weigall), Margaret Maxwell (née Weigall), Allan Willett and Malcolm Rose assisted with the chapter on Gerry Weigall and guided me through the dense foliage of the Weigall family tree.

David Wilson contributed much to the chapter on his uncle, Evelyn Rockley Wilson, while Venetia Lascelles (née Hesketh-Prichard) assisted with the chapter on Hesketh-Prichard. Stuart Trott uncovered valuable information about his great-uncle, Albert Trott. Brian Bassano gave assistance with the chapter on Aubrey Faulkner. Maurice Amon's first-hand experiences brought the Faulkner Cricket School to life.

I am indebted to David Foot's writings on Cecil Parkin. Jack Houldsworth of Church and Oswaldtwistle CC and Dave Appleton of the *Rochdale Observer* also contributed information about Parkin's career. Richard Greep came forward with his own research to assist with the chapter on Sir Arthur Conan Doyle and led me away from pitfalls like Sherlock Holmes taking an apprentice through Grimpen Mire. Articles on Conan Doyle by Geoffrey Staver and Clifford Jiggens also proved helpful. Roger Mann hunted down and made available several rare photographs. Greg Growden's biography of Chuck Fleetwood-Smith was of great assistance; it is superbly researched and intelligently sympathetic. Dorothy King of the Stawell Historical Society furnished information about Fleetwood-Smith's extraordinary family. Iain Wilton and David Kynaston shed light on Gerry Weigall. Brian O'Gorman contributed to the chapter on Basil Foster.

This list must include: Clive Fairbairn of the Melbourne CC, Bob Brenner of the New South Wales Cricket Association, Thrasy Petropoulos of *The Times*, Ian Wright of the Squash Rackets Association, Kathi Spinks, Helen Benacek, Richard Neville and Jennifer Broomhead of the State Library of New South Wales, Dr

Robert Grogan of the South Melbourne CC, Brian Graham of the Melbourne Transit Police, Reggie Salberg of the Salisbury Playhouse, Norman Fenner of the Richmond Theatre, David Hughes of Royton CC, Barry Taylor and Paul Booth of Bradshaw CC, Dr Neil Young and Roderick Suddaby of the Imperial War Museum, Russell Holmesby of the St Kilda Saints, Richard Owen of Portsmouth FC, Patrick Maclure of Winchester College, Penelope Hatfield of Eton College, 'Rusty' MacLean of Rugby School and George Chesterton of Malvern College.

The chapter on Raymond Robertson-Glasgow was enlivened by Pauline McCausland, Major Michael Edwards, Ronald Hope-Jones, Hugh Bulley, Anne Maier, John Willett, Michael Birley, Kenneth Kelman, John Garton Ash, Dr John Covell, Charles Selwyn and Captain Dacre Stroud, all of St Edmund's School.

Other correspondents included Paul Owen of Hindhead Golf Club, Charles Knott and Dick Moore of Hampshire CCC, Nicholas Sharp of Sussex CCC, Sasha Orivé of the Victoria State Library, Judith Murphy and Dellece Armstrong of the State Library of Queensland, Father Frederick Turner of Stonyhurst College, Simon Edginton of St Piran's School, John Janaway of Guildford Library, Viv Thompson of Peacehaven Library and Howard Milton of the Cricket Society.

Academics from universities and museums all over the world were generous with their time. The following gave help and encouragement: Dr Vincent Orange of the University of Canterbury (Christchurch), Lee Pecht of Rice University, Jonathan Smith of Trinity College, Cambridge, Jane Morris of Emmanuel College, Cambridge, Anthea Bundock of the Australian National University at Canberra, Andy Currant of the Natural History Museum and Yvonne Sarrington of the Royal Geographical Society.

Tim Clark, Dominic O'Byrne, John MacKenzie, Steve Poland, Stephen White, Richard de Costobadie, Tony Wakeley, Andy Cheesman, David Aiken, Rob Marshall, Dominic O'Byrne, Tony Harris, Roger Kay, Ron Coello, John Jenkins and Joe Webber all gave me support at different levels.

Introduction

There are heroes here, villains and a few buffoons. There are also three suicides, four alcoholics, the father of British socialism, the creator of Sherlock Holmes and one of the most outstanding individuals in the Allied forces during the First World War. Some of the essays are sentimental and they are often idolatrous. The abiding theme is that cricket is a prism through which a man's character is revealed. I believe that people show their innermost traits through what Denis Howell used to call 'the chivalrous unities of communal sport'.

Many of the players are surrounded by rich webs of lore and some of the anecdotes blur into the apocryphal. I have included these where they enlarge on the basic, prosaic facts, believing that it is more important that history should be romantic than precisely true.

I have tried to present these men in the round, describing both the splendour and the misery, the truculence and the generosity. Above all I have sought to breathe life into them through the regenerative power of anecdote. If the pieces have a theme it is the platitude that character is destiny.

Many of my subjects fell from grace and most of them descended far enough into the mire to have a look at the scenery on the way out. They would agree with Dostoyevsky's assertion that perennially happy people have no history. Some of them were lionized in their time, others have always been obscure. In a few of the better-known cases I have reluctantly chipped away a little at the monolith. I have written about these men because we will not see their kind again.

Paul Gallico told us that statistics never made anyone bleed or weep. I have little liking for them and am apt to make a hash of them. Those who want a detailed account of playing careers can turn to

Wisden. Many of the recollections are first-hand and several of my interviewees died during the three years it took to write this book. They remembered their heroes, relatives or team-mates with proud delight and with that intense concreteness of the very old recalling their childhood or youth.

I have avoided a few obvious candidates, most notably George Gunn. Sir Neville Cardus insisted that it required genius to be a biographer of genius but went on to leave little unsaid about one of his heroes. George was a fine pianist and had perfect pitch. While making a century in Australia to the accompaniment of a provincial orchestra playing Gilbert and Sullivan overtures, he strode over to the bandstand and complained that the cornet was flat. In a tense county game he suddenly gave his wicket away when nearing a century on a whim to 'go and sit with missus'.

The only criterion for inclusion was that the subjects should have played first-class cricket. Sadly this ruled out a few choice entries in J.J. Carr's *Dictionary of Extraordinary Cricketers*. The omissions include Hesketh K. Nayler (c. 1851), 'a New York millionaire impotent who derived sexual gratification by maintaining an establishment of ample women to play cricket before him with balloons and without clothes', and Karl Auty (c. 1911), 'a Chicago insomniac, who had a joiner make him an under-bed shelf on runners to accommodate his set of *Wisden*'.

There are several schoolmasters here though none of them displayed the distressingly sadistic tendencies of Dr George Heath. A headmaster of Eton and an enthusiastic follower of college cricket, he flogged the whole team (including the scorer) when it returned from Lord's after a heavy defeat by Westminster. Few things have tickled me more than an anecdote about Manley Kemp, captain of Oxford for the Varsity game of 1884. At a crucial stage of the match he was needed to bat but was found lying on his back in the dressing-room reading Molière.

Candidates who might well have sustained a chapter include Bert Ironmonger. As an orthodox slow left-armer he obtained prodigious spin from the stub of an index finger, having lost the top joint during a boyhood milling accident on his parents' farm. He came close to death from loss of blood until his 11-year-old sister had the sense to put his hand in a bag of flour. The glorious legend is that a decade later he lost another portion of the finger when demonstrating what had happened in the original accident. Ironmonger produced several fine Test performances for Australia on home soil but never toured England, blaming his omission on the fact that he made a slurping noise when drinking soup.

Other major omissions include The Hon. F.S. Jackson. As Governor of Bengal his administration saw much student unrest and he was lucky to survive an assassination attempt when a young girl fired five pistol shots at him. Jackson remained sanguine: 'Quickest duck I ever made. Lucky she didn't have enough for a full over.' Few cricketers have rivalled the eccentricity of Billy Buttress of Cambridgeshire. A brilliant leg-spinner, Buttress was also a gifted ventriloquist who would scare old ladies on trains by making them believe that there was a kitten under their seat. He was also a hopeless if gallant alcoholic who had to be locked in a cellar overnight at Lord's so that he would be sober for the morning. Billy was once called upon to bat but was found in a tree, blind drunk and singing ballads.

An unusual chapter could have been formed around Montague John Druitt, a first-rate club cricketer for the Gentlemen of Dorset and Blackheath. Druitt was a prominent barrister at the Inner Temple whose body was dragged out of the Thames at Chiswick on the night of 31 December 1888. Testimony from his brother and veiled hints in the memoirs of Sir Melville Macnaughton, a leading figure in the CID at the time, suggest that Druitt may have been Jack the Ripper.

I am not blind to the rich seam of eccentricity and flamboyance that has run through cricket in the last 20 years. Ian Botham, Phil Tufnell, Derek Randall and Greg Matthews are undoubtedly among the most colourful characters ever to have played the game. I leave them to another cricket historian at another time.

A preponderance of wrist-spinners here serves to underline Michael Parkinson's dictum that you must have a slate loose to even consider bowling in this manner. If this book has any merit it stems from the 300 or more correspondents and interviewees who generously contributed their time. The errors and misjudgements are my own.

Jeremy Malies
Peacehaven, East Sussex
1999–2000

Why do we like these stories so? Why do we tell them over and over? Our favourite people and our favourite stories become so not by any inherent virtue, but because they illustrate something deep in the grain, something unadmitted. Shoeless Joe Jackson, Warren Gamaliel Harding, the *Titanic: how the mighty are fallen.* Charles Lindbergh, Scott and Zelda Fitzgerald, Marilyn Monroe: *the beautiful and damned.*

Joan Didion, *Slouching Towards Bethlehem*, 1968

If you hang on to the past, you die a little every day.

Martin Scorsese, *Cape Fear*, 1991

And just ask yourself this: could you ever really love somebody who didn't cry, even just a bit, in *Field of Dreams*?

Roger Alton, *Guardian*, November 1994

1

Arthur Coningham

b: 14.7.1863, Emerald Hill, South Melbourne, Victoria, Australia.
d: 13.6.1939, Gladesville, Sydney, New South Wales, Australia.

Much Madness is divinest Sense –
To a discerning Eye –
Much Sense – the starkest Madness –
'Tis the Majority
In this, as All, prevail –
Assent – and you are sane –
Demur – you're straightway dangerous –
And handled with a Chain –

Emily Dickinson, 'Much Madness Is Divinest Sense', 1862

At 5.20 pm on 2 April 1901, an Australian Test cricketer leapt across a packed Sydney courtroom and grappled with a senior Roman Catholic priest before being overpowered and carried out of the building sobbing. Earlier, in more lucid if garrulous moments, he had quoted extensively from the redemptorist teachings of Saint Alfonso Liguori, but only after having been relieved of a pistol which he had brandished at his opponent's legal representatives. His outburst was the finale of a court case in which he had accused his wife of adultery with the Archbishop of Sydney's assistant, Father Denis Francis O'Haran, and alleged that they had frenzied sexual marathons on the floor of the Cardinal's Hall adjacent to St Mary's Cathedral. A rich cast of venal hypocrites, liars, perjurers and sophists had made the case scandalous, gaudy, exciting and incredible. The backdrop had been a trail of prevarication, deceit and falsehood.

Arthur's upbringing was unremarkable and gave little indication that he would become one of the most notorious Australians of his generation. He spent his childhood at Emerald Hill in south Melbourne and was the son of William Coningham, a brass finisher, and Jane Ann, née Wilson. Both his parents were Londoners. There is a family legend that Jane Wilson was an antecedent of the British Prime Minister. Arthur's grandfather, George Coningham, was the eighteenth and last beadle of Limehouse and is believed to have inspired Dickens's creation in *Oliver Twist*.

As a schoolboy Arthur excelled at rowing, athletics and cricket. He began playing senior cricket with Melbourne CC before moving to Brisbane at the age of 16. He travelled widely around Australia and worked sporadically as a chemist though there is doubt as to whether he received any formal training. In the mid- and late 1880s he played a few games for Queensland which at the time was the 'Cinderella' state of Australian cricket with little reputation or pedigree. In November and December 1887 Arthur captained XVIII of Queensland in two matches against Shrewsbury and Lillywhite's England touring team. In the first game he was dismissed for 18 and 0 but took three wickets in the visitors' only innings. In the second match he bowled superbly to take 8 for 135 over two innings but again failed with the bat, scoring 2 and 5.

In 1893 he formed part of the Australian touring party to England, though he was only selected after the short-lived and unpopular Australian Cricket Council insisted that a token representative of Queensland should be included. The tourists boarded the liner *Orizaba* on the afternoon of 11 March. Earlier in the day Arthur had been married at St Matthew's Anglican Church in Sydney. His bride was 23-year-old Alice Stanford Dowling. Born at Stanford Turnchapel in Devon and the daughter of a warrant officer in the British army, Alice had been educated at a convent and emigrated at the age of 16 to live in Brisbane with her married sister. As a Catholic she obtained a dispensation to marry Arthur, a Protestant, with an agreement that their children would be brought up in the Church of Rome.

Jack Blackham's tourists remain the most dispirited and quarrelsome group of Australian cricketers ever to visit England. A brilliant wicketkeeper, Blackham was too highly strung for leadership and lost several stone in weight through worry during the tour. To the embarrassment of journalists and cricket followers, he regularly slated his players during pre-season practice. The tour was generally unhappy, its manager Victor Cohen being incompetent and insensitive. Cohen had been instrumental in setting up the Australian Cricket Council and many regarded him as a spy. Cohen in turn levelled accusations of assault and drunkenness at the players and Thomas Horan noted: 'The manager had practically no control over the men from shortly after the commencement of the tour.'

In the first game Arthur found immaculate line and length against Lord Sheffield's XI to take 5 for 74 from 38.2 overs. *Wisden* noted: 'Lord Sheffield's side might well have represented England.' Arthur's victims included three of the best batsmen in the world, W.G. Grace, Arthur Shrewsbury and A.E. Stoddart. He was also successful with the bat, scoring 26 not out and 29. At a vast fireworks party in Sheffield Park, Arthur borrowed one of his Lordship's top hats and careered through the grounds lighting roman candles. He had already caught the eye of a correspondent from the *Cricket Field* who pronounced: 'Coningham, besides being a good bowler, is a useful bat. He indulges largely in pulls to leg, scoring the majority of his runs in this manner.' Relations between the players were particularly fraught at this time and the *Australasian* reported that when their train pulled into Brighton Station, a guard found blood all over the tourists' compartment.

A few days later Arthur made 43 against Gloucestershire. In the following game he curbed his aggressive instincts and made a patient 46 against MCC. He was used sparingly for the rest of the tour and was not selected for the Test matches. In its analysis of the season, *Cricket* concluded: 'A mistake was made in giving Coningham so little to do' while *Wisden* reinforced the point: 'Coningham had some cause of complaint against the managers of the team...We cannot help thinking that he might have been given a better trial.' The *Australasian* was more explicit: 'Coningham is pronounced to have an excitable temperament which perhaps stood in the way of his advancement.' The story may be apocryphal but there is a persistent legend that Arthur annoyed Blackham and spoilt his chances of regular selection when on a particularly cold day, he assembled a bonfire of twigs and leaves in the outfield, asked a spectator for a match and began ostentatiously warming his hands. He was certainly the most entertaining member of the team and drew large audiences when performing trick shots on the billiards table.

There were frequent press reports of rowdiness among the players and with discipline under Blackham and Victor Cohen at a low ebb, Arthur absented himself for long periods. However, he was at pains to advertise the fact that he was a teetotaller and in a retrospective interview with the *Australasian* he commented: 'When a man is full of champagne overnight, he is not fit for much the next day. One morning coming down the stairs we found one of them asleep with his clothes on, his head on the stair mat. Walter Giffen and myself never drank a drop on the entire tour.' In the same interview he was curiously sycophantic towards Victor Cohen: 'From what I saw of Mr Cohen he was a very hard-working fellow, but it was impossible for any man to manage the lot he had to deal with. They treated him disgracefully as well as quarrelling with each other.'

The *Cricket Field* described how, during a trip on the Thames, Arthur saw a boy about to drown in a strong current. He dived in and pulled the child to safety. Arthur came good in the second week of August when he took 6 for 41 from 18.2 overs in the second innings of a match against Liverpool and District. He also scored 23 not out and *Wisden* reported: 'Towards the finish Coningham gave the Liverpool bowlers serious trouble and carried out his bat for a very useful score.' In late August he took 5 for 21 from 9.3 overs against XVI of Blackpool, finishing the match with a hat-trick. His bowling put him second in the tour averages for all matches behind Charlie Turner, with 38 wickets at an average of 16.4 and an excellent economy rate of 2.35.

The tourists left England for a whistle-stop tour of America and Canada. This proved a commercial disaster and the players had a two-week vacation in Vancouver. Arthur got back to Australia in mid-December and set up home with Alice at Cordelia Street, South Brisbane. He played in few domestic games in the 1893–94 season, a highlight being his return of 5 for 46 for Queensland against South Australia in February 1894. In the following December he made his Test debut at Melbourne against an England side captained by A.E.

Stoddart. Amid mounting tension after a 20-minute delay for rain, Arthur delivered the first ball of the match to Archie MacLaren. It reared viciously from a length and MacLaren could do no more than spoon an easy catch to Harry Trott at point. Arthur had become the first man to take a wicket with his opening ball in Test cricket. Despite bowling economically, he did little else during a game in which Stoddart made 173.

The Australian selectors had discovered a more manageable if similarly eccentric bowler in Ernest Jones, and Arthur was one of four players dropped for the next match. He never played Test cricket again. However, he did appear against the English tourists as part of a combined New South Wales and Queensland side. While the crowd were marvelling at the fluent batting of Stoddart, who had raced to a score of 40, umpire Charles Bannerman no-balled Arthur for overstepping. *Cricket* described Arthur's reaction: 'That mercurial individual lost his head, and in his annoyance deliberately hurled the next ball at Stoddart. The English captain wisely and firmly called upon Coningham to apologize to the umpire and himself, and this the bowler ultimately did, but not for some time. The incident put Stoddart clean "off", Coningham's next ball bowled him off his pads.'

Early in the following season Arthur refused to go on a two-week trip to Sydney and Newcastle since the Queensland authorities would not reimburse him for loss of earnings (estimated at £10). At the last moment some Sydney cricket enthusiasts stumped up the money, and Arthur struck form against New South Wales with an innings of 151. Looking at the prospects for the forthcoming tour to England, *Cricket* reflected: 'Coningham maintained his reputation as Queensland's best man and one of the finest all-round players in Australia. Whether he will have a look-in for a place in the team for England is another question. He has an unfortunate temper which renders him anything but amenable to authority...'

He was not selected and in 1896 he moved to Sydney. He settled in Bondi and played for South Sydney CC. In September he failed as a tobacconist at Waverley, a suburb to the south-west of Bondi Bay. As the New South Wales side prepared to depart for Adelaide in the following December, a note from the Registrar of Insolvency advised that the permission of his creditors would be necessary before he was allowed to leave the state. Arthur was now playing club cricket for Glebe in Sydney and his aggregate of 655 runs in 1896–97 was the highest of the New South Wales grade season.

Two years later Arthur had another stint as a tobacconist but again he was unsuccessful. When his premises burnt down, the insurers suspected arson and would pay only half of the £250 policy. By November 1899, Arthur and Alice had lively aspirations but few prospects. They also had three children to feed: Arthur Jnr, Mabel and Vincent. Alice was able to earn a modest living as a hairdresser and Arthur tried his hand briefly as a barber. There is a story that he once left a bare razor embedded in the cheek of a customer when he realised that he had five minutes to make the four-mile journey to the Sydney Cricket Ground.

In November 1899 he set up as a bookmaker at Randwick Racecourse, his satchel displaying the proud legend 'Coningham the Cricketer' in white letters. In an interview with the Queensland *Sportsman* he explained his 'system' and described how he had 'made £5 on the day that every other bookie lost £20 or more'. However, it is likely that Alice's earnings formed most of his daily float. There is an old racing adage: 'You can't win with scared money.' Arthur took a trimming in the Villiers Stakes. He surrendered his licence and a few weeks later he was acquiring debts as a billiards hustler.

In desperation, Arthur and Alice hatched an extraordinary plan. Their target was Father Denis Francis O'Haran, a debonair and noto-riously vain Roman Catholic cleric who at the time was Administrator of St Mary's Cathedral, Sydney, and secretary to Cardinal Herbert Moran, the Archbishop of Sydney. O'Haran was much discussed by gossip columnists and known for what were probably innocent flirta-tions with female members of his congregation. He was also given to presenting his lady admirers with signed photographs of himself.

The Coninghams agreed that Arthur would allege, and Alice admit, that she had committed adultery with O'Haran during 1898 and 1899. Arthur filed for damages from O'Haran of £5,000, dissolution of the marriage and custody of his children Arthur Jnr and Mabel. He made no claim for the youngest child, Vincent, alleging that he was O'Haran's son. On 3 December 1900, the case came before Mr Justice Simpson at a packed Sydney courthouse in Macquarie Street.

Journalists circled like buzzards and there were shrieks of excitement from the public gallery when O'Haran's counsel, Jack Want QC, immediately branded the Coninghams as 'sordid blackmailers'.

Shortly after the trial began Arthur's lawyer, Hyman 'Smudgy' Moss, retired exasperated when his client admitted to having shared a bedroom with Alice after he had issued the writ for divorce. Arthur proceeded to handle his own case with competence and at times brilliance. He was frequently reprimanded for ignorance of legal etiquette and annoyed court officials with his theatrical gestures. However, he demonstrated a darting wit and his alertness in cross-examination was extraordinary. The *Australasian* described it as 'a wonderfully able effort on the part of a man unversed in law. He was as unfair as a big QC and as resourceful as a cat.' Arthur immediately suggested that Alice had met O'Haran at a concert in March 1897 and that their friendship had blossomed over two years. In May 1900, with his suspicions aroused, Arthur reported having found a signed photograph of O'Haran in Alice's vanity box. He then described how Alice had broken down and confessed to adultery on 3 July.

Arthur called his wife to the witness box. Inside a more than luscious arrangement of flesh, Alice obviously had a level head and the *Australasian* summarized her with: 'Tall, dark, rather handsome... absolutely self-contained and one of the coolest witnesses ever seen in a court.' Alice described how she next visited O'Haran in September and his words of welcome were: 'Now you are here, we may as well indulge.' Alice's graphic testimony detailed how the pair had indulged every Friday, a convenient day for O'Haran since he went to confession on Saturday. The pair had sex in various parts of the cathedral buildings, on the floor of the Cardinal's Hall and in the summerhouse but never within the cathedral itself. Alice then described how she fell pregnant in May 1899 and told O'Haran that he was the father.

By now the atmosphere in the courthouse was electric and 6,000 people queued down Macquarie Street for news of proceedings. Gilbert Smith wrote in the *Melbourne Age*: 'The strain on Mrs Coningham was great for on the first day when she went out to her cab, a mob of howling men and women hooted and used vile epithets.' Arthur was harassed by enraged Catholics as he left the court and had to be rescued by the police. Blanket newspaper coverage included full banner headlines and the case was only pushed off the front pages by the Federation of Australia ceremonies.

Proceedings soon became a bedlam of charge and counter-charge. It emerged that at the age of 17, Alice had believed that she was engaged to James Garrick Jnr, son of Sir James Garrick, the Agent-General for Queensland. She had an illegitimate child by him which died in infancy. Over the coming days Alice's dubious past was resurrected and she was branded as a former garrison harlot, known and admired for a feisty temperament, quick wits and a figure which, in the words of Raymond Chandler, might make a bishop kick in a stained glass window.

O'Haran denied all the charges and called on fellow clerics, who gave him alibis on the dates of the alleged assignations. Arthur even subpoenaed O'Haran's superior, Cardinal Moran, and plunged deep into theological debate. Was it possible, he asked, for a Catholic to commit a sin, confess it in return for absolution, and then maintain that the sin had never occurred? There was much criticism of the judge for allowing this kind of lengthy discussion, which was primarily responsible for extending the trial to 10 days. Arthur's breadth of reading proved extraordinary and he closed one speech with a quotation from Horace to the effect that even if punishment is slow, it seldom fails to overtake the guilty. However, in the worldly Cardinal Moran, who smacks of Trollope's Archdeacon Grantly, he was trying to pluck a bird of his own feather and the theological debates led nowhere.

Arthur would often stride across to the jury as though giving them the benefit of his innermost thoughts. At one point he brandished a pistol at his opponent's attorneys. O'Haran trotted out a series of plausible engagements on the dates of the alleged assignations with Alice, prompting Arthur to dismiss the alibis as 'cheap as bananas, fourteen in a box for sixpence'. He later complained that he was 'fighting the whole weight of the Catholic Church, backed up by an army of pimps and myrmidons anxious to do its bidding'. When O'Haran vehemently denied being the father of Alice's youngest child, Vincent, Arthur claimed that he had been made impotent by a blow from a cricket ball in January 1899 and called a doctor to confirm this. The trial was badly handled by Justice Simpson who added his own touch of opera with apposite but self-indulgent quotations from *Othello*. On 14 December, after a 12-hour deliberation, the jury declared itself hung and a retrial was ordered. The Melbourne *Argus* concluded: 'Father O'Haran is a martyr indeed, or else the cassock robes the rake.'

The second trial began on 11 March. Arthur was lucky to be in court at all; a few days earlier a piece of biscuit had lodged in his throat and he had been unconscious for four hours. The case had been marinating in sectarian strife between Protestants and Catholics, which at the time was inflamed over the issue of denominational schools. After allowing Arthur a few airy spontaneities, Judge Owen gavelled him down and declared that this time there would be no general theological discussions.

The defence then took a surprising turn. Between the trials Arthur had received valuable letters of advice from one 'Zero', a senior Catholic priest who had a deep hatred of his superiors at St Mary's Cathedral. O'Haran had employed two formidable assistants in Paddy Crick, a corrupt solicitor and politician with wide experience as a jury-rigger and evidence-faker, and Daniel Green, a scoundrel of the first chop and an accomplished manipulator of witnesses. The pair were reinforced by a small army of grafters and roughnecks. In his capacity as Postmaster General of New South Wales, Crick intercepted the correspondence between 'Zero' and Arthur. O'Haran identified 'Zero' and had him beaten up before carting him off to an up-country seminary and sending him to the United States. Daniel Green immediately employed somebody who could imitate 'Zero's handwriting and he and O'Haran continued the correspondence, in which they gave Arthur a stream of misinformation.

Initially they advised Arthur to dismiss the few members of the jury who might have been inclined in his favour. Gaining confidence, Green decided to impersonate 'Zero'. He disguised himself in clerical habit and dark glasses and met Arthur in a secluded area behind the courthouse. He was disturbed to see that Arthur was carrying a revolver but kept his nerve and gave Arthur two dates on which he said it would be easy to prove that O'Haran and Alice had enjoyed frenzied encounters. The dates turned out to be days on which O'Haran had cast-iron alibis. Witnesses and even journalists declared that O'Haran had been following public engagements many miles outside Sydney. In an even more audacious initiative, Green managed to drug Alice and steal some particularly damning letters which she had received from Arthur during the trial. Arthur and Alice's continuing correspondence was of course intercepted through Crick's contacts with the postal authorities.

O'Haran's defence immediately exposed Arthur and Alice as being in collusion and dismissed them as 'unscrupulous and blundering blackmailers', though Crick was obliged to apologize for the manner in which the evidence had been obtained. Arthur's final speech lasted five hours and he dwelt on the fact that he was in no position to employ a retinue of thieves and informers in the manner of the defence. His denunciation of O'Haran was virulent: 'Curse you! A priest of God, I call you a priest of the Devil. May you rot body and soul, you lecherous thing!' The judge concluded that the onus of proof lay with Arthur, who was obliged to convince the court that the alleged adultery had taken place. The jury retired on the afternoon of 2 April and returned two hours later with a unanimous verdict in favour of Father O'Haran. However, the foreman, taking his cue from Judge Owen, expressed distaste for the manner in which O'Haran's camp had obtained its evidence and concluded that there were no grounds to prove conspiracy.

A few months later, Arthur, Alice and the children moved to Westport in South Island, New Zealand. Arthur had a Panglossian optimism and was convinced that he could make his fortune as a bookmaker. After struggling for some time he found work as a travelling bookseller with the Brookes Company, selling their *Dr Muscott's Medical Guide*. He canvassed the Westport area under the assumed name of William Arthur. He was employed on a commission basis and received nine shillings for an initial order and a further nine shillings when the customer paid the cover price of £3 3s for the guide. As a businessman Arthur set himself very low standards which he failed to live up to. In the summer of 1903 he began to fabricate sales. His employers became suspicious and could find no trace of many of the people appearing on Arthur's order forms. On 2 November Arthur appeared at the Westport Magistrate's Court charged with fraudulent conversion of £6 3s.

Again he appeared for himself but the florid rhetoric had gone for good. Sadly, his evidence appears to have been shot through with falsity and he made a futile attempt to blame the fraudulent sales returns on an assistant, a Mr Moore, who could not be traced. After a few vacuous aphorisms which he took for wit, Arthur lapsed into bleating submission and resorted to a cringing jeremiad in which he appealed for leniency under the First Offenders' Probation Act and 'on account of his wife and three little ones'. The trial excited media interest and, harking back to the divorce case, the Sydney *Bulletin* quipped: 'It isn't any fault of Coningham's that he has a wife to base such an appeal on.'

Later in the same month, Arthur began concurrent six-month sentences at Hokitika Jail for larceny and false pretences. Known as 'Misery Hill', the prison was on the coast of South Island on the Tasman Sea. It had been built in 1896 to house hardened criminals and there were two hangings during his internment. The bulk of the prisoners were Maori insurgents from the wars of the 1860s. In the following year Arthur and Alice took rooms in an apartment block in Ghuznee Street in central Wellington. Alice opened a hairdressing salon on nearby Cuba Street but Arthur remained shiftless, working occasionally as a pharmaceutical sales agent and a land manager. The marriage was rocky and he spent much time away from home, lodging in Elizabeth Street. Alice would later recall that Arthur 'had not really maintained her for ten years'.

Relations worsened early in 1912 when Alice began to suspect that Arthur was having an affair with their neighbour, Mrs Mary Riman, who had expressed interest in studying to become a hairdresser. After consulting a solicitor, Alice was put in touch with a private detective, Samuel Free, who followed Arthur and Mrs Riman to a bathing-shed at Lyall Bay on the south-eastern side of the city. On the following evening Alice (complete with revolver) accompanied Free in a cab and found Arthur cuddling Mrs Riman. She immediately presented Arthur with a divorce petition.

The case was heard at the Wellington Supreme Court on 13 and 14 May 1912. For the third time in his life, Arthur conducted his own case but he was a shadow of his former self. He proved nervous in the witness box but made the best of a thin defence. At times he was incoherent: 'You say you called me a scoundrel, and yet you wanted me to help you with your bookkeeping. I wanted to get you in the evening.' The Wellington *Evening Post* carried extensive reports but it omits what it refers to as 'evidence of a somewhat disgusting character'. Alice obviously possessed much physical strength and she admitted knocking Arthur off his feet during an argument at their apartment, breaking a water bottle over his head during another fracas at the surgery of a local doctor and pointing a revolver at him.

Arthur consistently maintained that his relationship with Mrs Riman was platonic. 'There is not one atom of truth in the accusations made against me in connection with Mrs Riman or any other woman at any time during my married life. She [Alice] knows it only too well. I have almost shed tears of blood over that woman. I am fighting for one object. That is to protect an innocent woman [Mrs Riman] and her husband. For myself I do not care that [with a snap of his fingers].'

Justice Chapman was consistently annoyed by Arthur's ramblings, particularly his lengthy discourses on the ethics of private detectives. Alice's counsel also made much of the fact that if Arthur's prime concern was to defend the honour of Mrs Riman, it was odd that Mrs Riman did not see fit to attend the hearings or even submit written testimony. To this Arthur responded that his alleged lover felt her life was in danger. The directions to the jury were explicit; Justice Chapman stressed that since he was conducting his own case Arthur had been allowed a great deal of freedom and that his imputations against Alice's own sexual conduct should be ignored. The jury took less than an hour to find Arthur guilty of adultery, and Alice was granted a *decree nisi* together with custody of the children. Arthur obviously retained some vestiges of his old wit, telling reporters: 'In Sydney my wife said she did and a jury said she didn't. In Wellington, I said I didn't and a jury said I did.'

Arthur was 5 ft 7 in tall. He had striking pale blue eyes, a fair complexion, and sandy-coloured hair set off by an extravagant moustache. He was of a slight build but had much wiry strength. He appears to have been impetuous and ill-disciplined but vastly charismatic. A witness called by Father O'Haran during the first divorce case pronounced: 'Coningham has the audacity and cunning of an ape and the modesty of a phallic symbol.'

As early as September 1893 Arthur was making the mistake of

believing his own publicity and the *Cricket Field* included the following: 'It seems that Coningham is a great athlete as well as a cricketer. In conversation with one of our staff he said that he had done the 100 yards in $10\frac{1}{4}$ seconds; the mile in 4:24, and the 440 yards over 3 ft 6 in hurdles in 58 seconds (which would be a world record). His best long jump is 21 ft 10 in, while he has surmounted 5 ft 10 in at the high jump.'

Arthur's long jump claim is reasonable: some five months earlier, fellow cricketer C.B. Fry had equalled the world record with 23 ft $6^1/_2$ in. But the claim for his hurdling is indeed preposterous, the world record held by Godfrey Shaw being $59^3/_5$ seconds. Similarly, the contemporary record for the mile was 4 minutes $12^3/_4$ and Arthur's alleged time would have made him among the top half-dozen amateur middle-distance runners in the world.

There is no doubt that he was a fine athlete and for several years in the mid-1880s he performed superbly at athletics meetings in Brisbane sponsored by the St Patrick's Oil Company. In 1885 he won various flat and hurdles events and the *Australian* reported: 'The manner in which Coningham carried off the honours in the events in which he took part was the theme of general admiration.' Sadly the paper does not give any times. In 1886 he won a round robin event over distances of 100, 150 and 220 yards. Similarly, few would argue as to his agility. Early in the 1893 tour, having had W.G. Grace caught in the slips by Hughie Trumble, Arthur performed a cartwheel and travelled the length of the wicket on his hands.

As a left-arm fast-medium bowler, Arthur obtained exceptional bounce for his height. Among more recent players he might be classified as somewhere between Derek Underwood and John Lever. A preview of the 1893 tour in the *Morning Post* started with: 'He varies his pace and pitch well, and occasionally sends down a fast ball which is generally destructive. That he is a thorough tryer is admitted.' Arthur's delivery may have been a slinging action from his right hip since many contemporary magazines make surprising comparisons with Bobby Peel.

He batted left-handed and though highly unorthodox, he gave an impression of solidity at the wicket. He appears to have been a poor judge of a run. He was an erratic fielder and could become overexcited under pressure. On the 1893 tour he took a superb balloon of a catch to dismiss John Dixon off his own bowling in a game against Nottinghamshire. A few minutes later Arthur Shrewsbury hit another towering drive. Arthur charged after it though several other players were better placed and only came to his senses when he had knocked one of his colleagues over.

The 1915 Auckland census lists Arthur as running a grocery business. A year later the entry records that he was living in the resort island of Kawau near Auckland with no regular occupation. In 1916 or '17 Arthur settled in Rotorua to the south-east of Auckland. Here he worked as a corporal in the Salvation Army at the Convalescent Soldiers' Institute. He assisted with the rehabilitation of troops, including Arawa Maoris from the New Zealand Expeditionary Force who had been wounded on the Gallipoli Peninsula. Arthur escorted soldiers to the many spas in the area and on fishing and sightseeing trips on Lake Rotorua. It is also possible that he was able to put his modest pharmaceutical knowledge to some use. Light relief came in 1918 when an Australian film company made Rotorua the location for an early version of *Mutiny on the Bounty* and Arthur's patients acted as extras. Entertainment at the institute was provided by a group of young women known as the Cheer-O-Girls with whom Arthur must have been in his element.

His lifestyle at this time was mundane but he could at least take pleasure in the progress of his elder son, Arthur Jnr, who would become Air Marshal Sir Arthur Coningham. Arthur Jnr showed conspicuous gallantry during the First World War in Samoa and Egypt. He was discharged in 1916 after contracting typhoid fever but later in the year he travelled to England and joined the Royal Flying Corps. He assumed command of 92 Squadron and claimed 12 victories despite being shot down twice. Arthur Jnr remained in the services and became Montgomery's opposite number in the RAF during the Desert War. He also played a key role in supporting the Normandy invasion.

Arthur's movements in the 1920s are difficult to follow. In the early 1930s he returned to Australia and lived for some years at Nowra to the south of Sydney. In November 1937, at the age of 74, he was admitted to the Tarban Creek Mental Hospital at Gladesville in Sydney. It is interesting that his notes list two children, Arthur and Mabel. There is no mention of Vincent, an indication that he may well have been fathered by Denis O'Haran.

Arthur died in the asylum in 1939, the official cause of death being senility. He is buried at the vast and windswept Rookwood Cemetery on the western outskirts of Sydney where his tombstone bears the simple inscription: 'Arthur Coningham, International Cricketer.' Whatever the true nature of the man, his myth retains undying magnetism.

2

Don Davies

b: 13.3.1892, Pendleton, Lancashire.
d: 6.2.1958, Riem Airport, Munich, Germany.

Death cancels everything but truth, and strips a man of everything save genius and virtue.

Michel de Montaigne, *Essais,* 1588

Don's father, Richard Davies, was a cotton warehouseman and later a mill foreman. His mother was Elizabeth, née Ashton. Don spent his adolescence in Bolton and attended Holy Trinity School before winning a scholarship to Bolton Grammar School. He showed promise as a footballer, having been inspired by seeing Steve Bloomer at Burnden Park, and soon became a stalwart for Northern Nomads on the right wing.

Don also excelled at cricket and by the age of 15 he was playing for Halliwell in the Bolton and District Senior League. He left school in 1909 and became a pupil-teacher at St Paul's, Bolton. His timetable allowed him to pursue a wide course of studies and he attended open lectures at Manchester University where he came under the spell of the Belgian poet Emile Verhaeren. For many years, cricket, football and academia were to be conflicting loyalties. In 1912 he toured Eastern Europe with a team sponsored by the Lancashire Amateur Football League and fell in love with the architecture of Prague. He was proving an agile and quick-thinking winger with a powerful shot that belied his slight build. At this time he was also receiving cricket coaching from the ex-Test player Albert Ward, who encouraged him to take a trial with Lancashire.

By now he was a candidate for the England amateur football team and he was selected to play against Wales at Home Park, Plymouth, in February 1914. England won 9–1. Don produced some telling crosses and combined superbly with his inside forwards, Ivan Sharpe and John Raymond. The teams were grossly ill-matched and the game could easily have degenerated into a rout had the Welsh goalkeeper James Bowen not played superbly. Later in 1914 the England amateur side played a series of club matches in Austria and Eastern Europe. Don was injured at Temesvár in Hungary and was sidelined for much of the tour.

In August he agreed to give up teaching and play for Stoke City if the club would cover his tuition fees at Manchester University. By October he had completed one week of a BA degree in history when he joined the Royal Flying Corps as a flight lieutenant. Within days of his mobilisation he was shot down on the Western Front behind German lines at Douai. He was imprisoned at Karlsruhe in southern Germany where fellow inmates included the future Lieutenant General Sir Brian Horrocks. Don marvelled at the ingenuity of escape attempts by Russian officers and assisted in the tunnelling activity, which was performed with nothing more than small trowels. He was later interned at an improvised camp within Freiburg University where he was put in solitary confinement when he annoyed a guard by singing Puccini arias in the bathroom.

He spent the latter years of the war at Holzminden, a high-security camp near Göttingen, where escapees were often shot on sight or sent to Fort Zorndorf, the First World War equivalent of Colditz. Don was always reluctant to speak about his imprisonment, but the Imperial War Museum holds a graphic account of conditions in the camp by Lieutenant John Whale. Prisoners were responsible for preparing their own food but were lucky if they could improvise more than weak vegetable soup and a coffee substitute made from ground acorns. Occasionally there were feasts on Oxo stew, bully beef and chocolate when Red Cross parcels got through from Holland.

Discipline was strict and the camp's sadistic commandant, Franz Niemeyer, would impose a spell of solitary confinement for the slightest misdemeanour. The prisoners did everything they could to maintain hygiene, but were handicapped by the fact that the communal bathroom was a tiny outhouse used as a kennel by night for the camp's bloodhounds. However, morale seems to have been good; the inmates played cricket in the summer and created skating rinks in the winter. Don had made an impression on the Manchester University history faculty in his few days of study and throughout his captivity Professor Thomas Tout sent him books. He read Gibbon's *Decline and Fall* from cover to cover and also attended classes in French and German.

Don contracted a viral condition in the last months of his imprisonment and arrived home in 1919 weighing less than six stone. He was given a few months to live but rallied promptly and began courting Gertrude Quinn, a schoolteacher from Blackley. They married two years later and rented a cottage near the Bradshaw cricket ground. The couple had two daughters, Deirdre and Sheila. Don began playing cricket for Bradshaw in the following year and scored 427 at an average of 35, a highlight being an undefeated 114 against Westhoughton. He captained the club in 1922 and 1923, showing tactical astuteness and empathy with players of differing ages and backgrounds.

In the mid-1920s he was playing football for the Old Boltonians with such success that the *Bolton Evening News* ran a story entitled 'Is Donnie Davies right in refusing talent-money?' At the time his main employment was at the Manchester engineering firm Mather and Platt, where he taught English literature, mathematics and sport to apprentices on day release. Don took pride in the fact that many of his pupils progressed to the Manchester College of Technology. In the autumn of 1922 he began evening study for a combined arts degree at Manchester University, having repeatedly refused an ex-serviceman's grant which would have allowed him to attend Oxford or Cambridge.

He made his first-class cricket debut in 1924 when he played for Lancashire against Kent at Old Trafford. He showed a good deal of authority while making 46, and was particularly severe on 'Tich' Freeman. Neville Cardus described his innings in the *Manchester Guardian* as '...the most interesting feature of the day...Time after time he hit manfully to the off. He emerges from this glimpse Old Trafford had of him decidedly well.' It proved to be his highest first-class innings and it needs to be said that Don's form at county level was modest. In the following year he played a handful of matches deputising for Ernest Tyldesley. His innings of 44 was the highest score in the Lancashire vs Worcestershire fixture at Stourbridge.

A fortnight later he partnered Charlie Hallows on a difficult wicket at Hove and made 38 from an attack including Maurice Tate in his pomp. It was a stout effort, but Don was characteristically self-effacing when recollecting the innings: 'I was morally bowled on average three times every over. When anyone asks me if I ever batted against Maurice Tate I think of the mother who asked the headmaster if her son had done trigonometry. "Well, no, madam," replied the headmaster, gently, "it would be an exaggeration to claim that he has *done* trigonometry, the most we can say is that he has been exposed to it."' This run of form led to an offer of a professional contract with Lancashire. Don knew he would never play Test cricket and decided that he had more to offer in other walks of life.

Jack Cox has described how, in 1924, Don acted as tour guide for a party of amateur footballers visiting Antwerp. He made everybody climb the 900 steps to the top of the Cathedral of Our Lady and told them to remove their hats as the bells chimed: 'Boys, you've been listening to the Middle Ages.' A love of architecture permeated his whole life and in the following year he designed his own house at Blackley. He began playing for Manchester CC and travelled to away matches in a battered Humber coupé. In 1928 Don and Gertrude were devastated when their one-year-old son, Michael, died of meningitis.

Don found an outlet for his grief by submerging himself in the Scout Movement which became a vehicle for many of his values. His work caught the attention of Baden-Powell and in 1929 he was a moving force behind the third Boy Scout World Jamboree, during which 50,000 scouts from all over the world descended on Arrowe Park in Birkenhead. Don was in his element organising football tournaments and helping the boys to produce a newspaper, the *Daily Arrowe*, which had a circulation of 38,000. He also attracted attention with his proficiency at wheelchair basketball which he played with a group of disabled Canadian Wolf Cubs. In the following year he hung up his cricket and football boots for good at the age of 38.

Don had been writing scrupulously lucid prose since the late 1920s and his freelance journalism brought him work with the BBC. His output included Saturday evening talks on sport with Wilfred Pickles at the BBC's Manchester studio, where he interviewed the likes of Don Bradman, Aubrey Smith and Jack Hobbs. By the early 1930s he had resolved to write for the *Manchester Guardian*. Persistent applications resulted in an invitation to cover occasional football matches and he was given the by-line 'Old International'. He soon widened his subject matter and began filing copy on scouting and general sports issues. His work at Mather and Platt continued and he became headmaster at the firm's day continuation school. Summer vacations were often spent taking scouts to Hungary, where they would be dragged round the cathedrals of Budapest.

In the early years of the Second World War Don demonstrated consummate bravery when he nearly lost his sight as a result of the viral infection contracted at Holzminden. He tried to enlist with the RAF but at 47 he was turned down on the grounds of age. He formed his own Home Guard unit in Blackley and his home, 'Kelmscott', became a boarding-house and social club for American airmen.

Don was distressed when the Old Trafford cricket ground was damaged by bombing, and as a vice-president of Lancashire CCC he did much to finance repairs to the ground after the war. He increased his radio activity and co-hosted a lunchtime football preview programme on Saturdays with Eamonn Andrews.

In a letter to me, Michael Parkinson assessed Don's radio work: 'He was the first and the last of the radio sports reporters who created a performance out of a match report. His sense of theatre, his love of words, his scholarship but above all his distinctive voice made him into a star. He might object to the word but nowadays he would be priceless.'

In 1950 he became education officer at Mather and Platt, later serving as welfare officer until his retirement in 1957. The work demonstrated his ability to get on with staff at all levels, a gift which was underlined when the company lavatory cleaner left instructions in her will that he should be her pall bearer. Don enlisted a few stalwart members of the Lancashire cricket team and carried out her request with gravity and pride.

At 5 ft 2 in with a slim frame, Don weighed a shade under eight stone for much of his adulthood. He was graceful in all his movements and looked excellent in drag. This fact was not lost on him and he once dressed up in a lady railway porter's uniform to raise money for an impoverished scout group. He then climbed a ladder and began cleaning signal lamps, attracting wolf whistles from commuters not in the know.

As a right-winger he was fast, tricky and as elusive as a dog at a fair. According to an obituary tribute in the *Old Boltonian*, 'a clear, quick-thinking brain controlled his deadly right foot. Moreover, he never lost a moment in cutting into the penalty area if he opened a gap, whilst his judgement in controlling his centres through the air and along the ground was excellent.' Don was a classically correct batsman with a strong cover drive and a fierce square cut. He was also electric at cover point, where his movements were like those of a gull swooping on a fish. Don was also noted for superb anticipation and a strong, flat throw.

He was similarly blessed as a journalist. Whatever the subject matter, his style is characterised by economy, elegance and playfulness; no clearer voice has ever been addressed to football reporting. Like Henry Longhurst, Don attracted readers who had little if any knowledge of sport. A *Times* tribute picked up this theme: 'Probably no contemporary writer on sport was so widely read by people without any particular interest in football and this was the mark of genius.' If the deadline permitted, he would pause for an hour over the proper word or cadence and he often quoted Flaubert's 'There are no such things as synonyms.'

Don never lost sight of the golden rule, 'get the score in the first paragraph', and yet every word he wrote reflected – sometimes gratuitously – what he felt on the day. His analogies and figurative language are often inspired: Charlie Macartney is the Danton of cricket, Cecil Parkin its Falstaff, Victor Trumper like something out of Malory. Don had Hazlitt's priceless gift for digression and could drag a reference to Vaughan Williams's atonalism into a review of a Burnley League match. At other times he wrote as simply as St Luke. He was often delightfully playful: 'Billy Meredith is the Lloyd George of football. Both were hailed by friends as the highest product of Welsh genius, and by opponents as the lowest form of Welsh cunning.' Don's beloved Dickens was never far from his thoughts and after a cup-tie in which Manchester United beat Arsenal 6–2 he reported: 'Old Trafford on Saturday was like Mrs Fezziwig, "one vast substantial smile."'

Don was as passionate about Tom Paine as he was about Tom Finney, as informed about Richard Wagner as he was about Richard Tyldesley. Michael Parkinson's evaluation of Don's writing includes: 'His contribution to soccer was as important and distinctive as Arlott's to cricket.' Neville Cardus stressed the breadth of his perspective in a *Manchester Guardian* obituary: 'Old International always wrote with his eye on the ball. But because he was more than one-eyed, he also saw the drama and the scene, the crowd spending its passion, and the players, now masterful and godlike, now impotent, cast down and comic in their sudden exposure of moral fallibility... He produced the best literature the game has so far inspired.' Don is still occasionally feted as the sainted guru of a depleted generation of sports journalists and an abiding testimony to editorial standards of the time. Cardus's evaluation holds good. After a respectful nod to David Lacey and Brian Glanville, the verdict is inevitable. Don remains the greatest soccer writer we have seen.

Many recollections stress a Quakerish dislike of ritual, an almost disabling modesty, shrinking dislike of ostentation and innate courtesy. He was devout but never pious and his whole life remains testimony to why squareness is better than sham. Don never relaxed his standards, and in a quiet voice would expose false values and mixed motives. He had a hypersensitivity to the faintest aura of sycophancy and was an impossible man to make up to, cozen or impress. He once said he judged a city not by its civic officials but by the faces of its children. Jack Cox's eulogy was: 'He gave ordinary men and women in Lancashire a burning faith in themselves and their own capabilities...' while an anonymous obituary tribute in the *Boy's Own Paper* ended with: 'He pushed you into things you never dreamed you could do and, thereafter, he stood on the touch-line of your life shouting encouragement.'

Don's literary and artistic tastes were wide ranging but had consistently Germanic overtones. He was devoted to the poetry of Goethe and Heine and his study wall was covered with Dürer prints. He was a competent graphic artist and would make charcoal sketches when visiting his daughters at Oxford. Don's one material indulgence was the purchase of 78 rpm gramophone records. As a pianist his technique left much to be desired, but he could play almost anything by ear. His daughter Deirdre once described his tenor voice as 'untrained but lyrical'. Surrounded by a few friends, Don would cheerfully hammer out his favourite ballads which included *The Rose of Tralee*. He was also a devotee of Flanders and Swann and knew every number from *At the Drop of a Hat*. A regular party piece was a spirited attempt at the Prize Song from Wagner's *Meistersingers*.

His passion for Wagner was deep and unaffected. It can be traced to his days as a POW, when a waggish camp commandant provided the inmates with musical instruments but restricted their sheet music to Wagner. Sadly, he was not completely free from the usual exaggerated belittlement of every other composer without which no genuine Wagnerian seems to have fulfilled his mission. He was a born linguist and became near fluent in French, German and Spanish. He read Baudelaire and Cervantes in the original and would often recite Heine. His favourite English poets were Keats and Tennyson and he would quote snatches from the latter's 'In Memoriam'.

> With exuberance, dedication and idealism, went grace and courtesy. In the dark years of the depression his own strait-ened circumstances never restricted his generosity; when he died men wrote of how he had helped them out of poverty and unemployment into work and faith. But he was no easy-going and uncritical help-mate. His standards were exacting; he loathed and despised the sham and the crooked and I have known strong men shrivel before his blaze of contempt.
>
> Sheila Henderson (née Davies), March 1961

In February 1958 Don flew to Belgrade with Manchester United as the Guardian football correspondent. He was standing in at the last moment for his deputy, one John Arlott. He saw the visitors draw 3–3 with Red Star Belgrade and filed his copy by telephone, ending with a glowing evaluation of the youthful Bobby Charlton. Charlton's team-mates included Roger Byrne, Tommy Taylor, Jackie Blanchflower,

Dennis Viollet and Duncan Edwards. Their manager was Matt Busby. Don was travelling with the team and eight other journalists on a British European Airways twin-propeller monoplane, the *Lord Burleigh*. The return journey required a stop to refuel at Riem airport outside Munich.

At 14.31 hours, while making his first attempt to take off, Captain Ken Rayment found that his boost pressure was unsatisfactory. He tried again at 14.34 but began braking when he once more observed fluctuating boost pressures. Players, attendants and journalists trudged through the snow to the airport lounge. By 15.00 they were back in the plane and it has since emerged that the control tower instructed Rayment to be airborne by 15.04 or abort the flight. At 15.03 Rayment attempted to take off for the third time. As the plane was partially off the ground, the engines began to splutter. The rest you know.

3
Archie MacLaren

b: 1.12.1871, Manchester, Lancashire.
d: 17.11.1944, Bracknell, Berkshire.

'... For his bounty,
There was no winter in't; an autumn 'twas
That grew the more by reaping: his delights
Were dolphin-like; they showed his back above
The element they lived in; in his livery
Walk'd crowns and crownets...'

Shakespeare, *Antony and Cleopatra*, V, ii

The subject is a farrago, an extraordinary mass of contradictions and a character at once ambiguous, driven and revealing of his time. At turns Archie could be warm, insensitive, charming, and arrogant. He could combine – almost in the same deed, on the same day – the most staggering misjudgements and the most piercing insights.

MacLaren's upbringing was in Whalley Range, a genteel suburb of Manchester. It was comfortable but unremarkable. His father, James, was a cotton merchant who acted as honorary treasurer to Lancashire CCC for much of the 1880s. He was a competent club cricketer and rugby player and an energetic administrator, who served as president of the Rugby Football Union while also appearing on the International Board.

Archie received his first cricket tuition at the age of seven when a maiden aunt began bowling to him in the back garden. Two years later he was sent to Elstree, a feeder school for Harrow. After making 82 not out against Finchley School he gained his first XI colours.

Archie was put down for Harrow in the summer of 1885 and spent the vacation at Old Trafford, where his father arranged nets against bowlers of the calibre of Johnny Briggs. His cricket fortunes at Harrow were mixed and initially he proved incapable of scoring on damp wickets. As a gawky 15-year-old, he played superb innings of 55 and 67 against Eton in 1887 which *Cricket* described as 'invaluable displays of batting, worthy of unstinted praise...showing judgement and confidence'.

In 1890 Archie captained Harrow against Eton at Lord's and excelled with 76. In his *History of Cricket*, Harry Altham recalled: 'The wicket was difficult, he had no support but made his runs in 115 minutes without a mistake.' In his final year, Archie's acolytes at Harrow included an unusually precocious fag whom he later dismissed as 'a snotty little bugger'. The youth was Winston Churchill. Later that summer Archie stepped effortlessly into first-class cricket, making an elegant 108 for Lancashire against Sussex. The *Manchester Courier* reported: 'He did not give a ghost of a chance and his innings throughout was a most dashing display' while the *Manchester Guardian* enthused with: 'His hits were alike for good style, clean hitting and complete confidence.'

By his late teens Archie was 5 ft 11 in tall. An imposing carriage and a shark's fin of a nose gave an impression of hauteur and he occasionally lacked the common touch. Struggling for consistency, he approached his captain, Albert Hornby, for some technical advice. Hornby's response was characteristically terse: 'Keep your left shoulder up and say your prayers.' Of far more help was the former Lancashire and England wicketkeeper Dick Pilling, who had been forced out of county cricket in the previous season through inflammation of the lungs. He spent hours in the nets with his young pupil and Archie was distraught when his mentor died a year later at the age of 35.

Archie was one of seven brothers and the fees at Harrow had stretched his father's resources. There were no funds to send him to university and he took a menial job at the Manchester and Liverpool District Bank. He appeared irregularly for Lancashire over the next few years but met with reasonable success. In 1894 he played his first full season of county cricket and showed enough promise to be selected for A.E. Stoddart's Ashes tour to Australia.

At the age of 22, Archie shot to fame when he scored 228 against Victoria in a shade over four hours. He had endeared himself to the crowd by consuming several large whiskies during the innings and the *Australasian* reported: 'His cutting and off strokes were perfectly executed... the innings was faultless and is classed by the chief critics as one of the best ever played at Melbourne.' Archie was also exciting interest among the gossip columnists who were circling like vultures. On the voyage out he had met fellow passenger Maud Power. She would become his wife some years later and was much in evidence during the tour. Maud was elegant, wilful, vivacious and as trim as a trout. She came from the upper echelons of Melbourne society, being the daughter of Robert Power. Power was a wool and horse-racing mogul who played cricket for Victoria and founded the Victoria Racing Club. Archie was in poor form for much of the Ashes rubber but his maiden Test century came in the form of a resourceful though hardly chanceless innings of 120 in the final match at Melbourne.

Archie's inability to manage his finances was already apparent and there were several frantic telegrams to England. MacLaren Snr was unimpressed and eventually the Lancashire committee stumped up his expenses for the following season in advance. Archie squandered these during a stopover on a Japanese island on the voyage home. He returned in desperate need of funds and was forced to take a teaching job at a prep school in Harrow.

At the end of term Archie travelled down to Taunton to play for Lancashire against Somerset. His finest hour was upon him. By the end of the day he had scored 228. A stack of encouraging telegrams overnight included a heartfelt message from W.G. Grace. On the following day he had breezed his way to 424 when he tired and skied a drive from the bowling of 17-year-old Herbert Gamlin. (Gamlin would go on to be one of England's greatest rugby full-backs.) He had been at the wicket for 7 hours and 50 minutes during which he hit a six and 62 fours. At the time it was the highest score in first-class cricket, overtaking Grace's 344 at Canterbury in 1876. By any standards, it was a remarkable performance. Alan Gibson has noted that the same ball was used throughout and that it must have resembled a bath bun towards the end of the innings. As an individual landmark, his score was overtaken in 1923 when Bill Ponsford made 429 for Victoria against Tasmania. As a record on English soil, Archie's total was only overhauled 99 years later when Brian Lara scored 501 not out for Warwickshire vs Durham.

Amazingly, Archie's availability for Test matches against the visiting Australians in 1896 was restricted by his teaching commitments. When A.E. Stoddart – another amateur – withdrew from the third Test at The Oval in a fit of pique after newspaper speculation as to his expenses, MacLaren was drafted in as a replacement. Years later, when pressed as to why he had stood down, Stoddart mused: 'Archie needed the money.'

Archie played little in 1897 but finished the season with a jaunty 244 against Kent at Canterbury. He had plans to settle as a teacher in Sydney and was delighted when he was included in Stoddart's touring party. In the first Test at the Sydney Cricket Ground he was brilliant, with scores of 109 and 50 not out while deputising as captain for Stoddart, who was grieving after the death of his mother. The following anecdote reflects badly on Archie and we could charitably put it down to inexperience. In Australia's second innings, Charley McLeod had his wicket broken by a delivery from Tom Richardson. The whole ground had heard the umpire's shout of 'no ball' save for McLeod himself, who was as deaf as an adder. This was common knowledge. McLeod began walking towards the pavilion and – to his eternal discredit – the England wicketkeeper, William Storer, uprooted the remaining stump and claimed a run-out. Archie looked on and did nothing.

He received a slating in the Australian press but recovered some composure with an uncharacteristically patient 124 in the third Test at Adelaide, which he made in five hours. At the end of the tour Archie married Maud Power. Media interest remained high and in the following year Archie was interviewed at length by *Strand Magazine*. The piece ends with: 'He is equally at home with his gun as with a cricket bat, and if he has a weakness it runs in the direction of greyhounds.'

In June 1899 Archie captained England at Lord's in the second Test against Joe Darling's Australian tourists. He rose to the challenge and played what was probably the finest innings of his career, a resolute 88 on a crumbling wicket. In May of the following year he was able to give up teaching when Lancashire appointed him as assistant secretary. The position was a sinecure; he held it for the next three years and the arrangement allowed the county to treat him as a professional.

Archie's instinctive judgement of a player's potential seldom let him down. As captain of the 1901–02 tour to Australia he selected a 28-year-old medium-pace bowler with few graces and no real prospects who had hovered on the fringe of the Lancashire team and bowled brilliantly against Leicestershire at the end of the season. Archie took a quick peek at him and insisted that he make the trip. The selection resulted in surprise and much ridicule, but Archie had recognized a rare bloom. The newcomer was Sydney Barnes. Other quirky selections, widely questioned by supposed savants in the press-box, included Charlie McGahey. An ex-Tottenham Hotspur footballer who was trying to throw off tuberculosis, McGahey had touched a chord with Archie. He failed in the Tests but performed admirably in state matches.

Archie had an overriding concern for the physical fitness of his team and on the voyage out he introduced a rudimentary form of circuit training, forcing his players to skip round the deck to the amusement of other passengers. Archie's scores of 145 and 73 against New South Wales early in the tour prompted Clem Hill to pronounce him the finest batsman who had ever visited Australia. In the opening Test at Sydney, Barnes vindicated his skipper's confidence when taking 5 for 65, while Archie himself was superb, labouring to 116 on a difficult wicket. The tourists won this fixture by an innings and 124 runs but lost the remaining four matches. Archie played well throughout, making 67 and 44 in the third game at Adelaide, 92 in the following match at Sydney and 48 at Melbourne. He was also a success on the social circuit and one of his more interesting excursions was a day's shooting with the brother of the opera star Nellie Melba. He would later enjoy a half-hearted flirtation with Dame Nellie.

In the following spring Archie realised that his wife Maud was unsuited to the English climate and particularly to the rain of Manchester. She suffered from a succession of debilitating illnesses which prompted Archie to rent a property in Basingstoke where Maud could be near her sister. In a letter to *Cricket*, he outlined his domestic situation and announced his intention of playing for Hampshire in 1902. Archie was attractive to the opposite sex and spent much of his life fighting off the attentions of women of all ages. The brief dalliance with Nellie Melba was completely out of character. Archie's unflagging devotion to Maud over 49 years is one of the best things known about him. It was only when he was confident that her health had improved that he declared himself available for Lancashire in the 1902 season.

Archie captained England in all five Tests against Australia that year. The first two were ruined by rain. In the third game, at Sheffield, his scores of 31 and 63 could not prevent an Australian victory by 143 runs. It is in the fourth match, at Old Trafford, that we encounter a favourite MacLaren anecdote. On the first day, Victor Trumper scored a frenzied century before lunch, hitting numerous straight drives over the heads of Lionel Palairet and Stanley Jackson at long-off and long-on. Archie was widely criticised for his field settings and in later years it became a standing joke to taunt him about his strategy that morning. One evening over dinner, Archie sought to justify his tactics, using sugar cubes to illustrate the fielding positions: 'Well I couldn't put Lionel and "Jacker" in the bloody car park, now could I?'

In June 1903 Archie played a stunning innings of 168 for Gentlemen vs Players, much of it in partnership with C.B. Fry. In the following month he and Reggie Spooner put on 368 in 210 minutes for Lancashire's first wicket against Gloucestershire. Archie raced to 204 before being bowled by the journeyman medium-pacer Harry Huggins. The stand was made at 105 runs an hour or better and it remains a record for Lancashire's first wicket. In the following winter there was controversy when Pelham Warner was given the England captaincy in preference to several more established candidates, including Archie. Always fractious, he refused point-blank to tour under Warner and vented his frustration by spattering abuse in some graceless articles for the *Daily Chronicle* in which he made gloomy predictions about the forthcoming series which Warner won quite comfortably.

Archie spent the autumn of 1905 in India with Ranji and began working as his secretary. The pair played a great deal of lawn tennis and made some singularly unsuccessful attempts to sell Lanchester limousines to the Indian aristocracy. As a salesman, Archie had a gaudy line in patter and a sunny indifference to his customers' real needs. He was

overlooked again as captain for the 1905 domestic series against Joe
Darling's tourists but played with good grace under the leadership of
Stanley Jackson, who had been his junior at Harrow. In the first Test at
Nottingham, the Australian pace bowler Albert 'Tibby' Cotter unsettled the English openers with his fearsome pace and errant length.
Coming in at second drop, Archie was unimpressed as he strapped on
his pads: 'I'll Cotter him.' He went on to make 140 and the *Times* correspondent wrote: 'Mr MacLaren began to hit out and the Australian
bowling became completely collared.' At Lord's Archie made 57 and 79
on a damp wicket while in the final match at The Oval he became
unusually excited when his old crony Walter Brearley bowled Trumper
for 4 with a loosener in his first over: 'God, what a bloody ball, what a
bloody useless ball – oh, well bowled, Walter!'

In 1906, largely due to pressure from Reggie Spooner, Lancashire
organised a testimonial for its skipper. Archie immediately spent the
proceeds on a luxury car in which he and Reggie would hare around
the country, giving rise to the following doggerel:

> 'To Archie MacLaren quoth Spooner:
> 'I'm thinking of buying a schooner.'
> Said Archie: 'What rot!
> When a motor I've got
> We can get to the cricket ground sooner.'

> Anon.

Archie returned to England from India in the spring of 1908 suffering with acute rheumatism. *Cricket* announced: 'A.C. MacLaren will
not play for Lancashire next summer. He is acting as secretary to the
Jam of Nawanagar and finds that his time is occupied by affairs other
than cricket.' Ranji was even worse with money than Archie. He had
commissioned a portrait artist, Mary Tayler, to produce a likeness of
him but was unable to meet her bill. Tayler made regular visits to
Ranji's house in Shillinglee Park to extract her fee and Archie was
obliged to fend her off. At his lowest ebb, Ranji once lied through his
teeth to the effect that Archie had been involved in a motoring accident
and was unable to deal with his financial affairs. For quite some time
Archie remained indifferent to his employer's financial duplicity.

The pair were certainly up to their necks in various intrigues. Archie was living in a property attached to Ranji's estate and *Cricket* for 29 October 1908 described how Archie had appeared at Guildford County Court in the previous week for non-payment of rates. He explained at elegant if laborious length that he considered himself to be exempt from such taxes, being Ranji's secretary, and that Ranji was also exempt, being a ruling prince. For once the MacLaren hauteur cut little ice and he was told in no uncertain manner to pay up, which he did promptly. The pair never fell out, though Archie's candour and decency soon surfaced. He resigned as Ranji's secretary in the autumn of 1908 but immediately went back to India with him for a holiday.

At the age of 37 Archie was recalled to the England captaincy for the 1909 Ashes series. He knew he was past his best but bowed to pressure from the selectors. After his team was thrashed by nine wickets at Lord's, he asked Lord Hawke if he could stand down. With several matches left in the rubber, Archie gave an interview to the *Daily Despatch* in which he trashed the players and insisted that he had taken on the role against his better judgement. When the selectors ignored his advice he is said to have clutched his hands to his head and moaned: 'Look what they've given me now!' He would often take the field with an air of fatalism that would have done credit to Sydney Carton. Archie's own performance was poor; he scored 85 runs from seven innings while his bowling changes and field settings struck many as eccentric and misguided. In the second Test he dropped a depressingly simple catch from Vernon Ransford, which probably cost England the match.

There is a rather pathetic entry in *Cricket* for November 1911, which suggests that Archie was either suffering badly with rheumatism or more than usually hard up. 'Mr A.C. MacLaren has indicated to the committee of the MCC that should there be a vacancy in the cricket team that is to visit the Argentine in January, he would be glad to go.' Archie was finally included. He could not buy a run for most of the tour but came good with 172 at Buenos Aires against an Argentine-Born XI.

Relief from schoolmastering came in January 1914 when he set up a magazine, the *World of Cricket*, in association with J.N. Pentelow. It is likely that Pentelow did most of the serious writing but Archie plunged himself into the work with a will and pecked away at a battered Remington. Although given to labyrinthine sentences, by the standards of the time he was a competent journalist. Despite a tendency to facile generalisations, he writes with enthusiasm and prejudice. In turn he can be absurdly histrionic and devastatingly frank. Eight months later he was handling the massive obituary columns with sensitivity and flair. Sadly, the editors lacked financial acumen and the magazine folded soon after the outbreak of war.

In December Archie spoke at a recruiting rally in Manchester, sharing the podium with Gilbert Jessop. From 1914 to 1917 he served as a lieutenant and captain in the Royal Army Service Corps. He was invalided out but did valuable work as a P.T. instructor at an army gymnasium in Aldershot. Archie and Maud's finances were rocky at the end of the war. They gave up their house in Knutsford and took a cottage adjacent to the estate of Lionel Robinson at Old Buckenham Hall near Norwich. A Philistine of the first chop, Robinson was a vulgar if well-intentioned Australian millionaire who had made his fortune as a financial journalist and stockbroker. He was obsessed with sport and installed Archie as his racing and cricket manager. Archie knew as much about horses as a horsefly, seeing them only as a betting medium. He never allowed a little ignorance to stand in his way and after recruiting a team of experienced grooms, he blustered around the stables with a modicum of success.

As cricket manager Archie was inspired. His great coup came in 1921 when he persuaded Warwick Armstrong's Australian tourists to play their second match on Robinson's estate. They had thrashed England 5–0 in the previous winter and with the possible exception of Bradman's 1948 side, they remain the strongest Australian team of all time. Wanting to show that his favourite young amateurs were ready for Test duty, Archie got up a team of near international standard and amid rain and snow his players demonstrated that Armstrong's side was vulnerable.

And now to the most romantic match in the history of the game. It was Archie's last great moment and has sweetened into a legend. He had been pontificating in the press all season to the effect that he knew how to beat the Australians. In August he was invited to select and captain a team to play them at Eastbourne. He immediately instructed Neville Cardus to be there. (As the *Manchester Guardian*'s principal cricket correspondent, Cardus would normally have been covering the

Middlesex vs Surrey fixture which was going to decide the county championship.) Out of a hazy notion of loyalty to Archie, Cardus pitched up at the Saffrons. In a primitive press box inhabited by a few local hacks, he got the one and only scoop of his career.

Ronald Mason has described Archie's team as 'an interesting, gay, random, attractive, hugely vulnerable side'. Archie included three of the Ashton brothers, Gilbert, Hubert and Claude, who were among the most gifted university players of the time. At 21, Percy Chapman was also in the vanguard of promising youngsters. By contrast the team's all-rounder, the great South African Aubrey Faulkner, was 40, grossly overweight and had not played a serious game in years. However, he still had the remnants of an extraordinary talent. Incredibly, the strike bowler was Archie's old crony, the 45-year-old Walter Brearley. Brearley, Faulkner and Archie were all as grey as badgers and observing them in practice, Arthur Mailey sneered: 'Archie, old boy, you haven't got the Bolter's chance.' There was soon a moment of high comedy when, attempting to vault the pavilion rope, Brearley ricked his ankle. He was unable to bowl and was hidden in the field throughout the game.

When Archie and his boys were dismissed for 43 they looked dead for all money, and Cardus started enquiring about trains to London. However, the Australian reply was restricted to 174 as Faulkner and Michael Falcon bowled superbly. In the second innings Faulkner recovered much of his pre-war fluency to blast 153 in even time. He was supported by Hubert Ashton and the home side mustered 326. Falcon, Faulkner and Clem Gibson all bowled beautifully to dismiss the tourists for 167 and bring victory by 28 runs.

As the match went to the wire Archie proved nerveless and his courage in keeping Faulkner on at the death tipped the balance. The Saffrons overflowed with breathless holidaymakers and Archie was mobbed as he and Brearley hobbled off the field. Warwick Armstrong made an uncharacteristically graceful and complimentary speech and for once Archie was too emotional to respond. Armstrong and his men took an omnibus to Brighton, while Cardus finally got his train to London. Later, Archie wandered around the boundary rope blubbing and had to be supported by Faulkner. The pair picked up Brearley at the pavilion bar and proceeded to get blind drunk at the Grand Hotel.

The victory rekindled the blaze of Archie's legend and put his name back in the headlines, but he was still impoverished. In the following month he secured a contract with Lancashire to coach the side at the enormous salary of £550. As usual the terms stipulated that Archie should receive a large advance immediately. He spent two years at Old Trafford but ruffled too many feathers for the committee's liking and was replaced by Johnny Tyldesley. Archie remained quick in the memories of many at Old Trafford. He left a generation of young players with fond recollections and much technical insight, while his legacy to the catering manager was a huge unpaid bill for champagne.

Archie's playing career was more or less over. For many his batting was the sublimation of the grand manner. C.B. Fry concluded: 'He lifted his bat round his neck like a golfer at the top of his swing. He stood bolt upright and swept into every stroke, even a defensive backstroke, with dominating completeness.' 'Majesty' and 'grandeur' are the terms that appear most frequently in contemporary descriptions. Archie's batting was as spacious and opulent as the social circles he moved in. Essentially a fast wicket player, he was also superb in wet conditions, being catlike on his feet and resourceful in his tactics against a turning ball. He often chanced his luck when set, occasionally skying his drives and being caught in the outfield. Archie used a bat which resembled a railway sleeper and played most of his strokes after an imperious forward movement. The forward lunge did however make him vulnerable to high-class spin bowling.

It has become a slick judgement to suggest that Archie was among the greatest captains of all time. The statistics are hardly stacked in his favour. He led England in four Test series and never won a rubber. In 22 matches against Australia he obtained only four victories.

> His captaincy was a thing of romance as well as of science. He did things as they occurred to him, by intuition or analytical observation. They might be wrong, but they were his own.
>
> Raymond Robertson-Glasgow, *46 Not Out*, 1948

Of post-war cricketers only Ted Dexter approached Archie in combining the grand manner with inspired demotic gestures. It was Archie who scrapped the rule at Old Trafford that amateur and pro should enter like strangers from different gates. At a time when Lord Harris and Lord Hawke were treating professionals as though they had communicable diseases, nothing gave Archie more pleasure than skipping down the pavilion steps with his arm round Johnny Tyldesley. Archie was hardly weighed down by diplomatic niceties; he combined asperity with the brusque manner of a man used to exercising command but most of the professionals adored him. He was less popular with his peers and George Lyttelton's evaluation was: 'It is disillusioning to one of my youthful loyalties to realise that the Majestic MacLaren was an extremely stupid, prejudiced and pig-headed man.'

As a captain Archie let textbook axioms go hang and his last-minute changes in batting orders could be inspired. He would even change team selections at the eleventh hour; he once sprinted to the telegraph office on the morning of a Test match and sent a cable to Sydney Barnes ordering him to travel from Manchester to Sheffield only two hours before the start of play. (Barnes obliged with 6 for 49 from 20 overs.) In the field he was a colossus, despite endless banter with Walter Brearley that could cover anything from the chances of a gelding at Haydock Park to a pretty girl on the boundary rope. He was superb at first slip and inspired at square leg. In the slips he was known for superb anticipation and being equally competent with both hands.

Archie's lofty self-assurance could both annoy and amaze. In a Roses match David Hunter once appealed for caught behind when he believed Bobby Peel had found the edge of Archie's bat. MacLaren turned round immediately: 'Never within an ensanguined mile of it.' A.A. Thomson recalled that Archie's idea of a committee was 'a body consisting of himself and those who agreed with him'. He was certainly a maverick. Like his close friends C.B. Fry and Percy Fender, Archie had a healthy scepticism for received opinion. He knew his own mind and was alive to what it saw. He was never elected to office at MCC and the hypocrisy of his 'shamateurism' with regard to expenses brought him few friends in high places. (He may have consoled himself with the thought that lack of influence is more dignified than lack of talent.)

Archie's sense of humour could be sardonic and unworthy of his better nature. Spotting one of the more elderly and immobile

Lancashire professionals struggling to cut off a ball on the boundary, he once chortled to Reggie Spooner: 'He looks like a spavined cab-horse.' By contrast, he could be chivalrous to an extreme and the trait emerged in many revelatory gestures. Cardus recalled how he observed Archie rushing through torrential rain at Old Trafford while reporting a Test match for the *News of the World*. Archie finally took shelter in a sandwich bar where he spotted a waitress laden with a drinks tray. She was about to walk half the length of the ground to the Ladies' Pavilion: 'MacLaren stopped her, took off his raincoat and placed it over her shoulders. "*Now*, my dear."'

> However good a captain he was, he could be an obnoxious one. He was said to have been unpopular with the Players, intimidating them and often being severely critical of them to their faces with the rest of the pro side looking on. He was critical not only of Players but of fish. At the Hastings Festival I was seated on the next table to him at breakfast. He took one taste of his herring and shouted across the room at the waiter: 'Come here, you. Take it away. It stinks.'
>
> Ben Travers, *94 Declared*, 1981

Like his contemporary Gerry Weigall, Archie was an outstanding example of that frightening phenomenon, a rich man without any money. In his enduringly entertaining autobiography, William Howard recounted one of Archie's financial nadirs. Howard describes how at a county match he was informed that Archie was hunting all over the ground for him. '"Do you wish to see me?" I said. Turning his grey head quite unconcernedly, he replied, "Oh, it's all right, William. I only wanted to borrow five shillings from you to buy my wife some chocolate, but I found some money in your locker so I took that."'

Archie was plagued by rheumatism for much of his life and his trips to Australia helped him enormously. He once told Jimmy Catton that he used to break off at Naples when returning from a tour and buy an enormous box of powders from a monastery, the medicine doing him more good than anything prescribed for him in England. In the 1920s and '30s Archie wrote numerous articles for the *Cricketer* and other magazines. He frequently quarrelled with his editors, few of whom would cede to his requests for payment in advance. Archie lived largely off Maud's allowance from Australia, occasionally plunging this into a series of doomed business ventures. Maud and Archie ran a small hotel for several months but Archie's demeanour as a receptionist made a Basil Fawlty tirade look positively welcoming. Other unsuccessful schemes included a disastrous attempt at setting up a stud farm, importing Spanish willow in order to make bats and the manufacture of inflatable pads. Sadly, Archie had a Micawberesque sustaining illusion that he was always about to make his fortune.

In the mid 1930s Maud inherited a large fortune and the couple built themselves a house on 150 acres near Bracknell. Archie spent the rest of the decade entertaining his cronies in the style he had always craved. In 1938 he travelled to Hollywood to visit the former Sussex and England cricketer Aubrey Smith, now established as a successful character actor. Archie spent many hours on the set of Alexander Korda's *The Four Feathers*, finally appearing in a walk-on part as a monocled Crimean veteran.

Archie died of cancer in November 1944 at the age of 72. The judgements from contemporaries are mixed. Cardus once said that while watching Archie's follow-through he received the grace of art. Sir Neville equated Archie with Henry Irving: 'I first saw Irving and A.C. MacLaren at much the same impressionable time of life; they wakened the incurable romantic in me which to this day will not be exorcised even by the cynicism which saves a grown man from foolishness.' John Arlott's summation was: 'MacLaren's tragedy is that all his virtues bred their own faults. He was strong but inflexible, intelligent but intolerant: single-minded but humourless; impressive on the field but often disappointingly petty off it.' It is a characteristically tart verdict but hardly helps us in the final analysis.

Perhaps we should send Archie off in a glorious burst of anecdote. Back in 1905, after their failed attempts at promoting Lanchester limousines in India, Ranji and Archie turned to selling tyres. Business was slow and Archie was sent out one evening on a promise. He buttonholed a dyspeptic expatriate lawyer and after several hours his gaudy sales patter began to strike a chord. 'All right. I'll buy one of your tyres.' By now Archie was despairing: 'Heavens, has your car got only one wheel?'

4

Henry Hyndman

b: 7.3.1842, Paddington, London.
d: 22.11.1921, Hampstead, London

Like his, our lives have been coeval
With a political upheaval,
Like him, we had the luck to see
A rare discontinuity,
Old Russia suddenly mutate
Into a proletarian state.

W.H. Auden, 'New Year Letter', 1940

Regarded by many as the founding father of British socialism, Henry Hyndman is a striking reminder that one man's loose cannon is another's freedom fighter. He came from the upper echelons of London society and was born into a family which had a sizeable income from Demerara sugar plantations and an impressive intellectual pedigree. His father, John, was a talented barrister but rarely practised, while his mother, Caroline, née Mayers, was a fine mathematician and classical scholar.

Henry never attended Eton as is often stated but was taught at small academies in Leatherhead and Torquay. As a 16-year-old he went on an unaccompanied walking holiday in Germany where he acquired an abiding interest in Gothic architecture, being particularly impressed with Cologne Cathedral. He returned to Norfolk and spent two years at a crammer before entering Trinity College, Cambridge, in 1861 to study mathematics. He proved a desultory student but followed a course in political economy with interest. His ruling passion was music and he played the flute in the university orchestra. At 5 ft 6 in and a stocky 11 stone he was hardly a born athlete and in his first year he made little impression at cricket.

His first innings of note was 62 for Gentlemen of Sussex vs Gentlemen of Hampshire at Brighton in 1863. In the following year he met the novelist George Meredith at a village fete. Fourteen years older than Henry, Meredith was a cricket enthusiast and invited the rather intense undergraduate to literary dinners at Box Hill near Dorking, where guests included Dante Gabriel Rossetti. Henry's social poise improved but he showed no interest in the opposite sex. He did however become close to Meredith's wife, Marie Vulliamy, who encouraged him to improvise on the flute and accompanied him in Moritz Hauptman duets. In August his cricket blossomed; he made a polished 58 for Sussex against Hampshire before being run out while attempting a quick single. A few days later he was equally assured when scoring 62 against Middlesex, an innings which won the match for his county.

After leaving Cambridge he read for the bar with no great enthusiasm: 'I disliked the idea of battering out my brains over disputes as to other people's property.' He had a considerable private income and followed the country house cricket circuit in the mid-1860s, where he acquired a reputation as a wit. His first-class cricket career ended in 1865 when he played six matches for Sussex, the only performance of note being 48 not out against MCC. He played a few club matches in the late 1860s and dabbled with golf but was unimpressed with the game: 'It combines boredom and complications in equal measure.'

Early in 1866 Henry visited Italy. He rushed around Rome clutching a copy of Gibbon and became a competent Italian speaker within weeks. War was raging between Italy and Austria and he approached the *Pall Mall Gazette*, who offered him work as a correspondent. He followed Garibaldi's force into the Tyrol and showed remarkable stamina during a food shortage, sustaining himself for a fortnight on coconut macaroons and chocolate drops.

His reports are distinguished by vitality and candour. Like André

Malraux, he is one of few writers to describe the almost sexual arousal of men in battle. The pieces also offer much technical insight; he had acquired an excellent knowledge of military routines and could sum up the tactical possibilities of a piece of terrain at a glance. Towards the end of the campaign Henry displayed exceptional courage after the Battle of Bezzecca, when he spent several days tending the wounded at a typhoid-ridden dressing station. He returned to London in the autumn of 1866. Having met Garibaldi and become interested in Italian nationalism, he immediately interviewed the exiled Mazzini, who was now languishing at squalid lodgings in the Fulham Road.

Henry appears to have been as strong as an ox throughout his life but he was a hypochondriac and in February 1869 he decided he needed sunshine. He travelled to Australia, worked as a bushman in Victoria and cut a fine figure when hunting kangaroo. His conversion to socialism was some way off but by now he was certainly a maverick and he instigated a backlash against squatters at Glenormiston near Melbourne. As a competent all-round journalist he was head-hunted by the editor of the Melbourne *Argus*, who commissioned a series of articles assessing the merits of secular education in which Henry left readers in little doubt as to his views. He would later opine: 'I dislike and even fear the Catholic Church as an institution devoted to the misguiding of human intelligence into the jungle of superstition and misery.'

In June he travelled to Fiji on the *Marion Rennie*. He proved fearless when the vessel narrowly avoided shipwreck and endeared himself to the crew when he began rustling up excellent meals while standing in for an alcoholic cook. Henry left the boat a day before it was attacked by Fijians and every man aboard killed. In the summer of 1870 he toured the United States. He was unimpressed by the countryside and his hosts, the only highlight being a meeting with the humorist and poet Bret Harte.

Hyndman always fancied himself as an anthropologist. In the spring of 1875 he elbowed his way into the Royal Geographical Society. Here he met Henry Stanley and took an immediate dislike to him. Later in the year he wrote an article for the *Pall Mall Gazette* in which he criticised Stanley's treatment of African bearers during his search for Dr Livingstone. It is a masterpiece of invective, exposing what he considered to be 'the unscrupulous slaughter of miserable negroes merely for the sake of getting more quickly from one part of the country to another'. The quarrel continued at meetings of the society, where Henry berated Stanley with a virulence verging on slander. He often had to be silenced and was lucky not to be sued.

In February of the following year Henry married Matilda Ware, the daughter of William Ware of Newick, a stalwart of Sussex cricket. Matilda was hardly an intellectual but was noted for her spontaneity and a warm, rustic sense of humour. She was a tireless charity worker and did much to introduce free school meals in the mid-1880s. By now Henry was interested in Indian politics and soon after his marriage he published *The Indian Famine and the Crisis in India*, which received some scathing reviews. It is hardly an easy read: even the most rabid Hyndman fan would be catatonic by the end of the first chapter, though he is deeply and comprehensively right in his ideas on irrigation.

Hyndman Snr died in 1880 and Henry inherited a vast fortune, much of which had been invested in American mines. He was increasingly estranged from the social values of his class but had no qualms about his inheritance, which he managed with considerable acumen. Even a cursory study of Henry's autobiography reveals that his radicalism hardened into socialism over a period of five years. Sadly this punctures the two most persistent myths about him, which attribute his politics either to disappointment at not winning a cricket blue or frenzied enthusiasm for Marx's *Das Kapital*.

Henry had not bothered to read *Das Kapital* when he first met Marx in the spring of 1880. He was amazed when his interviewee showed a detailed knowledge of Henry's pamphlets on India. The meeting set up a profound admiration; Henry confided to a friend: 'I think he is the Aristotle of the nineteenth century.' His later evaluations are more measured. In a curiously intense piece contributed to the anthology *How I Became a Socialist*, Henry gives a forthright account of his early political experiences but is at pains to establish that his regard for Marx stopped well short of idolatry.

In 1880 Hyndman stood as an independent candidate for Marylebone, his platform being colonial reform. He could still be wildly rhetorical and self-regarding and cut an unsympathetic figure at the hustings, where he provoked Gladstone into slanging matches, later accusing his opponent of 'verbose rhetoric and dextrous casuistry'. Henry's interest in Indian politics was now an obsession. He believed implicitly in the desirability of British rule and never aligned himself with Indian nationalists but recoiled from the prevalent view of Empire being God's reward for work well done.

He was consistently critical of the quality of expatriate civil servants and the many examples of venality. Outlining British imperialism later in 1880 he speaks of 'our criminal and ruthless plunder at the beginning...and cold-blooded economic exploitation in the middle'. The greatest disappointment of Henry's life was the fact that Gladstone's second Liberal government of 1880 did not continue the reforms in India which his writings had done much to set in motion.

Hyndman was in the chair for a meeting of radicals at the Westminster Palace Hotel in March 1881 which resulted in the creation of the Democratic Foundation. The organisation had many middle-class members and its aims included adult suffrage, abolition of the House of Lords and legislative independence for Ireland. Some months later there was a change of name to the Social Democratic Federation (SDF), after which the designer and poet William Morris became the group's moving force. Later that year Henry fell out with Marx, who had misinterpreted his essay 'England For All'. The argument was fuelled by Friedrich Engels, who never liked Henry, describing him as 'self-satisfied and garrulous'.

Henry saw William Morris as a reincarnation of Chaucer. In the following winter they collaborated on *A Summary of the Principles of Socialism*. He was delighted when Morris showed a willingness to work at the grassroots of the SDF: 'Socialism was no longer the creed only of the scum of the earth.' In 1884 Henry began editing the Federation's newsletter, *Justice*, to which Morris contributed several poems. In June at a meeting in Sheffield he declared himself 'a Socialist unarmed with revolvers or any dynamite other than mental dynamite'. Henry was attracting interest among intellectuals though many, including George Bernard Shaw, were disturbed by his arbitrary and autocratic leadership. Relations with William Morris became strained and in December many members began rallying round the poet. A vote of no confidence was passed. Morris broke away to form the

Socialist League and took some influential members with him including Edith Nesbit, author of *The Railway Children*.

Henry had an abiding commitment to what Michael Foot once
called 'the civilized idea of full employment'. In February 1886, while
distributing mimeographed pamphlets on the unemployment problem, he incited a massive crowd to riot in Trafalgar Square. There was
looting of shops and an amusing slanging match with members of the
Reform Club, who were hanging out of the windows and screaming
abuse. Henry was tried and acquitted at the Old Bailey for his part in
the riots. He appears to have been dealt with leniently due to the influence of the Chancellor of the Exchequer, Randolph Churchill, who
always had a soft spot and grudging respect for him. Henry preserved
his sharpest humour for the witness box and proved capable of
convulsing judge, jury, and the massed ranks of journalists. There is a
persistent legend that while giving evidence he insisted on being
advised of county cricket scores. Sadly this is deflated by the histori-
cally inconvenient fact that the trial took place in March.

Hyndman was sued down to his socks in 1887 when his criticism of
conditions in the Welsh slate quarries enraged the owners. He had to
sell his luxurious Devonshire Street house and take modest lodgings in
Buckingham Palace Road. He describes himself as having been in
grave danger of becoming 'a trouserless socialist'. In the following year
he wrote a pamphlet proposing an element of self-government for
London, the technical details being uncannily similar to the principles
behind the GLC a hundred years later. By now he was feuding bitterly
with Engels, whom he described as 'the Grand Lama of the Regent's
Park Road'. The pair argued publicly during the London dock strikes
of July 1888, which were only quelled when Cardinal Manning did
superb work as an intermediary between workforce and management.

His finances took another battering in 1890 after the (first) Barings
collapse and he was reduced to jobbing journalism for the next four
years. He stood at Blackburn for the SDF in the general election of 1895
but by now the Federation was losing support to the Independent
Labour Party created by Keir Hardie and Ramsay MacDonald. To
Henry's immense joy, William Morris rejoined the SDF in 1896. Two
years later he was distressed when Marx's daughter, Eleanor, committed suicide. He believed he was close to her though he seems to have

been deluded; letters found after her death reveal that the irritable and anorexic Eleanor loathed Henry and had ridiculed him for years.

In July 1899 Henry organized a rally in Trafalgar Square to protest against the Boer War and as the keynote speaker he denounced British imperialism. He was pelted with bottles and suffered significant injuries. Recalling this in his autobiography, he concluded: 'There is nothing I have done that I look back upon with more genuine satisfaction than my opposition to that shameful campaign.' By now the second Dreyfus trial was at its height. Henry's admiration of Marx had occasionally been extreme but his one and only god was Georges Clemenceau. He spent much of 1899 following the trial with Clemenceau, came down firmly in favour of Dreyfus's innocence and used his excellent French to address 10,000 people on the subject. He would later write an admiring but intelligent and scholarly biography of Clemenceau which includes original reflections on the Dreyfus case.

Henry resigned from the SDF in 1901 as a result of continuing worries over his finances. These improved when he invested shrewdly after a mining boom on the Gold Coast. He was appalled by Joseph Chamberlain's plans for tariff reform in 1903, followed Chamberlain on the stump right around the country and drew comparable if not larger audiences. Henry rejoined the SDF in 1904 and in the following year he contested Burnley in the general election from a moderate platform of free trade, secular education and Irish Home Rule. He fought an excellent campaign and lost by only 324 votes to the Liberal candidate.

He was still capable of losing his head. In August 1907 he travelled to Stuttgart for a socialist congress, where a delegate from the British Dockers' Union was prevented from speaking. Henry began raving and invited the chairman to spit in his face. A Reuters report noted: 'Hyndman stood like Casabianca on the burning deck, amidst the flames of wrath, and would not sit down. He was flatly and transparently out of order; he was wildly and shamelessly anarchistic.'

Tension between the upper and lower Houses produced two general elections in 1910. Henry contested Burnley twice, concluding in *Justice*: 'I was beaten by ignorance, poverty and weight of money.' He consoled himself in the following year when, in a matter of weeks, he rapped out his jaunty and eminently readable autobiography, *The Record of an Adventurous Life*. It is a sustained joy; Henry describes his career with candour, digression and a lot of style. Later in 1911 the SDF merged with the British Socialist Party. By now Henry was speaking of his grave concern over Prussian militarism, describing the German people as 'hypnotised by the cult of scientific barbarism'.

In June 1913 Matilda Hyndman died after a long illness. Six months later, at the age of 71, we find Henry exchanging impassioned letters with Rosalind Travers. The daughter of Major John Travers of Arundel, Rosalind was a 38-year-old poet and an authority on medieval troubadour songs. She was undoubtedly a woman of remarkable intelligence, integrity and grace. Sadly her poetry is appalling; it has some original metre but is paralysed by self-conscious archaisms and irrelevant classical references. Five years earlier Rosalind had supported the Finnish struggle for independence and she had met her future husband at a rally in Trafalgar Square. Like Henry she had a shrinking dislike for ostentation and surprising phys-ical strength. (She once dragged a fully grown dock worker out of a British Socialist Party meeting after he had called Henry a liar.) With an atypical gesture, Henry sent his lover a diamond as big as the Ritz and they married in the late summer of 1914.

As hostilities loomed during his honeymoon, Henry threw himself solidly behind the war effort. His socialism was mellowing into a Fabian gradualism and he denounced wartime strikers as 'traitors to the whole nation'. His views at this time were very similar to those of his close friend H.G. Wells. In 1864 Henry had played cricket against Wells's father, Joseph, who was a competent professional for Kent. Henry retained his interest in socialism. In the middle years of the war he corresponded extensively with the American agitator John Reed. (Reed's life has been celebrated in Warren Beatty's superb biopic *Reds*.) He also gave Eugene Debs much support in his socialist candidatures for the American presidency.

In March 1916 Henry made wild claims that Arthur Bonar Law was involved in corrupt iron dealings in South Africa. As with the explorer Henry Stanley, he was lucky not to be involved in a crippling lawsuit. A month later the British Socialist Party denounced the war. Henry resigned immediately and formed the National Socialist Party. There is an old calumny that needs righting here. Henry took many young socialists with him to the new party. They have been regularly vilified as conscientious objectors while the simple fact is that most of them saw active service in France and Belgium.

Henry was thrilled by the Russian Revolution in the following year and his colleagues pleaded with him to visit Russia. However, the sea voyage would have been arduous and his finances had sustained yet another setback. He was obliged to take a modest cottage in Hampstead but was delighted to discover that previous occupants had included the poet John Masefield. By now he could be slightly dotty and he embarrassed his followers when he volunteered to root out 'German spy waiters' from the restaurants of London. Like his old cricketing adversary W.G. Grace, he appears to have been unfazed by the Zeppelins hovering over London. The Doctor used to shake his fist at them, while Henry simply stayed in bed, reasoning that 'it was the most convenient place in which to be killed'.

Henry suffered from heart problems in the final months of the war and Rosalind took him to stay with Thomas Hardy at Max Gate. The pair discovered common interests, including a passion for the poetry of Henry's old mentor George Meredith. Henry's interest in India resurfaced after the war. In 1919 he was appalled by the infamous massacre at Amritsar when, through the incompetence and savagery of General Dyer, British troops shot dead 379 unarmed civilians. His exposure of the British enquiry as a monumental cover-up brought much credence to the Home Rule movement in India.

In 1920 Henry was critical of the newly formed League of Nations and he was one of the first political observers to recognize Mussolini as a potential tyrant. In the summer of 1921 he visited Lord's, where he saw Warwick Armstrong's Australians destroy the home side by eight wickets and win their seventh consecutive Test match on the reel. He was unimpressed and pronounced that a straight bat and a stout heart would combat Gregory and McDonald. In the autumn of 1921 he visited Czechoslovakia and spoke widely at radical meetings.

Reviewing Henry's autobiography in 1911, *Cricket* concluded: 'His association with the game, though brief and not brilliant, was long enough and successful enough to show him a player of parts who might have done bigger things if other matters had not claimed his energies.' The piece also quotes Henry's rueful confession: 'I declare that I feel at this moment 50 years later, my not playing for Cambridge against Oxford as a more unpleasant and depressing experience than infinitely more important failures have been to me since.'

As a batsman Henry was an aggressive middle-order player with a fondness for lofted drives. He was addicted to quick singles, which often cost him his wicket. Few would make extravagant claims for his ability; in first-class cricket he scored 309 runs from 20 innings at an average of 16. He usually fielded at point or long-on, where he covered vast amounts of ground and proved safe under high catches. In club cricket he was a competent change bowler, producing gentle off-breaks from a round-arm action.

Henry's vision and integrity still hang heavily over British socialism. His personality was an odd mixture of crassness and extreme sensitivity which struck the imagination of thousands. Henry became so exhilarated by agitation that he adopted it as a profession. Hyperbole was simply his natural form of expression. However, he was never a mere iconoclast and might have echoed George Bernard Shaw, who once remarked that any rebel is obliged to replace the conventions he destroys with better ones. Henry is remembered by his contemporaries for the vitality of his conversation, the flow of ideas, the range of historical reference and intellectual curiosity. An abiding impression is that of a restless idealist and a tireless exposer of cant.

Chushichi Tsuzuki notes: 'Among all who contemplated him, there was a measure of bewilderment that such a mixture of incongruities should ever assemble in one man at the same time.' Henry once described himself as 'a vigorous and persistent enemy of Capitalism and Imperialism all over the world'. He thought nothing of consorting with Lavrenius the German anarchist, and would sit in Lavrenius's Paris lodgings while he tinkered with bombs and picric acid. He occasionally advocated assassination as a last resort and wrote a pamphlet on the subject in which he recommended strangulation and stabbing before bombs and poison. He could run amok with his political adversaries and was not above the strain of pure asininity that characterises the most earnest idealists. In a rare moment of self-deprecation he once described himself as 'a pestilent agitator and sanguinary revolutionist'.

Henry was fussy about his dress from boyhood; as a politician he was rarely seen in anything other than an immaculate frock-coat and top hat. His second wife likened him to 'a small polar bear in galoshes', while Bernard Shaw once quipped that he must have fallen out of the womb in morning dress. An extravagant grey beard heightened the grandeur in middle age and he would have cut a fine figure as an Old Testament prophet.

His literary enthusiasms were wide-ranging. As a young man he was close to Samuel Butler. It was Henry who advised Bernard Shaw to read Butler and the influence immediately became apparent in Shaw's work. He knew Oscar Wilde well and was intrigued by Wilde's *The Soul of Man Under Socialism*. His own writing can be emotionally exploitative, absurdly histrionic and devastatingly frank. One of his maxims was: 'Egotism may be pardoned; dullness is an unforgivable sin.' His historical works are more measured: 'There is something so fascinating and seductive in the effort to materialise in thought and in writing the insubstantial visions of history.'

Hyndman remained active to the last. In November 1921 he caught a chill while speaking in Enfield on 'Industrial Ruin and the Way Out'. The chill became double pneumonia. He recovered but his constitution had weakened and he succumbed to heart failure. Rosalind Hyndman noted: 'Quite suddenly and painlessly in the early morning of Tuesday, November 22, his heart gave way. I am not sure if he knew it, but he died in my arms as he had always wished to do.' In an obituary tribute, Rosalind quoted her husband's favourite epigram: 'Truth must ever be sectarian; error alone can afford to be catholic.' It is a suitable epitaph.

I consider Rosalind to have been one of the most extraordinary women of her generation and out of the same drawer as Eleanor Roosevelt. It was Lauren Bacall who said that being a widow is not a profession. Rosalind spent the next two years working for the SDF and writing a biography of her husband which has been dismissed by a contemporary critic as rhapsodist. It is in fact bright and graceful, anecdotal but perceptive. While the memoir occasionally degenerates into a roseate encomium, it is packed with insight and remains a balanced celebration of her husband's boundless faith in socialism as an international creed. She delivered the manuscript of *The Last Years of H.M. Hyndman* to her publisher, Grant Richards, at 4 o'clock on the afternoon of 9 April 1923. An agnostic veering towards atheism, she poisoned herself three hours later. The suicide note makes plain her dedication: 'If there is any sort of personal survival after death he may be wanting me. I must take the chance.'

5

Albert Trott

b: 6.2.1873, Melbourne, Australia.
d: 30.7.1914, Harlesden, Middlesex.

'Let no one say I was cleaning this gun:
I killed myself because
I wanted the sun
But got the moon.
Sanity came back too soon.'

Alan Sillitoe, 'Poem Left By A Dead Man', 1964

The subject remains among the most tragic cricketers we have seen and ultimately a grotesque parody of his own legend. He was brought up in Collingwood, Melbourne, where the Trott family was closely associated with sporting life in the city. His father, Adolphus, was a West Indies-born accountant and a keen cricket enthusiast, while his mother, Mary Ann, encouraged Albert and his brothers, Harry, Gus, Frederick and Walter, to play tennis. Harry would go on to captain Australia at cricket and Frederick became a club professional in Scotland. Albert played for Capulet Juniors before joining South Melbourne CC as a 17-year-old. His father was club scorer and Jack Pollard has recalled the florid eccentricity of his running commentaries: '"Another four to 'Arry... One more to 'Arry – an uppish stroke, I'll have to talk to him about that. A single to Albert, another four to 'Arry..."'

In the 1893–94 season Albert switched to East Melbourne CC where he was offered work as a ground bowler. He also played baseball for the club and acquired a reputation as a brilliant swerving pitcher who could throw a lamb chop past a wolf. Having watched how the prominent Test all-rounder George Giffen defended his wicket in a state cricket match, he determined to increase his powers of spin. His practice regime involved placing a tea chest in front of the wicket and forcing himself to turn the ball around the case and on to the stumps. Albert had made his debut for Victoria in the previous winter. He hovered on the fringe of the side for the next two seasons and performed competently, but was unable to hold down a regular place.

In November 1894 he showed much promise when taking 6 for 103 for Victoria against the England touring team. At the age of 21 he was selected for the third Test at Adelaide. Played amid temperatures of 105 degrees in the shade, the game saw Australia reach a total of 238 to which Albert contributed 38 not out. He bowled only three overs during the visitors' first innings of 124 while the English side was skittled out by George Giffen and Syd Callaway. Albert then breezed his way to an undefeated 72 in Australia's total of 411 and the *Melbourne Argus* congratulated him with: 'Even his comrades were astounded at the perfection of his play. With such a performance he jumps at once to the front rank of Australia's punishing batsmen.' In England's second innings Albert produced the finest bowling performance of his career, taking 8 for 43 from 27 overs. The *Argus* continued: 'No Australian colt ever came to the fore with such a rush, and it would be a waste of words to say how good his double was.' The *Sydney Morning Herald* enthused: 'Trott not only varied his pace with rare judgement but never once lost his length. It is not too much to say that his bowling was unplayable.'

In the fourth Test at Sydney Albert was laid out for several minutes by a bouncer from Tom Richardson. Three doctors and half a dozen undertakers forgot the game and were on their feet thinking they had a case on their hands. Albert recovered to score 85 not out in an hour and three quarters as part of a total of 284. The *Melbourne Leader* summarised the innings as '. . . a fine, free but never reckless game . . . it had the force and judgement of the most experienced of batsmen.' He was not required to bowl as his brother Harry, Charlie Turner and

Hughie Trumble skittled England out twice in the same day for totals of 65 and 72. The decisive fifth Test was at Melbourne and on the eve of the game, the Melbourne Argus noted: 'The popularity of Albert Trott is such that if he died at this moment – Heaven forbid! – there would be an irresistible demand for his immediate canonisation. Saint Albert would look well in a coloured window.' Albert failed with scores of 10 and 0 and he bowled indifferently. However, he had been the youngest player in the series and his career average for Australia of 102.5 remains a record.

Albert's performances for Victoria in the 1895–96 season were modest but his exclusion from the Australian team which toured England in 1896 under the captaincy of his brother Harry, fairly screamed for explanation. In this period a tour to England could keep a cricketer away from home for nine months. The Australian Cricket Board was anxious that players should be able to finalise their professional and domestic arrangements in good time, and had announced its squad before Albert's outstanding performances at Adelaide and Sydney. It seems to be a case of incredible intransigence, but Albert was never considered as a tourist.

Albert travelled with Harry and the rest of the team from Australia to England in the spring of 1896. His fare may have been paid by Lindfield CC, which he represented under the assumed name of 'Richardson' in several matches. Initially Albert lodged in Queen's Park, Brighton, with a family friend, John South. A retrospective piece in the *Sussex Daily News* described how in his first match for XVIII of Lindfield District, Albert took 8 for 12 against the Lindfield First XI. There was talk of him registering with Sussex but he gravitated to London, was offered a job on the MCC groundstaff and began to serve his residential qualification period for Middlesex. In his autobiography, Cyril Foley recalled how he stood alongside Albert in the slip cordon on a bitter morning at Lord's while Sir Timothy O'Brien was shivering in an ulster overcoat. Albert had no sweater and was wearing a flannel shirt that had been washed so many times you could see his skin through it. Foley observed that it was about to snow. Albert's response was characteristically disarming: 'I do hope so, I've never seen any.' Albert hardly set MCC alive with the bat and his bowling was inconsistent, a rare highlight being 6 for 103 against Oxford University.

He returned to Australia for the Australian season of 1896–97 and played for East Melbourne. In February he married 19-year-old Jessie Alveleta Rice. The couple left for England three days later after MCC sent out £70 for a first-class passage. Albert was unfaithful and wayward though never violent. The marriage was not a success. It was never dissolved but by 1906 the couple were going their separate ways. Albert and Jessie had two daughters, Jessie Annie and Hilda Mabel.

Albert spent the 1897 season qualifying for Middlesex and playing for MCC and Ground. He bowled competently and took 48 wickets at an average of 14. In the following winter he worked as a coach in Johannesburg and played for the Wanderers, taking all 10 wickets for 22 on a perfect pitch against the Pirates. By 1898 he had qualified for Middlesex. His extraordinary talent, high spirits and lack of guile soon made him the most popular man at Lord's. Despite missing the early part of the season when he hurt his hand during some horseplay in the pavilion at Fenner's, Albert took 108 wickets including 6 for 70 against Leicestershire. In the winter of 1898–99 Albert was selected for the England tour to South Africa. Before his decline he was widely admired for an incorrigibly cheerful temperament and team-mate Frank Mitchell noted that at the time Albert had a perpetual grin and a lead stomach. He failed with the bat in the two Tests but bowled superbly, his aggregate analysis being 17 wickets at 11.6. Playing against teams of as many as 18 players in up-country matches, he took 187 wickets at 9.46. He made one century, a ferocious 101 not out against Transvaal at Johannesburg during which he was particularly severe on Jimmy Sinclair.

Albert contributed much to team morale; he was regularly asked to speak after dinner and proved a superb deep-sea fisherman. However, he was ill-disciplined and wayward, building up huge debts with local bookmakers. At one point he approached Lord Hawke for a loan saying he wanted to send money to his brother in Australia, a deceit which Hawke found transparent. On the voyage home, passengers included the George Edwardes Gaiety Company, which took much pleasure in dressing the cricketers for a fancy dress ball. Pelham Warner went as a girl and was so convincing that he was obliged to fend off amorous advances from his team-mate Willis Cuttell. Albert came as a Russian Orthodox priest and cut a dashing figure on the dance floor.

In May 1899 he played the finest innings of his career, 164 for Middlesex vs Yorkshire at Lord's. He started quietly but began hitting Ted Wainwright ferociously and the last 137 runs came in 90 minutes. A Reuters report described how he hit a drive into the pavilion rails with such force that it bounced back to within a few yards of the stumps where an astonished Stanley Jackson meekly handed the ball back to the bowler. In the following August the visiting Australians played MCC. Albert had a few points to prove and Pelham Warner described how he 'found his range with a couple of sighting shots' off Victor Trumper. When Monty Noble served up a peach of a half-volley Albert laced it over the pavilion and into the garden of Number 6 Grove End Road. *Cricket* noted: 'The ball went just over the roof, hit a chimney behind it, and disappeared for the time being.' Albert loathed Noble and blamed him for his omission from the 1896 Australian touring party. As the ball sailed out of the ground he waved his bat around in exuberance. A few minutes later Albert dipped into the well once too often and holed out at third man for 43. To date nobody else has hit a ball over the Lord's pavilion.

The feat did him few favours. The resulting publicity went to his head; he started using ridiculously heavy bats and quickly degenerated into a slogger. Albert tried to replicate the hit in every subsequent innings with blind swiping which restricted what had been a wide repertoire of shots. Pelham Warner observed his antics and told him that he 'had sawdust for brains'. Albert scored 1,175 runs in 1899 and his unique mixture of medium pace and spin brought him 239 wickets at an average of 17.09. Writing in this year, C.B. Fry noted: 'He may be regarded as the most original, inventive and enterprising performer with the ball at present engaged in first-class cricket.'

On a drying pitch at Taunton in September of the following year, Albert took all 10 wickets for Middlesex against Somerset in 14 overs. His victims included Lionel Palairet, Sammy Woods and Jack Daniell. He took 211 first-class wickets in the season at 23.33. However, by 1901 he was degenerating into an alcoholic. He was also becoming musclebound and had lost the ability to bowl his killing faster ball. *Cricket* mused: 'He is a bowler who is wildly exciting and vastly disappointing by turns.'

Albert had a happy knack of picking up lucrative employment at the end of the English season and he spent the winter of 1901–02 in New Zealand as a coach at Hawke's Bay, Napier. By now he was drinking heavily, putting on weight and suffering from dropsy. The highlight of the following season was a ferocious innings against Somerset at Lord's. He gave a sitter to Len Braund in the slips when he had scored 5 but went on to savage 103 in 70 minutes. He returned to Napier in the winter and played against a visiting team led by Pelham Warner. He was co-opted into the touring side when it travelled to Australia but did nothing with bat or ball.

Albert returned to England with Warner's tourists in the spring. Sir Pelham recalled: 'Now Trott though he had travelled much, had no gift for foreign languages, certainly not French, and on his way home to England via Marseilles, Paris and Dover, he was asked by a fellow-professional which was the first stop between Paris and Dover. Taking his ticket out of his pocket, on which was written, "Prix" so many francs, he replied: "Why, Prix (which he pronounced as if it were spelt pricks), you fool!" "Pricks" was good, but "you fool" was even better.'

Albert's overall form in 1903 was modest, though his occasional brilliance helped Middlesex to win the championship under the captaincy of another future alcoholic, Gregor MacGregor. Recognising Albert as an underachiever, MacGregor once berated him with: 'If you had a head instead of a turnip, Alberto, you'd be the best bowler in the world.' By now Albert's alcoholism was developing from a fitful malady into a permanent disease. His marriage broke down in 1904 soon after the birth of his second daughter, Hilda Mabel.

There was a slight recovery in the winter of 1905–06, during which he stayed off the sauce and held down a lucrative job as coach in the indoor nets at Camberwell Baths. By the spring of 1906 he was living near the bone and his intake of beer and whisky had made him balloon to 18 stone. Albert was at the thin end of a familiar wedge. In the following summer he began to lose his bowling action and at times his best prospect of getting rid of a batsman was by breathing on him. Albert soon went off the rails, becoming a barfly and worse. After taking a wicket at Lord's he would rush to the tavern under the grandstand where one of his cronies would always stand him a scotch.

The remnants of Albert's extraordinary talent surfaced during his benefit match in May 1907, the fixture being Middlesex vs Somerset at

Lord's. On the final day, Albert took four wickets with successive balls, his victims being Albert Lewis, Edward Poyntz, Sammy Woods and Ernest Robson. Six minutes later, Osbert Mordaunt, Prebendary Archdale Palmer Wickham and Albert Bailey were back in the hutch; Albert had taken another hat-trick. His analysis was 7 for 20 from 8 overs and he also took two catches. A good deal of tripe has been peddled to the effect that by curtailing his own benefit, Albert 'bowled himself into the bankruptcy court'. He may have cost himself a few gate receipts on the final afternoon but he found consolation by getting blind drunk on whisky with fellow Anglo-Australian Sammy Woods. Albert still possessed the relics of a beguiling tenor and the pair spent the evening singing Gus Ellen numbers. Later that year a well-known prostitute was murdered in Taunton. It emerged that Albert was a regular client. He was never even remotely implicated in the killing but the newspaper coverage did his public persona little good.

Albert had an accordion of a forehead. His John Newcombe moustache was set off by a pair of syrupy eyes and he could have been mistaken for a music-hall comic. In his pomp he was boundlessly powerful, and before it became inflated by dropsy he relied on an exceptionally powerful upper body. Albert's simplicity, candour and decency endeared him to many in English sporting society. His nicknames included 'Alberto', 'Turnip-head' and 'The Albertrott'. Pelham Warner is unusually warm in his summation: 'Poor Alberto. He was a good soul. He had a heart of gold and was as simple as a child, and he was one of those people who compel affection.'

His intelligence was limited and at times he could appear simpleminded. A revealing obituary tribute in the *Referee* concluded: 'I think Trott's misfortune was that, with a true genius for cricket, he had no resources outside the game.' Albert's social skills were excellent and he mixed comfortably at all levels. He certainly nourished his own myth and the contemporary journalist Jimmy Catton noted: 'The "Albertrott" was a strange bird. A cricketing genius; but most eccentric both in action and speech. How Trott did orate, how he told me everything he ever did, the date on which each event happened, and the exact figures he established. What a marvellous memory, thought I. When I came to write Trott's story, I discovered that it was teeming with inaccuracies, and that scarcely a date or a figure was correct. He was undeceived in print.'

When in form Albert scored freely all round the wicket. His bat resembled a club and Albert Knight once described it as 'a savage beast of a thing'. Many of his runs came from front-foot drives which he hit cleanly with a huge follow-through. As a bowler, Albert generated a unique mixture of leg-breaks and off-cutters at a healthy pace from a low but sideways-on action. He swung the ball prodigiously in the air and had a vicious swinging yorker which he could bowl at will. This was complemented by a funereal slower ball which he disguised superbly. C.B. Fry's summation of Albert's bowling described it as '...exceptionally interesting to deal with, since it is quite impossible to deduce what to expect from each successive ball'. Despite being profoundly unintellectual, he had an enduring preoccupation with the technicalities of his art and spent many hours discussing ballistics with Middlesex team-mate Bernard Bosanquet, populariser of the googly.

Albert took 100 wickets in a season on seven occasions and deafened umpires with his appeals. If he found himself on a damp pitch he would resort to off-breaks which he bowled with an extraordinary grip akin to that employed by a baseball pitcher delivering a 'knuckleball'. His baseball experience gave him the ability to pull the ball back in the air and force the batsman to play early.

With hair-trigger reflexes and hands like landing nets, Albert pouched extraordinary catches throughout his career and he fielded superbly to his own bowling. His favourite position was second slip but he was secure under high catches and had a terrific arm when he went out into the country. Again, his baseball background proved invaluable. He would often slide into the ball before picking up and throwing in one movement, a technique that was 90 years ahead of its time. Albert expected high standards of fielding from everybody and Brian Bearshaw recalls that after a young and dandified Middlesex professional lost a match through careless fielding, Albert put him across his knee in the dressing room and spanked him with a hairbrush.

By 1910 Albert was in abject decline. He was playing from memory and Middlesex dropped him after two matches. The last flicker of the lamp came in 1911 when he took 9 for 89 over two innings for MCC and Ground against Leicestershire. Knowing that he was a spent force, the *Wisden* correspondent was puzzled and commented on his 'unexpectedly deadly bowling'. In November 1913 Albert was devastated by the death of his father. Between 1912 and 1914 he put up a creditable fight against the onset of severe dropsy and he stood as a first-class umpire. His eyesight and hearing were unimpaired and he combined a superb technical knowledge with an ability to empathise with players. There is little doubt that he was a highly competent umpire. However, staying on his feet for long periods was a problem and his last match was Surrey vs Somerset at The Oval in May 1914.

The dividing line between an icon and a relic is a thin one. By July Albert was receiving intensive care at St Mary's Hospital in Praed Street. He was barely sentient; according to a *Daily Telegraph* obituary, 'A more pathetic figure in later days than Trott it would be difficult to imagine. He was a broken man, young yet old, and for many months terribly conscious that he had already squeezed the best out of life.' At the time the chief consulting physician at St Mary's was Sir John Broadbent, whose speciality was heart disease. As a keen club cricketer and a member of MCC, he took much interest in Albert, spending many hours at his bedside. While Albert recalled his cricket career and complained about the tedium of hospital life, Broadbent uncovered a hulk of fallen, bloated muscle. Albert was suffering from congestive cardiac failure with complications from nephralgia. He never understood his precise condition; as Cara says of Lord Marchmain at the end of *Brideshead Revisited*, he was 'dying of a long word'.

On 28 July Albert decided that he would go out with his dignity intact. Despite protests from his nurses, he checked out of St Mary's and took a cab to his lodgings in Harlesden, tapping a hospital orderly for the fare. Over in Austria a massive army was being raised to attack Serbia while memorial services were being held all over Europe for the murdered Archduke Ferdinand. If Albert had been in any state to look at the newspaper billboards as he left central London he might have seen a *Pall Mall Gazette* placard: 'Entire Continent Arming.' There was a *Götterdämmerung* flavour to the whole week; it ruined the rest of the twentieth century for all of us. Albert spent the next 48 hours in extreme discomfort from dropsy, insomnia and related melancholia. In the early afternoon of 30 July he asked his landlady, Mrs Crowhurst, to get him a sleeping draught. She trotted down Denbigh Road to a pharmacist but was told that her tenant would need a prescription. Albert's anguished reaction was: 'Oh, dear! I can never go through another night.'

Albert loved life too much to let it go off easily so the end was messy. Mrs Crowhurst cooked him some lunch and he retired to his room where he drank a huge quantity of cheap beer. At about four o'clock he shot himself through the head with a small Browning revolver. He was spared additional trauma. A week later the lamps went out all over Europe.

6

Cecil Parkin

b: 18.2.1886, Eaglescliffe, County Durham.
d: 15.6.1943, Manchester, Lancashire.

A Bowler there was name of Parkin
Who had too much liking for larkin';
He made people stare
And provoked a 'Lord's' prayer
And he set all the little dogs barkin'.

Cecil Parkin, 'Pome' on Himself', 1923

Cecil Parkin will be remembered not just as a great spin bowler but as an even greater entertainer. As a character he was a rare bloom and an outstanding embodiment of what Alistair Cooke's father used to call 'a card and no mistake'. 'Cec' was a unique figure who struck the imagination of thousands indelibly.

In the 1920s he was one of few bowlers on the county circuit willing to stand up to the equally eccentric George Gunn. In his prime Gunn would often stride several paces down the wicket as the bowler approached the crease. On a famous occasion Cec held on to the ball, advanced up the pitch and stared at Gunn as long as Scrooge recognising Marley's ghost: 'Was there something you wanted to say to me, George?'

Cec was brought up at Norton near Stockton-on-Tees. His father, Henry, was employed by the North Eastern Railway as stationmaster and the family lived on the premises. Henry was a competent club cricketer and recalled that his son's first gurglings sounded like 'How's that?' By the age of 12 Cec was playing senior cricket for Norton-on-Tees. He held his own, and noted in his memoirs: 'As a youngster my principal qualifications were my batting and fielding; indeed, I was regarded as the best outfield the club possessed for I was a fast runner and had a safe pair of hands.' At Norton Cec came under the tuition of the England leg-spinner Charles Townsend, whom he described as 'the best left-hand batsman I ever saw and the man who taught me more about cricket than anyone else'. As an aspiring pace merchant Cec weighed only eight stone and was prone to over-tax his strength.

He was spotted by a talent scout from North Ormesby CC who offered him a professional contract when he was 16. His father was anxious that he learn a trade and insisted that Cec finish his apprenticeship as a patternmaker. Three years later Cec signed as a professional with Ossett CC in West Yorkshire. He took 116 wickets in his first season and impressed the great slow left-armer George Hirst, who suggested he have a trial for Yorkshire.

In July 1906 he made his debut for Yorkshire against Gloucestershire at Headingley. The match was ruined by rain but Cec adapted well to the first-class game and bowled eight overs, taking 2 for 23. He also fielded superbly in the covers. Sadly, there were complaints from MCC, its committee having somehow spotted that he had been born in Durham. Yorkshire were obliged to release him but the county was not exactly devastated by the loss. Cec was an individualist from the cradle; his high spirits had already ruffled a few feathers at Headingley and Lord Hawke, the supremo of Yorkshire cricket, was heard to remark: 'That fellow Parkin is very sure of himself, I must say.'

In the following season Cec signed for Tunstall CC in Staffordshire. Here he saw Syd Barnes in his pomp and resolved to make himself into a spin bowler. Cec decided that his wife, Jennie, should act as a batting guinea pig and he paid extravagant tributes to her in his memoirs, recalling how she would often return from net sessions with chipped fingers, bruised thighs or a black eye. Jennie cried when the ball rapped her on the hands but nothing would make her leave the wicket. None of this is to Cec's credit: his desire to excel as a bowler was now approaching mania.

In the spring of 1910 he demonstrated his experimental spin bowling to Syd Barnes. Barnes recognised Cec as one of his own and recommended him to Church and Oswaldtwistle CC in the Lancashire League. The club paid Cec handsomely and set him up with a grocery shop at the tram terminus. Cec attracted much attention with his performances for Church but he would not bowl spin in a serious match and continued with fast medium. He began playing for Lancashire in 1914. His debut for the county was sensational; on a pitch giving him little help he took 7 for 65 and 7 for 34 against Leicestershire at Aigburth. The *Manchester Guardian* enthused: 'His good style, his accuracy, the remarkable variety of balls he has command of, his briskness and enthusiasm, and the amount of life he threw into every delivery would have picked him out in any company.' Cec played five more games that year in between league commitments and finished with 34 wickets at an average of 15.73. By the end of the season the acting Lancashire captain, Jack Sharp, had warmed to him considerably. As the pair arrived for a fixture at Canterbury, Sharp ushered him towards a dressing-room, where they came upon the veteran Kent wicketkeeper, Fred Huish. Sharp warned Huish: 'Fred, just wait till this lad gets at you; you'll wonder what day it is!'

Cec spent the war working as a fuel overseer at a chemical company near Oswaldtwistle. He played cricket on Saturdays for the Bradford League side Undercliffe alongside two Test players, Charlie Llewellyn and George Gunn. In 1919 he signed for Rochdale. At the first home fixture of the season he was about to open the bowling when a brass band struck up with a Sousa march in nearby Dane Street. Cec stopped his run-up and started over again, making sure that his movements were in time to the music. His antics shocked many but endeared him to the club's president, the millionaire financier and theatrical impresario Jimmy White. White controlled Daly's Theatre in the West End and made sure that the hospitality tent featured leading actresses and a bevy of chorus girls. During the annual grudge match against Littleborough, White paraded round the boundary rope with Evelyn 'Boo' Laye. Earlier in the year she had been an enormous hit in Noël Coward's *Bitter Sweet* and she was celebrated for her recording of 'I'll Be Seeing You'. Cec was taken with her and the pair performed the song as a duet.

In the same season Cec appeared in the Gentlemen vs Players fixture at Lord's, where he took 6 for 85 from 39.5 overs in the Gentlemen's first innings. By now he was confident enough to bowl spin in major matches. He dismissed the first five players in the amateur batting order, his victims including Donald Knight and Pelham Warner. Another highlight in 1919 was a haul of 14 wickets in the Roses match at Old Trafford. The *Manchester Guardian* noted: 'Parkin was most resourceful, seeking out the weak points in the batsmen's defence audaciously.'

Spectators at Old Trafford in 1920 included a 12-year-old future journalist. Now 92 years old, he still has pin-sharp memories of Cecil and recalled in a letter to me: 'Parkin was a born clown. We awaited his arrival as if he were George Robey. I learned to do the trick for which he was most famous: tipping the vamp of his right shoe and letting a rolled ball run up his trouser leg till he collected it at the waist. With the Blackpool School XI, this was probably the most distinguished feature of my bowling.' The youngster was Alistair Cooke.

In May 1920 Cec made national news when he walked off the pitch during a game between Rochdale and Littleborough after having three plumb lbw appeals turned down. His action was premeditated and not petulant. Cec was making a statement about the lbw law. At the time batsmen could pad up safely to anything pitched outside off stump without offering a stroke. (The law was not changed until 1937.) Cec could turn his off-break a yard on most club pitches and in the manner of Jim Laker some 30 years later, he often bowled round the wicket on a pitch that was taking spin. Even rudimentary geometry indicated that this would make his break less acute and give him a better chance of trapping batsmen lbw. Sadly, at the time there was prejudice amongst umpires against giving any lbw decisions to a bowler coming from round the wicket, regardless of the type of spin or mode of delivery.

Cec received widespread support in the press. Jimmy White withdrew Rochdale from the Central Lancashire League and the side played friendly games for the rest of the season. White even considered plunging some of his fortune into creating a rival league. The dispute was settled by town councillors during the winter and Rochdale, with Cec as its professional, returned to the fold in the following year.

Cec was a surprise selection for Johnny Douglas's England touring party to Australia in the winter of 1920–21. He was chosen as a last-minute replacement for the irascible Syd Barnes, who had rejected the terms of his proposed contract. Cec's broad North Country humour and Sid James laugh sent shockwaves through some of the first-class passengers on the SS *Osterley*. He had not travelled by sea before and was seen as a greenhorn and fair game for burlesque. Soon after he boarded, the Yorkshire amateur Rockley Wilson told him that there was a fire in the stokehold and poor Cec rushed down to the engine room with a bucket of water. When the ship was sailing on the Red Sea, Percy Fender advised him that flying fish might come through his porthole and bite lumps out of him and he should keep the window closed at all times. As a result Cec nearly passed out in sweltering heat. In an uncharacteristically frisky mood, Johnny Douglas joined in the fun and informed Cec that there would be an enormous bump when the ship crossed the equator. Cec spent hours consulting a map and trying to calculate when this would occur.

It is of course possible that to an extent he was playing the faux-naïf. Nothing could dampen his high spirits and on the night that the ship left Naples he decided to observe the eruption at Stromboli. Cec reasoned that there was no point in doing this alone and kept other members of the party awake by organising a singsong. Cec employed his resonant baritone and cavernous lungs to lead the cricketers, and even persuaded some of the more urbane amateurs like Rockley Wilson to join in his favourite numbers. These included 'Lily Of Laguna' and the Al Bowlly classic 'You're A Sweetheart'.

Like so many cricketers, Cec was an accomplished conjuror. Johnny Douglas appreciated his abilities and often invited him to entertain lady passengers. Employing Jack Hobbs as his stooge, Cec's show-stopper was a trick called 'The Fallen Belgian Soldier' that involved a clay pipe. Cec had a myriad variants on the three-card trick and was showered with presents of chocolates and cigars after his perform-ances. He seldom got to enjoy these, since Jack Hobbs and Harry Makepeace would steal them from his cabin. Cec also excelled at deck tennis and acquitted himself well against Gerald Paterson, the Australian Davis Cup player.

Cec was uncomfortable on his arrival in Australia. He had little liking for the intense heat and was obliged to wear dark glasses for the first week. He suffered with a variety of skin infections and was further unsettled in Brisbane when he came within inches of being impaled by the shaft of a butcher's cart. His bowling in the opening games was unimpressive and the Australian press corps was disappointed with the player who had been hailed as England's 'mystery bowler'. A wag from the *Sydney Morning Herald* suggested that the only mystery was when he was going to get a ball to turn. He was wayward with his faster ball and Herbert Strudwick needed all of his agility when keeping wicket to his erratic bowling.

Cec came good in the third Test at Adelaide, where he took 5 for 60 from 20 overs in Australia's first innings, his victims including Herbie Collins, Jack Ryder and Bertie Oldfield. It was during this game that Cec watched Charlie Kelleway labour to 147 in seven hours and commented: 'Kelleway might be a good player in the next world where time does not matter.' Cec was successful in state and up-country games and with 73 victims he took more wickets than any other MCC bowler. Cec was tetchy about occasional newspaper criticism of his performances and developed a lifelong hatred of E.H.D. Sewell, a correspondent with the *Morning Post*. He was also annoyed by a Sydney cub reporter who was trying to confirm rumours that Jack Hobbs was consumptive. Cec's comment was: 'Yes, but only at mealtimes.'

He later complained that in serious matches Johnny Douglas cramped his style by instructing him to aim outside off stump. Cec adored his captain all the same and had considerable rapport with him. The following anecdote is a peach and warrants quotation. However, given the prevailing relationships between amateurs and professionals the story should be treated with suspicion. Many commentators noted that Douglas frequently over-bowled himself. One of these protracted spells came at the Melbourne Cricket Ground, which boasted a scoreboard giving a full breakdown of performances. Douglas was bowling with his back to this and there is a legend that Cec screamed: 'Mr Douglas, if you won't stop bowling, put yourself on at the other end where you can read your analysis!'

There was another Ashes series during the summer of 1921 and the teams travelled back to England on the same ship. The voyage was a riot. Cheered on by his colleagues, the Australian captain, Warwick

Armstrong, popped down to the boiler room on a daily basis and shovelled coal into the furnace in order to stay at what for him was a positively svelte 21 stone. Cec contributed to much of the fun and the Australian all-rounder Charlie Macartney recalled: 'Parkin kept the ship alive with his vitality. He operated the "tote" every day and was the most successful auctioneer in the Calcutta sweep that I have met on any voyage.'

In the Old Trafford Test Cec opened the England attack and took 5 for 38 from 29.4 overs. The match featured an extraordinary innings by Herbie Collins who, much to Cec's disgust, spent almost five hours making 40 runs. Lionel Tennyson, a grandson of the poet, had replaced Johnny Douglas as England captain. A.A. Thomson recalls: 'It was during Collins's Methuselah-like effort that a spectator in his agony called out to England's skipper: "Hey, Tennyson, read him some of thi Grandad's poems." And Parkin called back: "He *has* done. The beggar's been asleep for hours!"' Rain on the first day ruled out a victory for either side and as a jape Tennyson asked Cec to open England's second innings. He produced some consummate clowning and made 23 before being caught by Herbie Collins from the bowling of Tommy Andrews. Cec played his first full season for Lancashire that year and turned in several fine performances including 7 for 83 against Sussex at Old Trafford. He was the first bowler in the country to reach 100 wickets and the *Cricketer* picked him out as an exceptional talent but cautioned: 'He is a man of moods and requires careful supervision.'

In county championship matches Cec took 172 wickets for Lancashire in 1922 at an average of 16.52. By now he had befriended the *Manchester Guardian* cricket correspondent, Neville Cardus. In May 1923 Cardus was enjoying the excellent wine cellar at the Granby Hotel in Gravesend during the Kent vs Lancashire fixture. On the morning of the first day Cec took a look at the wicket and strolled into the press tent: 'Mr Cardus, you can cancel your hotel booking for tomorrow night.' Lancashire struggled to 203 all out on a crumbling pitch whereupon Cec took 7 for 24 to dismiss Kent for 72. Lancashire then increased their lead by 125. Supported by Cec, Dick Tyldesley turned his leg-breaks square to skittle out Kent for 131 and give the visitors victory by 125 runs inside two days.

Cec's career received an almost fatal jolt during the Edgbaston Test against South Africa in June 1924. He had a quiet game and bowled only 16 overs in the whole match. At the time he had a ghosted column in the *Weekly Despatch*. After the game Cec asked a Manchester-based journalist, Johnny Clegg, to wire some copy for him. Cec did not ask to see a proof and did not even bother to suggest a subject. A few days later he was appalled to read the *Weekly Despatch*'s 40-point banner headline: 'Cecil Parkin refuses to play for England again.' The article suggested that Cec bitterly resented being under-bowled in the Test. Cec had no strong views on the matter and was known to have a wealth of affection and respect for his captain, Gilligan.

Cec's county colleagues advised him to send a disclaimer to Reuters and the other wire agencies but the damage had already been done. Pelham Warner read about the incident, rubbed his pious hands and immediately exercised a witless spleen in the *Cricketer*: 'Something more than a private apology is necessary...A frank public apology, and he will earn the respect of cricketers. Otherwise the world will regard him as the first cricketing Bolshevist.' No student of socialism and an indifferent student of cricket, Warner was forgetting Henry Hyndman and Charlie Parker.

Cec was hauled in front of the Lancashire committee who demanded to know the name of the offending journalist. There were widely held suspicions that it was Johnny Clegg but the club could only take action if Cec named him, something which he steadfastly refused to do. Fortunately the committee did not adopt Pelham Warner's McCarthyite technique of establishing silence as an admission of guilt. With his mind in turmoil, Cec managed to produce one of the finest bowling spells of his career when he took 9 for 32 for Lancashire against Leicestershire at Ashby de la Zouch. However, he was devastated by the Clegg incident and it was his last performance of real note. As a player Cec descended into a dazed parody of his younger self and team-mates noted that the spring had gone from his stride for good.

Arthur Gilligan was a popular figure throughout cricket circles and fans in his home county of Sussex were enraged by the perceived criticism of their captain. Cec received an assortment of telegrams, some of which are choice: 'Brighton, July 28 – Cecil Parkin, Esq, Old

Trafford. Will you accept engagement for pantomime? Own terms. Fred Karno.' The same day from Hove: 'Selected to play for *Weekly Despatch*. Will you bowl first? Gilligan not playing. Lewes Ladies' Stoolball Association.' Gilligan, the Lancashire committee and the serious cricket journalists were all supportive, but Cec took the matter to heart and convinced himself that he was no longer in favour with the public. Much of his natural gaiety disappeared permanently.

He remained his own worst enemy and later in the year he wrote an asinine article which attacked the most powerful figure in the cricket world, Lord Hawke. Hawke had just made an infamous speech at a Yorkshire CCC meeting in which he ended his remarks with: 'Pray God no professional will ever captain England.' At this stark level the sentiment was certainly offensive but Cec read the quote out of context. All Hawke was saying was that he would rue the day when there were no amateurs capable of holding down a place in the England side on playing ability. Cec may well have been deliberately fattening his myth as a maverick.

At the time the All Blacks had begun a visit to England under the captaincy of Cliff Porter, and Jimmy White had invited Cec to attend a welcome dinner for the tourists at the Piccadilly Hotel. Cec was followed down to London by a posse of North Country journalists, all of them anxious to inflame his perceived war of words with Lord Hawke. Cec made it to the dinner, but became distraught later on when a photographer forced the door to his hotel room and took a picture of him in bed. David Foot has recalled Cec's reactions when he got back to Lancashire: 'At home he buried his head in his hands and turned to his wife: "I feel unwanted for no just reason. I think I'll chuck county cricket. There's no joy in being cold-shouldered..."' Cec had always been touchy about his brief career at Headingley and was further upset when Hawke issued a press statement which declared: 'If Parkin was still a Yorkshire player I would make sure that he never stepped on to a cricket field anywhere in the county.'

The authorities at Old Trafford now felt that perhaps Cec was more trouble than he was worth. Despite all the support that the club had given him, he remained inordinately aggressive in his wage demands. He stayed with Lancashire for another two seasons and played his last county matches in June 1926. The final cause of his departure was his refusal to act as twelfth man in a game against Warwickshire. He was still bowling well and in his penultimate county match he took 4 for 47 from 19.2 overs against Gloucestershire. There were mixed feelings on both sides and during a meeting with the Lancashire president, Sir Edwin Stockton, Cec became hysterical, telling Stockton: 'God has given me these hands to work with, and I will carry on with them even if I have to be a tramp.' Cec later confessed: 'I am not ashamed to say I have cried often about that parting...' He had between five and ten years' first-class cricket left in him and his departure was widely regarded as a sad waste of talent.

Cec once said to Neville Cardus: 'As soon as Ah stop playin' Ah'll do as them Roman Emperors used to do. Ah'll get into a hot bath – and cut me ruddy throat, so Ah will.' After leaving Lancashire Cec spent several months in a fog of bewilderment and cynicism. However, he rallied and went on to enjoy a reasonably happy retirement. In the following year he acquired the lease of the Lord Nelson in Blackpool. His social skills had not deserted him and he was a success as a publican. Cec became a popular figure in the area and played Saturday afternoon cricket for Blackpool as an amateur until 1929 when he joined East Lancashire.

In 1931 he moved to Stockport where he managed the Dog and Partridge. Cec made good newspaper copy throughout his life and he hit the headlines in October of the following year when he was fined for serving drinks out of hours. Cec pleaded not guilty and wept in court: 'I can stand in any pulpit in the town and as a Christian can honestly say that no beer was served in my house before 12 o'clock. It has broken my heart after all I have done for the police.' Cec was persuaded by his wife Jennie to leave the licensing trade when he began to show too much fondness for his own stock and was plagued by attacks of gout. He is known to have consumed large amounts of white curaçao, which was responsible for him putting on much weight.

Cec could still bowl competently and returned to club cricket as a professional in the mid 1930s, turning out for East Lancashire, Tonge and Levenshulme, for whom he played his last game in 1935. By now he was a respected lay preacher with a nice line in revivalist rhetoric. He gave talks all over the north of England in which he combined sporting and religious topics and quoted at extraordinary length from the Bible. He had become less mercenary and refused to take a fee, describing himself as a 'missionary'. His rift with Lancashire CCC finally healed and in 1938 he was employed by the county as a bowling coach. During the early part of the war he organised charity matches, standing in them himself as umpire. He was a resourceful administrator and persuaded many of his cronies to turn out for the games. Cec also wrote extensively for Sunday newspapers in the north, reporting on rugby league as well as cricket. He had acquired an understandable fear of ghost writers. Cec invested in a typewriter the size of a small printing press and insisted on being able to dictate his (surprisingly literate) copy direct to the sports desk.

Cec died of throat cancer in June 1943 at the age of 57. With a last extravagant and macabre gesture, he demanded that his ashes should be strewn over the Old Trafford wicket as a prelude to the next major game at the ground. A.A. Thomson once mused about Cec's ghost: 'Scatter me from the Stretford End, lads; I could always find a spot from there.' In July 1944 the North of England played the Royal Australian Air Force. At the ages of 72 and 66 respectively, the great England and Yorkshire all-rounders George Hirst and Wilfred Rhodes crossed the Pennines together by train to pay their respects. The journey exhausted them, and the pair appeared so frail when they arrived at the Old Trafford pavilion that Reggie Spooner, the Lancashire president, was reluctant to let them walk out to the middle. Cec's widow Jennie assessed the situation and offered each of them one of her sturdy arms. The trio made its way to the square, scattered the ashes and placed red and white roses on the wicket.

Subsequent proceedings were simple but equally poetic; Flight Sergeant Cyril Washbrook eased his way to 133 not out, observed by an unknown 24-year-old Flight Officer, one Keith Miller. Hirst and Rhodes watched proceedings from the press box and were put on a train by Don Davies. They blubbed all the way home.

Cec's general characteristics included spontaneity and impulsiveness, tempered by an incongruous mercenary streak and lack of subtlety in his financial dealings. Making a wages offer to Cec for a season of club cricket was like the first bid you make for a rug in a Middle East bazaar. He had seven children and was acutely aware of the need to support them. Brian Bearshaw recalls how one of his fans produced a newspaper review: 'It says here, Ciss, that you're the best bowler in England.' The response was characteristically pragmatic: 'Ay, but that doesn't feed my young devils, does it?' Cec was undoubtedly mercenary but any criticism of this angered him. With fellow maverick Syd Barnes he was one of the few players to represent England while not attached to a first-class county, believing he could make more money as a club professional.

Cec was an oddity in that he was both a humorist and a wit. He is best remembered for verve, candour, innate decency and uncontrollably high spirits. One of his charms was that you never knew what he was going to do or say next. Cardus once described him as 'a clown in the tradition of Grock'. Now a forgotten figure, Grock (christened Karl Adrian Wettach) was a Swiss-born circus and variety hall performer at the turn of the century who achieved fame throughout Europe playing 24 musical instruments as part of an extraordinary mime act.

Cec's own slapstick could be creasingly funny. Occasionally when beaten in the field he would pretend to stop the ball, using his excellent sleight of hand to produce an orange from his pocket and splatter it into the gloves of wicketkeeper George Duckworth. Cec once turned up at a cricket debate only to discover that he agreed with the opposing speaker. He spent the rest of the evening doing card tricks. His patter when performing these was superb and in his flat, North Country accent he could keep both adults and children amused.

Cec was only too happy to play the goat but had an agile intelligence and saw through anything resembling pomposity. The hatred of Lord Hawke is hardly surprising. Cec could disarm rational judgement with his charisma. He was by no means inept socially; he knew when and at whom to throw the pie and mixed successfully at all levels. He was fond of the Somerset amateur Guy Earle, whom he once berated for hitting him out of the Taunton ground. At the post-match dinner Cec approached Earle and claimed 4s 6d: 'I needed a taxi to get the ball back!' Cec treated much of life as theatre and Raymond Robertson-Glasgow recalled: 'He enjoyed fantasy, experiment and laughter. He loved cricket from top to toe and expected some fun in return.'

> I found fun in cricket and made fun for the spectators, not
> as a buffoon but as an entertainer who never forgot that
> the public go to cricket matches to be entertained. Cricket
> should not be dull, or merely a battle of wits; it should be
> as bright as the players can make it.
>
> Cecil Parkin, *Cricket Triumphs and Troubles*, 1936

Commenting on Cec's many indiscretions, Rex Pogson reflected: 'His repentance was usually sincere and disarming and his hold on the public's loyalty never wavered.' It is a tribute to Cec's personality that even after the incident involving Arthur Gilligan, the Sussex captain had no hesitation in writing the foreword to one of Cec's volumes of autobiography. When reviewing Lancashire cricket in the *Manchester Guardian*, Cardus often likened Cec to Henry Machin, hero of Arnold Bennett's *The Card*. The abiding impression is of a man with deep and stubborn convictions but considerable mental confusion and a fatal streak of impulsiveness. Cec was characterised by innocence, turbulence and a capacity for wonder.

Sadly, all three volumes of Cec's autobiography are evasive as to his home life and activity outside cricket. Like Sir Donald Bradman's memoirs, they are tinny with self-justification. Cec goes through every thing ever said against him and there is a tedious 'Je ne regrette rien' theme running through the books. Much of it is very sorry stuff and brings to mind Clive James's quip that ideally a trilogy should consist of two volumes. What does emerge is that Cec worshipped George Hirst and Maurice Tate. He hated the distinction between amateurs and professionals, particularly the use of 'Mr' or its omission in scorecards and newspapers. Cec wanted to be accepted as a gentleman not a genius: 'The only distinctive mark of class worth a cricketer's attention is *character* – honest nature and that decency of behaviour which is inborn and given to the poor man as abundantly as to the rich.'

In conversation Cec rated Charlie Macartney as the consummate all-rounder. His opinion of contemporary batsmen is harder to gauge. In his early memoirs he recalled having seen both Grace and Ranji, though both were in the twilight of their careers. He placed them above Bradman but in a subsequent book he rated The Don as the finest batsman of all time. The inconsistency suggests that the memoirs were heavily ghosted. Cardus noted this and pondered: 'It is wise not to be rude about autobiographies; you never know who has written them!'

As a youth Cec was slim to the point of being gawky. In middle age his drinking made him overweight but in evening dress he could still look as sleek as a seal. Cec had a face only a mother could love, with a lantern jaw, ears like a bat and a hairline as low as Boris Karloff's. During his first few years as a pace bowler he was genuinely quick but he eventually settled for an extravagant mixture of spin and swerve. Johnny Moyes recalled: 'When I first saw him at Melbourne in 1920 I rubbed my eyes in wonder.' Just occasionally he seemed bent on demonstrating his own virtuosity rather than dismissing the batsman. As a mature bowler his stock delivery was an off-break and he varied the pace and flight of this superbly. In his dotage, Ranji is said to have watched Cec on a turning pitch and confessed: 'I'd have had to be at my best to stop him.'

Cec had an ungainly run-up and arrived at the stumps in a flurry of limbs but the final arc of his arm was high and graceful. Alistair Cooke recalls: 'He had a unique and rather grotesque approach to the wicket – his left arm going high in a sort of Hitler salute.' In charity and festi-val matches Cec would occasionally bring his right hand over empty and deliver an underarm lob with his left. His appeals were deafening and Ronald Mason described them as 'a statement of fact rather than a request for information'.

As a cricketer Cec belongs with 'Chuck' Fleetwood-Smith and Herbert Hordern. He was a spin bowler of massive if not unique talent who only realised a fraction of his potential. Cec spent much of his life in cap and bells and was rarely taken seriously, but nobody in their senses could fail to be captivated. His blunt integrity and transparent honesty were ultimately his downfall. Cec may have displayed some self-conscious gaucherie but it was always part of the whole man.

7

Richard Barlow

b: 29.5.1851, Heaton, Bolton, Lancashire.
d: 31.7.1919, Stanley Park, Blackpool, Lancashire.

For the field is full of shades as I near the shadowy coast,
And a ghostly batsman plays to the bowling of a ghost,
And I look through my tears on a soundless clapping host,
As the run-stealers flicker to and fro,
To and fro:-
O my Hornby and my Barlow long ago !

'At Lord's', Francis Thompson, 1907

The title of the poem is a misnomer. Thompson was not at Lord's in 1907 when he wrote it and his tears were the by-product of an addiction to opium that would kill him in the same year. He had been invited to the Middlesex vs Lancashire fixture but illness had prevented him from attending. The piece was written as a gesture of thanks to friends who had issued the invitation. As a 19-year-old truant from medical school, he had been a spectator at Old Trafford in 1878 when Lancashire played Gloucestershire and the 'run-stealers' put on a first-wicket stand of 108.

Ten years later, having failed in attempts to join the medical profession and the priesthood, Thompson was sleeping under newspapers and eating vegetable refuse in Covent Garden. (Philip Larkin once said that he was seeking to avoid crushing responsibilities like getting up in the morning.) Thompson was rescued by the journalist, Wilfred Meynell, who tracked him down through a laudanum supplier and published his poems in *Merry England*. His work is characterised by sentimental and occasionally mystical pronouncements. It is frequently rhapsodic and can be arrestingly beautiful. Many of the poems concern the tension between sacred and profane love and it is strange that he should be best remembered for a piece on such a prosaic subject as a pair of Lancashire batsmen.

Thompson's hero, Richard Gorton Barlow, was brought up in Bolton where his father, Richard Snr, worked as a pharmacist's assistant. Richard attended St George's School and proved a dutiful if reserved pupil. He notes in his memoirs: 'I took instinctively to cricket almost as soon as I could walk.' Later, his love of cricket would prove to be as profound as that of any man in the game's history. His mother encouraged him and even provided sick notes so that he could attend net sessions. He and his brother Robert would challenge any other pair of colts in the district at twopence a game but soon ran out of opponents. Richard first carried his bat through an entire innings when he was 10 and would perform the feat another 50 times in all classes of cricket. Even as a child his defence was almost impregnable and he began playing for the Bolton senior club side at the age of 11. His bowling soon developed and he took a hat-trick when he was 13. For a while he had aspirations to be a wicketkeeper, but he lost his enthusiasm when a young batsman swung wildly at a long hop and knocked him senseless.

Richard left school at 14 and went to work as a compositor. In 1865 his parents moved to Staveley in Derbyshire where Richard Snr became a moving force in local sporting circles, acting as secretary of the Staveley Cricket and Football Club. Richard accompanied his parents and worked as a foundry assistant before serving an apprenticeship as a stonemason.

His first match of any consequence was for XXII of Staveley District against George Parr's All-England XI. With his third ball he had Robert Carpenter caught in the slips, later recalling: 'I did a little step dance without knowing if I was on my head or my heels.' In 1871 he was given a trial by Lancashire. This proved successful and he was pitched into the Roses match in July. On a lively wicket at Bramall

Lane he was hit on the hand by Bob Clayton having scored 6. He retired hurt but returned with his finger in a splint and made 28 not out in acute pain. In Yorkshire's first innings the tail-enders proved stubborn and Richard was given a spell with the ball. He took a wicket with his opening delivery when he clean bowled Johnnie West.

In the summers of 1873 and '74 Richard turned out as a professional for Saltaire CC near Bradford. As a young man he had an exceptional turn of speed and in 1876, at the club's athletics day, he won the 100 yards, 220 yards, 440 yards hurdles and the sack race. In a retrospective interview he commented: 'I won many prizes on the track in my younger days. For some years I ran as an amateur, afterwards turning professional for a short time. My quickest time was 122 yards in 12.5 seconds.'

In 1875 Richard produced some fine opening partnerships with his county captain, Albert Hornby. Against Yorkshire at Old Trafford, they had their finest moment. In a tense Roses encounter, Lancashire were set a target of 146 against the clock, whereupon the pair knocked off the runs without offering a chance.

Richard appears to have had much business acumen and in 1880 he set up a sports shop near Old Trafford. He introduced rubber-faced gloves and removable spikes but neither innovation caught on. He also pioneered a ticker-tape system and would post sports results on his shop window. Richard even patented a laceless football, and designed wicket covers which were later adopted by the MCC.

His form for Lancashire brought him a berth on the 1881–82 England tour to Australia under Alfred Shaw. The party sailed via America and on the boat from San Francisco, Richard and Billy Bates formed a two-man glee club to entertain fellow passenger King Kalakana of Honolulu. Richard excelled at dominoes, cards and quoits and was in great demand at the many impromptu concerts. He was reluctant to shave as the ship bobbed about in rough seas and arrived in Australia sporting a healthy beard. In the second Test at Sydney he made 62 which the *Sydney Morning Herald* described as: 'A patient, steady innings…his driving and shot selection were admirable.' In the fourth Test at Melbourne he made an assured 56 and played some imperious drives off the great Frederick Spofforth before being run out after an appalling call by John Selby.

He was somewhat accident-prone and at Newcastle in New South Wales he and Dick Pilling set fire to their mattress while trying to fend off mosquitoes with candles. At Dunolly Richard was thrown from a coach and was lucky not to sustain serious injuries. Four years earlier he had been involved in a bizarre incident when, trying to ground his bat in a tight run-out decision, he fell on the handle and knocked himself unconscious. As a teetotaller he was unhappy when his colleagues threw brandy down his throat, but his first question when he came round was: 'I'm not out, am I?'

In Brisbane Richard was deeply moved when an expatriate cricket enthusiast from Bolton who had known his father travelled 100 miles on foot through the bush and swam across rivers in order to wish him luck in the Tests. Richard was a poor sailor and on the return journey he was only too happy to leave the ship when it reached Naples. He had a gift for languages and soon picked up a smattering of Italian. Armed with a guidebook he marched up Vesuvius with James Lillywhite Jnr and Dick Pilling in his wake.

In the following summer he made 856 runs for Lancashire at 30.16 and took 73 wickets at 9.72. This topped the Lancashire batting and bowling averages and *Wisden* commented: 'He is fairly entitled to be reckoned the best all-round cricketer in England.' Richard began writing an occasional column for *Cricket* in this period and his views include: 'A wicket-keeper must be bold as a lion, nimble as a cat, tough as a rhinoceros, cool as an iceberg and as elastic as indiarubber.'

He was one of only four professionals who toured Australia in the following winter under the captaincy of the Hon. Ivo Bligh. On the journey out he proved irrepressible and excelled at deck games, winning the 100 yards, hurdles, and egg and spoon. He also came second in the high jump. On leaving Colombo the tourists' vessel, the *Peshawar*, collided with a large cruiser. Initial reports suggested that the whole team had drowned. In fact all of the passengers and crew survived but Fred Morley the Nottinghamshire pace bowler sustained chest injuries that would contribute to his death less than two years later. Bligh was unable to motivate his side in the field and the team consistently shelled depressingly easy catches which, as the Robertson-Glasgow poem has it, 'a child would take at midnight with no moon'. Richard was a notable exception and fielded superbly at point.

He had never ridden a horse but at Tamworth he proved fearless during a kangaroo hunt. He was thrilled by the stunning scenery along the banks of the River Peel and insisted on making regular excursions and taking numerous pictures, photography being one of his hobbies. Richard had little success with the bat but in the third Test at Sydney he took 7 for 40 in Australia's second innings and was carried shoulder-high round the ground.

He was a superb mixer and at Maryborough he joined in an aboriginal corroboree (a dance and sports display) with much gusto. On the return journey he was a stalwart of the ship's concert. His performances on the field had been modest and he was amazed to find a welcome party of several hundred people when he stepped off the train at Manchester Central Station. Richard made a short speech and wept openly. He was becoming one of the most popular professional players in the country and a contemporary profile in *Cricket* included the observation: 'He is civil and unassuming in his demeanour as well as earnest in his attachment to the game.'

In 1884 Richard appeared in the Gentlemen vs Players fixture at Lord's. He made 43 in the Players' first innings and also took the prized wickets of W.G. Grace and A.G. Steel. In the same season he made a sparkling century for the North against the Australians at Trent Bridge, playing Spofforth confidently on a crumbling pitch. The *Manchester Guardian* lavished praise: 'He scarcely gave a chance or made a bad hit. His judgement was as sound as his defence was admirable.' Richard also took 10 wickets in the match. Brian Bearshaw has noted that a wealthy mill-owner was so delighted with the result that he insisted on taking Richard to a jeweller's shop and buying him a diamond tiepin. In 1885 Richard scored two centuries, 117 in 3 hours and 5 minutes against MCC, and 108 in 5 hours and 25 minutes against Gloucestershire.

Richard made his third trip to Australia in the winter of 1886–87. Sailing out on the *Cuzco* he formed an unbeatable whist partnership with Johnny Briggs and sang duets with William Scotton. There was the usual plethora of deck games in which Richard won the hopping race and came second in the three-legged race partnering Billy Bates. Richard, Johnny Briggs and William Gunn put on a weekly nigger minstrel act, which was variously impeded by the accompaniment of

Mordecai Sherwin on tambourine and George Lohmann on comb and paper.

Travel across Australia proved difficult and the players were disturbed when they saw the suffering caused by a major earthquake at Cootamundra. There were only two Tests, both at Sydney, where Richard made scores of 2, 4, 34 and 42 not out. At Armidale the hosts organised a concert. Richard monopolised the stage, singing 'How Beautiful Upon The Mountains' and the Flaxington Harker ballad 'When Other Lips'. He received an encore and performed what he describes as 'his cricket song'. This was his own (dreadful) composition; the lyrics include: 'Captain Hornby is the finest man for many miles around/And all his men have brawny arms.'

Richard played his last match for Lancashire in 1892, an insignificant fixture against Cheshire. He had fallen out with the committee in the previous season when he was asked to stand down for a match against Essex at Old Trafford. The visitors had yet to attain first-class status and the selectors were anxious to blood new recruits. Richard said that he would play against Essex or never play for the county again. He was taken at his word and made no more first-class appearances. There was uproar in the local press and a *Manchester Evening News* correspondent wrote: 'He still has a lot of cricket left in him and might do worse than shave off his beard and come out as a colt at next season's trials.' In the following summer he became a county umpire. He proved successful and was widely respected by the players.

In 1899 he stood as umpire in the Nottingham Test against Australia. Sadly, he was far too highly strung to officiate at international level and his loyalties got the better of him. In England's second innings Prince Ranjitsinhji batted superbly to score 93 and stave off defeat. However, with his score on 30 he was palpably run out by Frank Laver and started to walk to the pavilion. To general astonishment Richard screamed from square leg: 'You're not out!' Ranji had no option but to continue his innings. Earlier, Richard had made a correct decision to give Clem Hill run out but had jumped several feet in the air and flapped his arms in excitement as he raised his finger. The worst mistake was an lbw decision against Monty Noble despite an inside edge that could be heard right around the ground. Joe Darling reported him to Lord Harris and it was agreed that he would not stand in any more Tests. As England captain, W.G. Grace apologised to Darling for some of Richard's excesses. There was an informal press conference, during which Richard became distraught and did not trust himself to speak.

In 1901 Richard played his last season of club cricket when he acted as professional at Blackpool CC. In 1907 he startled many by designing his own tombstone. He was in good health and would live another 12 years. The matter was treated as a joke until a photograph of the edifice appeared in a Manchester newspaper. Richard was unamused when he received a wreath and a note inscribed 'with deep regret'.

In the following summer Fred Reynolds retired as ground manager at Old Trafford and the club advertised for a replacement. The salary of £200 attracted over 300 responses. Many of them were wildly inappropriate, and Albert Hornby had to sift his way through a raft of applicants including unemployed actors and even two ventriloquists who sent in photos of themselves with talking dolls on their knees. The choicest letter came from a man who said he knew nothing about cricket and had never been to Old Trafford but had a brother who kept a pork pie shop in the neighbourhood and would provide a reference. Hornby gave the job to Richard and though he proved innovative in his ideas, he was unable to delegate. After a spate of burglaries in the area Richard became convinced that the ground was going to be vandalised and he resigned after only nine months.

In 1908 Richard wrote his autobiography, being one of the first cricketers to do so. He showed the manuscript to the Lancashire journalist Jimmy Catton who made various suggestions which he studiously ignored. Catton recalled: 'I ventured a few modifications, because it was plain that he was perfectly unconscious of being self-centred. However, he preferred it as it was.' The memoirs are dedicated to Albert Hornby. They are sprightly and show no evidence of a ghost writer. By now Richard's sports shop had made him a wealthy man; he subsidised the print costs and the volume is beautifully produced. He took on promotion of the book himself, advertised it widely and invited postal applications to his home.

The Francis Thompson poem has preserved Richard in a peculiar aspic with Hornby, and their relationship warrants discussion. Hornby died six years after his opening partner and in his dotage he often said that Richard's memory became increasingly precious to him. The partnership is the subject of widespread misconception; much tripe has been peddled portraying Hornby as a Quixotic figure and Richard as his Sancho Panza. The analogy is as inaccurate as it is hackneyed. They were by no means an antithesis; Richard was devoted to his captain and regularly shielded him from difficult bowling, but he was never servile.

Richard and Hornby are best remembered for spectacular running between the wickets. A contemporary newspaper review described how they would 'scamper about like rabbits near their burrow'. They played 'tip and run' for hours on end and frequently caused panic in fielding sides, who would concede overthrows. In an interview with *Cricket Field* in 1894, Richard noted: 'I liked the excitement as much as Mr Hornby did.' However, he is known to have lost his temper during the 1887 Surrey vs Lancashire fixture when he registered a platinum duck, Hornby running him out before he had faced a ball.

Richard's sporting talents were not limited to cricket and he played in goal for Manchester FC and Manchester Wanderers. In February 1880 he appeared for Lancashire against Ayrshire. Lancashire lost 9-1, but Richard performed competently in a strong crosswind and prevented the game from descending into even more of a rout. Ayrshire were a much stronger side; describing one phase of sustained attack, the *Manchester Guardian* reported: 'Barlow met the onslaught bravely and defended his citadel with great skill.' He was by no means the first-choice Lancashire goalkeeper at the time and this proved to be his only appearance at county level. Richard maintained his interest in football and in 1887 he refereed the extraordinary FA Cup tie in which Preston North End beat Hyde United 26–0.

Richard was 5 ft 8 in tall and weighed 10 st 10 lb for most of his adult life. He was thickset, but graceful if economical in his movements. Arthur Haygarth noted: 'Barlow is a cheerful, active-looking fellow. He is a teetotaller and abjures the fragrant weed.' (Ever the businessman, Richard would later introduce his own brand of cigars which he never smoked.) He was somewhat vain and took great pride in his appearance. He changed his facial growth regularly, finally settling for a naval-looking full beard that set off his pale blue eyes and brown hair.

As a batsman he was the dourest 'stonewaller' in the history of the game. He could be unhurried to the point of immobility and for W.G. Grace he was 'monotony incarnate'. Richard himself referred to his stonewalling as 'playing the old man's game'. However, when the mood took him he could bat fluently, a fact which he is at pains to point out in his autobiography. His nadirs included 5 runs in 90 minutes against Sussex in 1876 and 5 not out in 150 minutes against Nottinghamshire in 1882. His style was hardly memorable though his defence was superb. He was an excellent judge of length and played predominantly off the front foot. This made him vulnerable to high-quality leg-spin and in Gentlemen vs Players fixtures he was often dismissed by his county colleague A.G. Steel.

Richard bowled left-handed and possessed a deceptive inswinger and a killing arm-ball. He kept an immaculate length and from our own day he appears to have been similar in pace and method to John Lever. He was able to constrain W.G. Grace's scoring even on good wickets and is said to have reserved a special delivery for him. Richard loathed Grace and was terribly upset by W.G.'s condescending evaluation of his batting in *Cricket*. A few years later Richard gave Grace out lbw in a county match and Brian Bearshaw recalls the ensuing exchange: 'Barlow, I played that ball.' 'Yes, I know, Doctor, but it was after it hit your leg.' As a fielder Richard was alert and energetic. He was competent in any position but usually stood at point. He took four hat-tricks in first-class matches and almost 1,000 victims as a bowler.

At his core Richard was highly strung and very emotional. He was intelligent and articulate but became obsessed by cricket to the exclusion of anything else. Richard was orderly in his habits and fussy about his food. He refused to eat in the Old Trafford pavilion and his wife would bring a potato pie lunch wrapped in a handkerchief. During a Roses match his team-mate Alex Watson took a taste of the pie, demolished the lot and left a small piece of turf in its place. Richard blamed it on the visitors and stomped round the boundary in high dudgeon: 'If I've said it once I've said it a thousand times, something's sure to go wrong when these Yorkshire fellows come to Old Trafford.'

Richard's mania for cricket permeated every aspect of his life. In 1891 he moved from Staveley to Raikes Parade, Blackpool, where he had a house built to his own design. The residence became little more than a cricket museum. The pillars at the front gates were adorned with concrete cricket balls while the front door contained a piece of stained glass depicting Richard, Albert Hornby and Dick Pilling. He constructed a net in his back garden, kept every bat he ever used and collected the autographs of county players with a determination bordering on mania. His wife Catherine had to put up with many vagaries, including a row of cricket bats in the bathroom. The following is a chestnut and has been variously ascribed, but there are reports that in his sleep, Richard used to nudge Catherine and bark: 'Run up, there's two there!'

Richard often gave recitals at post-match dinners. His repertoire included 'By The Fountain' and his favourite, 'Tom Bowling'. He was an accomplished tenor and correspondence in the *Manchester Evening News* after his death described his voice as 'strong in the middle register with a marked clarity of tone in the upper octaves'. He could hit the top notes like a mallet hitting a chime and was not above blacking up as a minstrel. Having batted for three hours while making 29 against Leicestershire he sang 'Then You'll Remember Me', after which one of the opposition assured him that they would.

In a characteristically urbane essay, Eric Midwinter notes that Richard's grandson was christened Leslie Barlow Wilson; the acronym will become apparent after a moment's thought. At the turn of the century Catherine began suffering from a severe mental illness and the marriage was effectively annulled. Richard maintained his looks and charm into late middle age. In 1909, while walking along the esplanade on Blackpool's north shore, he met and became enchanted by Elizabeth Thompson. She was a book-keeper at the Imperial Hotel and some 25 years younger than Richard. At 58 he was hardly love's young dream but his feelings were returned.

The couple embarked on a love affair and had an illegitimate son, Reginald Gorton Barlow Thompson. Reginald inherited Richard's integrity and passions and was a regular visitor to Old Trafford until his death in 1981. He was a keen supporter of motor racing in Lancashire and was fiercely proud of his father's achievements. Richard's legitimate daughter, Alice, would have nothing to do with Reginald and she was particularly ungracious and mercenary when selling off Richard's cricket memorabilia.

Richard was depressed by the First World War, but did sterling work at a home for convalescent soldiers in Lytham St Annes, where he gave lectures on cricket. He remained fit and active almost to the last and his relationship with Elizabeth was an extremely happy one. He was proud of his physical fitness and in his mid-sixties he would challenge any man of a similar age to play him at single-wicket. Richard spent over £2,000 modifying his house and built an extensive gymnasium. He even had an indoor net at the rear of the building and taught his wife and daughter to bowl competent round-arm deliveries to give him practice.

In the spring of 1919 he began to suffer from a heart murmur. He died in the following July at the age of 68. We already know that as a former mason he had designed his own tombstone which can be found in Layton Cemetery. The inscription is unrivalled in its simplicity and pertinence and reads: 'Bowled at Last!'

Neville Cardus once remarked that 'poets do not write lovely and immortal songs about mediocrity'. Richard could be direct, spontaneous and impulsive about the things he loved. However, as a batsman he set new standards of dreariness. The abiding impression is of a clear-minded man of deep and quite stubborn convictions. Richard was characterised by remarkable candour, an occasional pleasant touch of self-deprecating humour and unflagging devotion to the traditions and courtesies of his trade. He was respected throughout society for his sincerity, sweet manners and immaculate appearance. A *Manchester Guardian* obituary ended with: 'In private life Barlow was a quiet, chatty, neighbourly man. He was thoroughly content with the world and his own place in it.' Richard must be thoroughly content with his place in immortality.

8

Julius Caesar

b: 25.3.1830, Godalming, Surrey.
d: 5.3.1878, Godalming, Surrey.

Mushlike memories perform
a ritual on my lips
I lie in stolid hopelessness
and they lay my soul in strips.

'Remembering', Maya Angelou, 1988

At around six o'clock on the morning of 3 October 1876, while working on a stretch of line near the Peasmarsh and Compton Bridges between Godalming and Guildford, Arthur Boxall, a plate-layer employed by the South Western Railway Board, discovered the mutilated body of a 17-year-old youth, Julius Caesar Jnr. He had thrown himself from an embankment on the previous evening. The suicide marked a low point in the pitiful decline of his father, one of the most tragic cricketers we have seen.

Julius Caesar Snr was known throughout society as 'Julie'. It should be noted immediately that his name was not an affectation. He always insisted that it should appear in full and would become incensed if he was ridiculed for it. Julie's father, Benjamin, was a baker and a fine club cricketer who played for Surrey against England in 1829.

Julie served an apprenticeship as a carpenter and in his youth he was respected for his work in the Godalming area. He excelled at many sports and his wiry physique made him an excellent boxer, with darting movements which meant that few amateurs could lay a glove on him. At the age of 16 he made his debut for Godalming CC, where he attracted the interest and patronage of Henry Marshall, a future mayor of Godalming and president of Surrey CCC. After Julie impressed all during a single-wicket match in July 1846, the *Surrey Gazette* enthused: 'This lad promises to be as noted in the game of cricket as his ancient namesake was in the art of war. The Godalming Club is willing to back him against any lad of his age in the County of Surrey.'

Julie married in June 1850, his bride being 20-year-old Jane Brewser, the daughter of William Brewser, a Godalming carpenter. The marriage came only a few weeks before the birth of their first son, Frederick. In August Julie played for XII of the Caesar Family against XI Gentlemen of Godalming at Broadwater Park. The match attracted 2,500 spectators and there was heavy betting among local gentry. The Caesars lost by 17 runs, Julie contributing scores of 5 and 11. He and his brothers were berated by their elders after the Caesars were bowled out for 54 when chasing 71. Julie had done his bit for family honour by taking five wickets with his fast round-arm bowling during Godalming's first innings. In major cricket his bowling would prove to be negligible.

In the following year he hit form with a fine innings of 51 for Surrey against Yorkshire at The Oval. *Bell's Life* noted: 'Great Julius appeared and a truly great score he made, his splendid driving eliciting shouts of applause.' He spent the latter part of the season touring with William Clarke's All-England XI, a highlight being an innings of 39 against XVI of Sussex.

In July 1852 Julie made a pair for Surrey against England, being clean bowled by William Clarke and Jem Grundy. He worried that a temporary loss of form would see him dropped by the county and he was often unsteady when facing Grundy, who would dismiss him many more times in coming years. A major game in the following season was England vs Sussex at Lord's. In front of 4,000 spectators Julie made scores of 35 and 43. He looked well set for a half-century in his second innings but was brilliantly caught and bowled by James Lillywhite Snr. A report in the *Brighton Herald* stated: 'Julius, who laboured under the disadvantage of an injured hand, played "fast" and gave some chances but made some beautiful drives.'

A few weeks later he produced one of the finest knocks of his career when he scored 101 for England against Kent at Canterbury. The innings was hardly chanceless and he gave a sitter to Alfred Mynn early on, but *The Times* commented: 'Caesar displayed his powers in the best style, striking the ball in every direction to the astonishment and discomfiture of the fielders.' A report in the *Kentish Gazette* concluded: 'A most masterful innings. Caesar hit the ball right around the ground, completely puzzling the opposition.'

He spent the spring of 1854 giving cricket tuition to undergraduates at Oxford. In May he played for the All-England XI vs XXII of Upton Park and his innings of 21 and 31 not out were the top scores for his side, *Bell's Life* noting: 'Caesar's hitting as usual was brilliant – principally drives.' It should be remembered that at the time wickets were often appalling and team totals averaged around 150. Surrey played few games that year, being racked by internal bickering and disputes with the landlord of The Oval. However, in late June and early July he made 77 and 43 for Surrey against Sussex at the Brunswick Ground, Hove. In the first of these innings his square cut proved murderous and he combined superbly with William Caffyn.

There was more squabbling at The Oval in 1855 when Julie and Heathfield Stephenson were suspended after a disagreement over travelling expenses. Julie appears to have expected the county to subsidise his rail fares with the All-England XI and in his *Surrey Cricket*, Lord Alverstone recalled that 'the other players felt annoyed and disgusted at his demands'. At the time Gentlemen vs Players was among the major fixtures of the year. In 1856 Julie made top score in the match (51) and helped the players to a two-wicket victory. He would represent the Players on a further nine occasions. In the following winter he sat on the committee of the newly formed Cricketers' Fund, which sought to provide its members with financial support and a decent burial in times of hardship. One of the most popular players in the country, with a comfortable lifestyle, Julie was blissfully unaware that he would later find himself in dire need of such support.

The first misfortune occurred early in 1859 when his daughter, Ann, died of whooping cough at the age of 18 months. He spent the summer attending to his grief-stricken wife and played little county cricket. However, at the end of the season he was offered a £50 fee to tour

North America with George Parr's XI. The party sailed from Liverpool on the *Nova Scotian* and Julie proved an excellent sailor. The diaries of fellow tourists recall that despite rough weather he never missed a meal, sustaining everybody with his vitality and practical jokes. He was the last to leave the whist table in the evenings but would be up to organise the morning roll-call. Julie's superb hand-to-eye co-ordination allowed him to beat all comers at deck games, particularly shuffleboard for which he won regular prizes of Moët champagne.

Few of the cricketers liked the gale-force winds and John Wisden observed that the sea needed an application of 'the heavy roller'. Julie was intrigued by his surroundings and had an almost childlike compulsion to share the excitement of his discoveries. He sketched the porpoise that swam near the ship and was thrilled by icebergs off Newfoundland. While making hot toddies he upset a kettle of boiling water over George Parr and relations between the pair became strained. The mishap was the final straw for Parr who was not a good traveller and spent the rest of the voyage drinking himself into a stupor on gin and water. Julie appears to have been omnipresent and cheerfully turned out for the *Nova Scotian* Harmonic Society though few appreciated his appalling voice. Oblivious to criticism, he bawled his way through duets with Jem Grundy, his favourite number being 'The Jew In The Corner'.

Despite his rudimentary education, Julie was reasonably literate and with help from Fred Lillywhite he began cabling reports for the *West Surrey Times*. The sentences can occasionally be Byzantine, but at other times the authors show a light touch and are skittish when describing the 'cat-like propensities in the field' of some of the less athletic tourists. The pieces have no by-line, and in detailing his duck against XXII of Canada when he simply played down the wrong line, Julie reflected: 'Caesar was as ever very unfortunate to be bowled off his legs.' The tourists travelled by express trains to Montreal but their progress was hampered by Lillywhite's enormous printing press, which caused the railway porters much inconvenience. Fred was accompanying the team as a reporter and self-styled typographer, priding himself on being able to produce immaculate scorecards during the games.

To entertain spectators at the Elysian Fields Sports Ground in New

York the tourists split into two teams and invited local players to make up the numbers. Julie played under the captaincy of his Surrey colleague Tom Lockyer and scored a fine 52 in front of a crowd of 12,000. The *New York Times* reported: 'Julius Caesar played a skilful game, being quite in his old form. The masterly manner in which he timed the ball was the admiration of all good judges.' The Englishmen were hitting all the front pages and Julie's high spirits had attracted attention as the team paraded around the city. A profile of Julie in the *New York Herald* ends: 'A very dangerous bat who will punish loose bowling most severely.'

The team was soon travelling by train to Philadelphia at the terrifying pace of 30 miles per hour. At Rochester the tourists encountered severe weather and were obliged to field in muffs and greatcoats. Julie's attacks of gout suggest poor circulation and he certainly felt the cold terribly. Having lurked in the pavilion drinking bourbon for much of the game, he was persuaded to bat at number nine but was dismissed for 11. However, he excelled at short-stop during an informal game of baseball with some young spectators.

A well-known anecdote comes from his contemporary Richard Daft. George Parr had instructed the players to take everything in their stride and praise American hospitality and customs to the hilt. Julie was conscientious in this until one evening he discovered a bar serving authentic London porter and had a skinful. Daft takes up the story: 'Julius managed to pick a quarrel with one of the natives, and after a good deal of strong language, threatened to punch the Yankee's head if he would but step outside. The American told him that sort of thing was not in his line, but said, "Here is my card!" and at once held the muzzle of a revolver close to Julius's nose; he was terribly alarmed, and immediately began to make friendly overtures to the American, pretending to treat the whole affair as a joke, and presently succeeded in smoothing matters over. However, he took the earliest opportunity of getting out of the place. "The first Yankee I meet on British ground," said Julius the next day, "I will give a hiding to even if I get three months for it."'

In June 1861 he blasted 50 and 111 for Surrey vs Cambridgeshire at The Oval. The *West Surrey Times* described the batting of Julie and Frederick Lee as 'some of the finest play recorded in cricketing annals'.

However, he was now suffering from repeated attacks of gout that caused him great pain, restricted his mobility and would plague him for the rest of his life. In August 1861 he made 72 for the All-England XI vs the United All-England XI.

Julie visited Australia in the winter of 1863–64 with another team led by George Parr. The tour would have been to the United States but for the small matter of the American Civil War which was raging at the time. The cricketers travelled out on Brunel's masterpiece the *Great Britain*. The Yorkshire player George Anderson kept a diary and he described how the 865 passengers entertained themselves with dances, concerts, magic lantern shows and even mock trials. Julie sang his favourite ballads to the accompaniment of William Caffyn's cornet. This may not have been a pleasurable experience for the other passengers, since E.M. Grace noted in his own journal that the ship's piano was appallingly out of tune. Grace also recorded that early in the voyage he had to treat Julie for a severe attack of gout. Julie could be disarming in his qualities of freshness and simplicity; he became very excited when he saw a large whale and was permanently entertained by the flying fish that swam alongside the vessel.

While he fielded superbly and contributed much to team morale, he could not buy a run and was often dropped to number nine in the batting order. His highest score was a sedate 40 in two hours against XXII of Ballarat. The tourists had been complaining that lunches during their matches were proving over-elaborate, and in its preview of the game the *Ballarat Star* commented: 'It is to be hoped that the orators will spice their speeches with the acceptable wit of brevity.' The tour included a trip to New Zealand; after a match in Dunedin the hosts organised an athletics contest, in which Julie beat William Caffyn and a dozen locals to win the 100 yards sprint. At Lyttelton near Christchurch, he was lucky not to be killed when his horse turned frisky and galloped down a slope, nearly throwing him over a 300-foot cliff-top. Julie kept his nerve and allowed his mount to come to a stop of its own accord a few feet from the precipice.

He proved highly strung in minor matters, but there was more evidence that he could keep his head in a crisis when the team left Sydney in April. In his *Seventy-One Not Out* William Caffyn describes how, as the team sailed out of harbour, their boat the *Wonga Wonga* collided with a small yacht. The players were taking tea and observed the crew attempting to save the occupants of the yacht, which had sunk within seconds. Caffyn records that George Parr and George Tarrant lost their heads completely but 'Julius Caesar behaved in a manner worthy of his name, keeping very cool and collected, and doing all he could to assist...' The *Wonga Wonga* returned to Sydney for repairs and when it docked the players discovered that John 'Foghorn' Jackson had slept through the whole affair, having over-indulged during a send-off lunch at the Post Office Hotel. Jackson was much feared as a pace bowler and acquired his nickname through the habit of blowing his nose loudly whenever he took a wicket.

In 1864 Julie left the All-England XI to play for the United South of England XI, which was predominantly composed of Surrey professionals. It was a successful season and in July he made the highest score of his career, an undefeated 132 against Sussex at Hove. The *Brighton Herald* correspondent wrote: 'This innings, considering the excellent fielding and bowling of the Sussex side, is one of the finest ever made.'

Two months later he was given a benefit by Godalming CC, the teams coming from the Sussex and Surrey squads with a few strong club players. The contest was ruined by rain and Julie did little with bat or ball, but there was a handsome post-match collection and the *Surrey Advertiser* reported: 'What Robin Hood was to archery, so is such a man as Julius Caesar to cricket.' Peter Mayne, a historian of Godalming CC, recalls that when receiving a massive gold watch and Albert chain, Julie made a graceful speech of thanks noting that 'having played for 15 years, his motto had always been in cricket as well as in the relations of life to play straight'.

Julie was 5 ft 7 in tall, and with a stocky physique he weighed 11 stone 6 pounds. William Caffyn once described him as 'a big man in a little room'. As a batsman he was a wonderfully sweet striker of the ball who played predominantly off the front foot. He had a superb lofted on-drive, though he occasionally gave a return catch when misjudging this. His timing was superb and he could usually hit across the line effectively. He was one of the first exponents of the pull shot but also played the old 'draw' or 'dog shot', in which the ball is hit through the legs. Richard Daft's evaluation was: 'His hitting was as smart and clean as anything that could be witnessed.' However, Julie's nervous disposition made him a poor starter and he scored his fair share of ducks, which depressed him immensely. After getting a king pair against Nottinghamshire in 1851 he came close to retiring from the game. He could be extravagant in his praise of others and seeing a stroke from Lord Lyttelton flash past him at point, he commented: 'That cut ought to be preserved in a glass case.'

Julie was a competent fieldsman in any position and excelled at point and long-stop where he intimidated batsmen with his hard, flat throw. He could bolster up a club attack with his medium-pace round-arm deliveries but in major cricket he was of no consequence as a bowler. However, he had a high opinion of his abilities and often pleaded to be given a turn. As a last resort he was once brought on in a Surrey vs MCC game when Reginald Hankey was scoring freely. When told he was going to bowl, Julie suddenly became diffident and his first delivery was a pathetic half-volley on leg stump. Hankey gave the ball an enormous clout, only to see the Rev. Charlton Lane take a blinding catch on the boundary. Julie turned to William Caffyn and grinned: 'Well, I soon found out *his* weak point, didn't I?' Caffyn recalled that in an 1849 match between Gentlemen and Players of Surrey, Julie bowled 11 wides in three overs and could not be relied upon.

The abiding impression of Julie is his extreme nervousness. He is said to have wept if he had to sleep in a room on his own and he was always worried that the hotels he stayed at would burn to the ground. Richard Daft described how he invariably travelled with a huge portmanteau of which he was very proud, telling everybody that it was solid leather. However, he did not have enough equipment to fill it; the bag was frequently squashed flat in carriages and occasionally mislaid as a result. Julie was hyperactive and extremely witty. He took great pride in his personal appearance and was an inveterate practical joker.

In *The Walkers of Southgate*, Walter Bettesworth gives a rare anecdote: 'In the early days of the United Eleven, [Tom] Lockyer and Caesar were playing in a match against a twenty-two on a small ground, on the outskirts of which, and not very distant from the wicket, coconuts were set up for spectators to throw at. Evening was approaching; it began to rain, and it looked as if the last two men of the twenty-two would play out time. One of them hit a ball past Julius Caesar at cover-point. Caesar ran after it with tremendous energy. "Now Julie," cried Tom at the wicket, "let us have it," upon which Julie picked up a coconut, threw it in full toss to Lockyer, who, whipping off the bails, pocketed the nut, and ran off to the pavilion.'

In August 1865 Julie made 82 for Surrey vs Hampshire at The Oval. It was the last flicker of the lamp. From now on the line of this memoir is simple and its tragedy unrelenting. The rest of Julie's life could be the outline for a bad Thomas Hardy novel. On the morning of Wednesday 18 October 1865, Julie was part of a shooting party on Munstead Heath to the south-east of Godalming. His companions included Lieutenant-Colonel Frederick Marshall and his brother, Murray Marshall. A 45-year-old beater, William Foster, began 'working a hedge'. This would have involved moving along the hedge and hitting it with a stick in order to drive game towards the marksmen. Soon after 11 o'clock a gun went off and Foster fell forward. Geoff Amey describes how 'A trail of smoke extended from Caesar about six yards behind. He was heard to exclaim: "Oh God, what have I done?"'

Julie collapsed in a gibbering heap while the Marshall brothers carried the wounded man to a cottage and called for medical assistance. At the inquest two days later, Dr Arthur Balchin testified: 'I never saw anybody in such a state as Julius Caesar was when we heard of Foster's death. He sobbed like a child and was dreadfully agitated by the intelligence.' Another member of the shooting party, Richard Dickenson, stated: 'The gun was, I imagine, on full cock. So far as my observation can go, I am satisfied the explosion resulted from an accident.'

Frederick Marshall later noted that Julie was 'the most careful man with a gun I have known'. In his history of Godalming CC, Peter Mayne records Julie's testimony: 'I wore a shot-pouch and possibly the strap might have touched the trigger, but I felt nothing so I cannot account for it. I have carried my gun a thousand times in the same manner.' William Caffyn concluded: 'Julius was one of the best shots I knew. I could hold my own with him at the traps, but he could beat me at ordinary shooting in the open...He never got over the shock till the day of his death.'

Julie's cricket was effectively finished. He played only a few games in 1866 and in 1867 his gout became acute. He turned out in a few festival matches before retiring to become an occasional umpire. In 1867 he installed himself as a cricket outfitter in Ockford Road, Godalming. However, he was innocent to the point of unworldliness and showed little business acumen.

In April 1872 he was employed as cricket coach at Charterhouse immediately after the school moved from central London to Godalming. Here he worked alongside his brother Fred, who was a competent medium-pace bowler and a solid middle-order batsman. A colourful character, Fred was a respected umpire and occasional club professional who also worked as a prison turnkey at Horsemonger Jail and as a publican in Southwark. Pupils at Charterhouse during this period included the future England cricket captain and Hollywood film star Aubrey Smith.

Julie stood as a county umpire during the vacations and once caused a furore at Brighton when he gave Henry Charlwood out for hitting the ball twice amid what *Wisden* describes as 'unpleasant excitement'. He appears to have been popular with staff and pupils at Charterhouse and in June 1873 he was persuaded to play for The Masters vs The School. A little of the magic remained and he breezed his way to 53 not out. Julie may even have rallied for a while but in July of the following year there came another grievous blow when his wife Jane died of cancer at the age of 45. Increasingly he sought solace at the bottom of a bottle and by 1876 he was unable to continue his work at Charterhouse. A horrible twilight was following in the wake of his high noon.

In October 1876 came the suicide of his son. Julius Jnr was proving successful as a ground bowler at Charterhouse and his father had high hopes of him. He had been courting Laura Whittle, the daughter of a Guildford publican, and at the inquest it emerged that she was heavily pregnant. Both were 17 years old and the youth, who had inherited his father's nervous constitution, did not know what to do.

The *Surrey Advertiser* reports that several trains passed over Julius's body before it was removed from the line and the corpse was almost unrecognisable. Detailing the inquest, the same paper noted: 'His father is completely prostrated and unable to attend.' A coroner concluded: 'The boy was afraid of his father hearing of the position he was in and the idea of getting married at the early age of seventeen evidently upset him.' It emerged from evidence given by other family members that Julius Jnr was on extremely good terms with his father. A letter written to Laura suggested that she was pressurising him for a marriage proposal. The jury concluded that Julius had 'committed suicide while labouring under temporary insanity'.

By the end of 1876 Julie was a dropsical wreck. He gave up his post at Charterhouse and soon declined into a travesty of his own legend. Early in 1877 he cut his losses and his hopes and moved into the Railway Tavern at Godalming as a complete invalid. He was suffering from a horrific combination of paralysis, heart disease and gout together with mental torment that we can hardly imagine. However, he had a staunch friend in Richard Yate, a cricket-loving doctor and fellow freemason, who tended to him regularly for no fee.

In December 1877 Frederick Marshall launched an appeal. The fund was administered by Charles Alcock, a talented cricket writer and a popular and forward-thinking secretary of Surrey CCC. The initial appeal came in the form of an open letter to *Bell's Life*: 'Julius Caesar... is in the depths of poverty. Illness and family troubles have produced this state of things... All who remember him will acknowledge him to have been a plucky, straightforward, honest man, full of fun, yet always in his place. It will be an act of real kindness if his old friends will remember him now in the days of his decadence.' The response was considerable and it allowed Julie a measure of financial security in his final days. He lingered for some three months and died at the Railway Tavern at the age of 47 on 5 March 1878.

An obituary in the *West Surrey Times* describes his decline: 'The name of Julius Caesar was at one time the emblem of all that was honourable in connection with our national game of cricket... As a player he was bold, skilful and withal honest.' There were only two cricketers at Julie's funeral, Harry Jupp and James Street. Perhaps few of them could bear to be there.

To the abiding shame of Surrey County Cricket Club, Julie's remains are in an unmarked grave in the old Godalming Cemetery, although action is being taken to remedy this. Next to him lies Philip Heseltine, better known under his pseudonym of Peter Warlock. A similarly tragic character, Warlock committed suicide in 1930 at the age of 36. As a composer and music critic he had found considerable fame in the 1920s with choral works and part songs and he is justly celebrated for his many inspired tributes to Delius. Warlock was a keen cricket fan and one of his more charming compositions is a setting of Bruce Blunt's 'The Cricketers Of Hambledon'. By contrast, Julie is now a shadowy figure. He is occasionally remembered for his manifold eccentricities, extreme sensitivity and outstanding talent.

9

Sir Arthur Conan Doyle

b: 22.5.1859, Edinburgh.
d: 7.7.1930, Crowborough, Sussex.

'Mediocrity knows nothing higher than itself, but talent instantly recognizes genius.'

Arthur Conan Doyle, *The Valley of Fear*, 1914

Conan Doyle was born into a devout Catholic family that included many talented artists. His grandfather, John Doyle, was a portrait painter and lithographer who was celebrated for his caricatures of the Duke of Wellington. Conan Doyle's father, Charles Altamont Doyle, was an architect and builder for the Scottish Office of Works and a gifted draughtsman. He was also an epileptic who descended into alcoholism and spent his final years at the Montrose Lunatic Asylum. In his autobiography Sir Arthur would recall: 'My father's life was full of the tragedy of unfulfilled powers and of undeveloped gifts.'

As a child he proved precocious, curious and chivalrous. In his memoirs Conan Doyle claims to have grown up 'in the hardy and bracing atmosphere of poverty'. The family certainly lived in a lower middle- if not working-class suburb of Edinburgh and Arthur's studious nature was at odds both with his surroundings and his own high spirits. He recalls how he once beat up a bully in a notorious slum area, went home and was reading Walter Scott's *Ivanhoe* a few minutes later. Despite straitened circumstances, his family found the money to give him a private education and in 1868 he was sent to Stonyhurst, a prominent Catholic public school near Preston. The school has always been known for its Spartan regime. (Reflecting on his lack of self-discipline, Sebastian in *Brideshead Revisited* speculates as to how he would have turned out if he had gone to Stonyhurst instead of Eton.)

Being sociable and good at sport, he was a popular member of the school, though his academic performance was never more than middling. Arthur's first exposures to cricket included an unpleasant incident; while watching an exhibition by the England all-rounder Tom Emmett he was struck on the head by one of Emmett's boundary hits and was carried off to the infirmary.

He had a healthy scepticism for received opinion and soon turned against the unremitting dogma of the school's religious teaching which gave him a lifelong distrust of sectarianism. He did however find kindred spirits among fellow pupils, and his close friends included the future detective fiction and short story writer A.E.W. Mason. Mason would prove fearless as a First World War spy and went on to play much club cricket, including several matches alongside his old classmate.

Stonyhurst combined conventional cricket (which it referred to as 'London cricket') with its own bizarre variant of the game which was something akin to korfball and stoolball with underarm bowling on a gravel pitch. Similarly, conventional rugby was combined with another game peculiar to the school and having much in common with Australian Rules. Conan Doyle excelled at all these sports. By the age of 15 he was 5 ft 9 in tall, and strong almost to the point of being muscle-bound. During vacations he held his own at senior league cricket in Edinburgh. His contributions to school life were not limited to sport. After seeing Henry Irving play Hamlet at the Lyceum he became a leading light in the dramatic society and also edited the school magazine.

Conan Doyle left Stonyhurst in the autumn of 1875 to finish his school education at Feldkirch, a Jesuit academy on the Swiss-Austrian border. Again he edited the school magazine and his articles indicate that he was already exceptionally well read. A profound influence was Edgar Allen Poe, particularly Poe's detective stories including *The Murders in the Rue Morgue*.

In October 1876 he entered Edinburgh University with a small bursary to study medicine. Here he came under the influence of a lecturer in clinical surgery, Dr Joseph Bell. An authority on criminal psychology and an engaging polymath who could make amazing deductions as to the backgrounds and professions of patients by analysing their dress, physique and posture, Bell would become the model for Conan Doyle's most famous literary creation.

In 1880 he took a break from medical studies and spent seven months as surgeon on a Greenland whaling ship. The crew was fond of boxing and his performance during some heavy sparring made an immediate impression on his colleagues. He was also respected for his vitality and a display of courage when he slipped on an icepack and nearly drowned. He returned to university in September 1880 and graduated in August of the following year. He had been a conscientious though hardly brilliant student and was often distracted by his extra-curricular reading which included the complete works of the American essayist Oliver Wendell Holmes. He was also a keen member of the university photographic club. Photography would later become a major theme in his promotion of spiritualism.

A need to earn money quickly and support his family prompted him to make another voyage as a ship's surgeon soon after he graduated. This time he sailed to the Gold Coast where he spent three days with the American Minister to Liberia, Henry Highland Garnet. A black abolitionist and Presbyterian minister who had escaped from a plantation at the age of nine, Highland Garnet was dying of tuberculosis but made a lasting impression on his visitor. Conan Doyle's own life came under threat during an acute bout of malarial fever and he recalled: 'I lay for several days fighting it out with Death in a very small ring and without a second.'

In January 1882 he settled in Southsea and set himself up as a medical practitioner in some squalid lodgings. In his first week in the town he won much respect when he beat up a sailor who had been mistreating a young girl. However, business was slow and he was devastated when what he thought was going to be his first patient turned out to be a representative of the gas board who wanted to read his meter. Empathy with his neighbours ensured that within six months the practice began to prosper and an increase in his disposable income allowed him to join the local bowling club and play billiards at the Bush Hotel.

He had been writing short stories for several years and a significant breakthrough came in the spring of 1883, when *Cornhill Magazine* accepted a piece based around the notorious ghost ship the *Mary Celeste*. In the following summer he started playing for North End CC, which would soon rename itself Portsmouth CC. His debut season was hardly outstanding but in 1884 he began opening the batting and made a fine 44 against the Hampshire Regiment. He also acquired an interest in soccer at this time and in October he became a founding member of the Portsmouth Football Club.

In February 1885 he was elected captain of Portsmouth CC. As a reliable stock bowler with an excellent technical knowledge of the game together with good communication skills, he proved a successful skipper for the next four years. In May 1889 he scored a century against the Royal Artillery and the *Portsmouth Times* enthused about '... the magnificent form of Dr Conan Doyle, the captain, who made no fewer than 111 not out'.

Four years earlier he had begun courting Louise Hawkins, the sister of a patient who had died of cerebral meningitis. They were married in August 1885. Louise was 27 years old and a model, doting Victorian wife. She was no intellectual but was a competent musician and graphic artist.

In November 1887 came one of the most significant events in Conan Doyle's life and a turning point in the history of detective fiction: *Beeton's Christmas Annual* included the novella *A Study in Scarlet*. Much of the story is an American flashback set among the Mormons of Utah, but the central character in the main narrative is one Sherlock Holmes. A few months earlier Conan Doyle had published his first novel, *Micah Clarke*, a treatment of the 1685 Monmouth Rebellion that owes much to Macaulay. The manuscript had been commercially unattractive but was eventually published by Longmans on the recommendation of Andrew Lang. An essayist and poet with a keen interest in fairies and the supernatural, Lang was also a cricket enthusiast and would later befriend and encourage an adolescent Douglas Jardine.

As the creator of Sherlock Holmes, Conan Doyle was invited to speculate on the Jack the Ripper murders in the autumn of 1888, but restricted himself to the suggestion that the Ripper might be posing as a midwife in order that bloodstained clothes should not attract attention. In August 1889 the American magazine editor Joseph Marshall Stoddart travelled to London in the hope of commissioning stories from two promising English writers. Stoddart took the pair for dinner at the Langham Hotel and both authors immediately signed contracts. The result from Conan Doyle was the extended Holmes story *The Sign of Four*. The second writer was hardly second rate: his contribution was *The Picture of Dorian Gray*.

By 1890 Conan Doyle was becoming increasingly interested in comparative religion, mesmerism, the paranormal and spiritualism. He was also tiring of general practice and attended classes at the Portsmouth Eye Hospital with the intention of specialising in ophthalmology. With this in mind he travelled to Vienna in January of the following year, but he was disappointed to discover that his German was not good enough for him to understand the lectures. He returned to England after a few months and settled in London, setting up as an eye specialist. A lack of patients allowed him to write extensively, and by the spring people were queuing outside the offices of *Strand Magazine* to read the next Sherlock Holmes story.

Conan Doyle was fortunate to survive a severe bout of influenza in the spring of 1891. While convalescing he decided to leave the medical profession and write full-time. He also moved away from the smog of central London to South Norwood, where he took to tricycling and played club tennis. By August he had recovered his strength sufficiently to tour Holland with a cricket team composed mainly of schoolmasters, his colleagues including the future Scottish rugby international Walter Neilson. The tourists struggled in intense heat against All Holland at The Hague and as the game entered a crucial phase, Conan Doyle persuaded the captain to let him bowl for the first time on the tour. The Dutchmen needed 15 runs to win with four wickets in hand. He proceeded to toss up full-length deliveries to a packed off-side field and the remaining batsmen were all caught in the covers. His team-mates attempted to carry him off the field but, underestimating his bulk, they dropped him several times on the way to the pavilion.

In the following summer he played regularly for Norwood. As an opening batsman he scored over 500 runs at an average of 23. He also sent down 200 overs and took 44 wickets at an average of 10.72. The games were serious, being against some of the strongest club sides in London, and as a relief he arranged lighthearted fixtures between Norwood and *The Idler Magazine*. He played for *The Idler* in these alongside his brother-in-law E.W. Hornung, the creator of Raffles, who kept wicket. The whole editorial staff would turn out for the games and enthusiastic supporters included Jerome K. Jerome and Israel Zangwill, the novelist and Zionist.

With shared interests of cricket and spiritualism, Conan Doyle soon gravitated towards J.M. Barrie and began playing for his cricket team, the Allahakbarries. The matches were noted for low playing standards, much frivolity and the presence of some glittering literati. The Allahakbarries published a booklet with pen portraits of the players and the entry for Conan Doyle describes him as: 'A grand bowler... knows a batsman's weaknesses by the colour of the mud on his shoes.' Team-mates included P.G. Wodehouse and his Stonyhurst contemporary A.E.W. Mason. Under Barrie's influence, he renewed his interest in spiritualism and joined the British Society for Psychical Research.

In 1892 his wife Louise contracted tuberculosis. Her condition stabilised over the next three years but in the mid 1890s the couple moved to Hindhead in Surrey, an area known to be suited to convalescent consumptives. Conan Doyle played village cricket and took a keen interest in sport at the local prep school, St Edmund's. Some years later its pupils would include the future cricket correspondent Raymond Robertson-Glasgow, who noted in his autobiography: 'Sir Arthur was a roughish determined batsman, with a vigorous design on short and improbable runs, not always answered by static and calm-browed partners.'

By now Conan Doyle was a wealthy man, the Holmes stories having increased the circulation of *Strand Magazine* to half a million. In September 1896 he made his first appearance at Lord's, scoring an undefeated century for Authors vs Press. His team-mates included J.M. Barrie and George Duckworth (the architectural historian not the Lancashire wicketkeeper!) The game was played in a quagmire and he showed a good deal of resolve while making 101 in partnership with C.A. Tyssen. The mud-encrusted bat that he was using became a talisman and took pride of place at his various homes for the rest of his life.

Perhaps Conan Doyle sought relief from sexual tension in sport. In

1898 he played for Barrie's Allahakbarries against the Artists at Broadway, Worcestershire. He scored 46 not out and Jim Coldham noted that Barrie, who had just taught himself to bowl an effective leg-break, took seven wickets to win the match. The Artists were captained by the 46-year-old Edwin Abbey. A Philadelphia-born mural painter, Abbey had been sent to England by Harpers to gather materials for his illustrations of the poetry of Robert Herrick. He is best remembered now for his decoration of the Boston Public Library. In a similar game two years later, Conan Doyle not only took eight wickets but also scored 91. Whatever his ability as a leg-spinner, Barrie was a hopeless batsman. When Conan Doyle saw him coming to the wicket at number 11 he decided to hit out immediately for his century but was caught on the boundary. As the pair left the pitch Barrie quipped: 'Careless of you to get out like that when we were both going for our hundred.'

On the outbreak of the Boer War, Conan Doyle volunteered for the Middlesex Yeomanry but was rejected on the grounds of age; he was now 40. He continued playing cricket and in 1899 he took 7 for 51 for MCC against Cambridgeshire at Lord's. It was among his best performances in a serious match and he reflected in his autobiography: 'I had some cause to hold on to the game as I had lost so much of it in my youth. I was now fulfilling a secret ambition by getting into the fringe of first-class cricket.'

He got his chance to take part in the South African war when in February 1900 he was asked to join a medical unit destined for Bloemfontein. The unit had been organised and privately financed by his friend John Langman and as senior physician he was asked to select personnel. The group travelled out on the same boat as a battalion of the Royal Scots Regiment and they played deck cricket until their only ball was hit overboard.

In April 1900 he took over a grossly overcrowded fever hospital which had been set up in a cricket pavilion. The backdrop was bizarre: prior to the outbreak of war the pavilion had been used to stage a production of *HMS Pinafore* and much of the scenery was still in place, a detail that could hardly have helped patients already delirious with enteric fever. The hospital was soon fighting a losing battle with dysentery and the death rate was such that men were simply lowered into the ground wrapped in blankets, at a rate of 60 a day. Conditions improved when a supply of clean drinking water was recovered from the Boers and by July the surviving patients were recovering rapidly. Conan Doyle widened his activity to act as a war correspondent for the *Pall Mall Gazette* and organised football competitions which did much to improve morale.

He was back in England by July 1900 and keen to resume his cricket career. In August he made his first-class debut for MCC against London County at Crystal Palace where he dismissed W.G. Grace, having him caught behind by William Storer. Arthur had packed the off-side field and induced the Doctor to get a leading edge when sweeping. It was hardly a major triumph; he bowled only 2.1 overs and it is possible that W.G. gifted his wicket having already scored 110. However, Arthur was elated and wrote a tongue-in-cheek 19-stanza mock epic poem: 'With the beard of a Goth or a Vandal/His bat hanging ready and free/His great hairy hands on the handle/And his menacing eyes upon me.' Grace would prove to be his only wicket in first-class cricket.

By March 1901 his sporting interests had widened to include golf and it was during a golfing holiday in Norfolk that Bertram Robinson invited him to Devon to investigate the legend of spectral hounds wandering the marshlands of Dartmoor. The result was the most famous Holmes story of them all. Two months later he played for a strong MCC team against Leicestershire at Lord's, his team-mates including players of the calibre of Grace, Billie Murdoch and Gilbert Jessop. In MCC's second innings he came in at number 10 and made 32 not out.

In July 1902 Conan Doyle again played for MCC vs London County at Crystal Palace, where he batted fluently and raced to 43 with successive boundaries off W.G. The Old Man decided he was getting over-confident and tossed up a slower ball. Arthur was deceived in the air and was stumped by Edward French. In August he reluctantly accepted a knighthood under pressure from his mother. He had never quite lost his boyish irreverence for pomp and office, and complained that the ceremonial uniform made him look 'like a monkey on a stick'.

Sir Arthur continued to be a mainstay of the annual Authors vs Artists fixture and one of the most notable matches was in May 1903, when the Authors included Doyle, A.E.W. Mason, P.G. Wodehouse, J.M. Barrie, E.W. Hornung and E.V. Lucas. In addition to Edwin Abbey and George Hillyard Swinstead, the Artists included the architect Reginald Blomfield, who is best remembered for the Menin Gate Memorial at Ypres. The Authors won by 101 runs, Sir Arthur scoring 28 and P.G. Wodehouse making a dapper 33 before being run out.

An odd incident occurred in the same season while he was playing for MCC against Kent. An inveterate pipe-smoker, he always carried a tin of matches and when he was hit on the thigh by a delivery from Bill Bradley the matches ignited. There was much merriment and W.G. squeaked from the pavilion in his odd falsetto: 'Couldn't get you out— had to set you on fire!' Sir Arthur recovered his composure to make a respectable 16 not out in MCC's second innings. His relationship with W.G. was excellent and 12 years later he would recall the Doctor in a perceptive and graceful obituary for *The Times*: 'Few men have done more for the generation in which they lived and his influence was none the less because it was a spontaneous and utterly unconscious one.'

Louise succumbed to tuberculosis in July 1906. Perhaps looking for diversion from his grief, Sir Arthur became interested in the case of George Edalji. A Birmingham-based solicitor of Parsee extraction, Edalji had been accused of mutilating farm animals in 1903. He was sentenced to seven years' hard labour but released without pardon or compensation in 1906. Sir Arthur took up the case, enlisting help from Jerome K. Jerome. After exposing police racism and inefficiency he cleared Edalji's name in the following year.

In September 1907 Sir Arthur married Jean Leckie. Jean was an elegant, urbane 23-year-old from a distinguished Scottish family that claimed a direct link with Rob Roy. She was noted for an hourglass figure, excellent dress sense and a superb singing voice. (There appears to be much of Jean in Irene Adler, the only woman to arouse the romantic interest of Sherlock Holmes.) Jean had first met Sir Arthur while organising one of his lecture tours several years earlier. The pair had been deeply attracted to each other at first sight but Conan Doyle would not divorce the ailing Louise nor would he have anything to do with Jean sexually. His integrity stands out here, given that in partnership with his close friend Thomas Hardy, he had been championing a relaxation of divorce law for many years and would later serve as President of the Divorce Law Reform Union. The couple set up home a few miles outside Crowborough in East Sussex. There they built a lavish house adjacent to Groombridge Place, which is the setting for the Sherlock Holmes story *The Valley of Fear*.

As a prominent member of the British Olympic Association, his main interest in 1908 was the London Olympiad. The meeting is best remembered for dramatic film footage that shows the Italian Dorando Petri collapsing only yards from the finish of the marathon and being helped across the line by officials. (He was later disqualified.) As a correspondent for the *Daily Mail*, Sir Arthur is visible within a few feet of Dorando at the finishing tape, encouraging him if not assisting him physically.

In February 1910 Sir Arthur staged his play *The House of Temperley* at the Adelphi Theatre. Based on his 1896 novel *Rodney Stone*, it is a Regency mystery story set against a backdrop of professional prize-fighting. He directed the fights himself and ensured that they were realistic even to the extent of having to cover the actors' bruises with make-up. Later in the year he was approached by the lawyers of Oscar Slater, a Silesian Jew and small-time pimp, who had been sentenced to death for allegedly murdering an 82-year-old woman with a hammer in Glasgow on ludicrous circumstantial evidence. The sentence was commuted to life imprisonment with hard labour, but after many appeals over the course of 17 years, Conan Doyle could take much credit for Slater's release.

Sir Arthur was distraught when his spiritualist friend William Stead died on the *Titanic*. After George Bernard Shaw exposed the inefficiency of the White Star Line in various British newspapers, he leapt to the defence of Captain Smith, claiming that he had swum to a lifeboat carrying a child but refused to clamber on board himself. At the time he was also campaigning for the construction of a Channel Tunnel and in April he wrote to *The Times*: 'The matter seems to me to be of such importance that I grudge every day that passes without something being done to bring it to realisation.'

Early in 1914 Sir Arthur was quick to see that war was imminent and he was almost clairvoyant in his predictions as to the devastating use that the German navy would make of U-boats. In the spring he visited America and attended a World Series baseball match between the New York Yankees and the Philadelphia Athletics. Later, in Canada, he was invited to start a baseball game. At 55 he still cut an athletic figure; he looked sprightly as he hopped up to the plate but the pitcher decided to be gentle with him. He was shocked when Sir Arthur – treating the ball as a full toss at cricket – simply opened his shoulders and laced it between first and second base into the packed press gallery.

As soon as war broke out he organised his own unofficial Home Guard battalion at Crowborough. He was disappointed when officialdom disbanded it but became a member of the Crowborough Company of the Fourth Royal Sussex Volunteer Regiment, happily serving as a private. He and Jean turned part of their house into a recreation centre for Canadian soldiers posted nearby and Arthur assisted in supervising German POWs at Lewes Prison. He spent the summer of 1916 on the Western Front as an observer for the War Office, making comparisons between British, French and Italian operational techniques. He is said to have proved nerveless under heavy fire at Bellenglise near St Quentin. The experience also inspired some of his best poetry which is otherwise almost universally mediocre: 'Behold all Europe writhing on the rack/The sins of fathers grinding down the sons!/"How long, O Lord?" He sends no answer back/But still I hear the mutter of the guns.'

In 1916 Sir Arthur publicly announced his belief in spiritualism. This explodes the popular myth that his judgement was unhinged after the death of his brother Innes and son Kingsley in 1918. However, much embarrassment would follow. In the summer of 1917 the spiritualist Edward Gardner told Sir Arthur about the Cottingley fairy photos. These were pictures taken by 15-year-old Elsie Wright and her 11-year-old cousin Frances Griffiths at their home on the outskirts of Bradford. The prints showed extraordinarily realistic images of fairies and elves; they had been taken to the London offices of Kodak, whose staff found no evidence of superimposition. Harold Snelling, a prominent photographer and the leading darkroom technician of the day, declared that the plates were a single exposure, that the figures were not made of paper or fabric, and that they had even moved slightly while the shutter was open.

Sir Arthur examined the pictures, was completely taken in and used them in an article in *Strand Magazine*. More embarrassing still, two years later he wrote a book entitled *The Coming of the Fairies*, which was greeted with ridicule. The pictures are undoubtedly the greatest photographic hoax in history. The saga has recently inspired Charles Sturridge's *Fairytale*. The film takes a few liberties with chronology but is beautifully shot and cast. Peter O'Toole and Harvey Keitel turn in superb performances as Sir Arthur and Harry Houdini respectively. In 1982, at the age of 83, Elsie Wright admitted to the *British Journal of Photography* that the pictures were fakes, the fairies being magazine pictures attached to hatpins, while Frances Griffiths confirmed as much a few months later in a letter to *The Times*.

There is a fascinating evaluation of Sir Arthur during this period in Cynthia Asquith's biography of J.M. Barrie: 'Conan Doyle has been our chief newcomer. Burly, unpretentious, loveable, ingenuous, he looks like a country doctor – he is a doctor. I'm sure the reason why people accept his word on Spiritualism is that they confuse him with his own creation. Surely, they think, Sherlock Holmes would be able to sift evidence. So, crediting Conan Doyle with the faculties of his hero, they are confident that he couldn't be imposed upon by frauds; whereas, really, he is, I'm sure, a touchingly credulous man – a King Gull! If Conan Doyle's presence attracted any of those mundane-looking fairies of whom he showed me photographs, none showed her horrid self to me.'

In the final weeks of the war Sir Arthur's son Kingsley died of pneumonia while trying to resurrect his medical studies. He had served with distinction as an observation officer with the Hampshire Regiment but had been invalided home suffering from acute debilitation. This had occurred after he showed exceptional courage while crawling through no-man's-land marking out uncut barbed wire for gunners. Sir Arthur immediately began seeing him at psychic seances. In February of the following year, Sir Arthur's younger brother, Innes, succumbed to influenza. Innes had also been severely weakened by active service. Sir Arthur never escaped the shadow of these losses; he spent the rest of his life trying to articulate his grief and find solace.

In 1920 he saw the American magician and escape artist Harry Houdini at Portsmouth and was immediately attracted to him, believing his powers had spiritualist origins. Houdini was an agnostic but he empathised with Sir Arthur and visited the family home at Crowborough. Two years later Sir Arthur embarked on a lecture tour to the United States promoting spiritualism and was disturbed when several members of his audiences committed suicide in a rush to enjoy life on the other side. He met Houdini again and in an unimpressive seance, Jean Conan Doyle claimed to intercede for Houdini with his dead mother. Houdini was unconvinced but handled matters with tact.

Physically, Conan Doyle was an outstanding example of Victorian manhood. His biographer Charles Higham talks of a 'physical massiveness and brass-band optimism'. His height was 6 ft 2 in and in his prime as a footballer he weighed 15 stone. He prided himself on his strength and stamina and took bodybuilding courses designed by the American physical culturist and Vaudeville strongman Eugene Sandow, the Charles Atlas of his day.

He proved relentlessly curious throughout his life and was something of a dilettante, music being about the only art form at which he did not achieve some competence. It appears that he was almost tone deaf, though he once purchased a banjo and tried to accompany Jean's superb mezzo-soprano, with pitiful results. Contemporaries recall that he was generous to a fault, rarely criticised anybody and was unfailingly courteous to servants and social inferiors. He was also chivalrous towards women and once slapped his son Adrian across the face when he remarked that a woman was ugly: 'Just remember that no woman is ugly.'

Sir Arthur was interested in many forms of religion and tolerant of all. He carried his learning lightly and was admired for his strong sense of mission coupled with a romantic stubbornness. He lived for the outdoors and had much in common with Teddy Roosevelt, with whom he enjoyed a long friendship that verged on hero-worship. At times he could be an inspired practical joker and he loved to frighten guests with a clockwork snake.

In his autobiography, he describes cricket as: 'A game which has given me more pleasure than any other branch of sport'. He batted right-handed and his natural inclination was towards defence, but when needed he could score rapidly with a variety of unorthodox shots. Many contemporary references suggest that he was addicted to quick singles. In his ten first-class games he scored 231 runs with an average of 19.25. He appears to have been intolerant of left-handers and in *Strand Magazine* for August 1909 he recommended (quite seriously) that left-handed batting should be banned: 'The left-handed batsman is undeniably a nuisance, delaying the game and giving the field an immense amount of trouble. Why should he be permitted to do this when he is in so immense a minority?' Sir Arthur was a spin bowler and the *Wisden* obituary describes him as having 'a puzzling flight', but little more is known about his mode of delivery. Given the hatred of left-handers and the fact that he appeared to gain speed off the wicket it is probable that he was a leg-spinner.

There is little treatment of cricket in Sir Arthur's fiction. A posse of literary sleuths has shown that Sherlock Holmes never so much as mentions it. However, there is some cricket content in the Brigadier Gerard stories, and in 1928 *Strand Magazine* published 'The Story of Spedegue's Dropper'. Conan Doyle based the piece on the experience of having been bowled in bizarre circumstances by the Essex and England player A.P. Lucas. Lucas slipped in his delivery stride, the ball followed an almost vertical trajectory to a height of 30 feet and then fell plumb on to Sir Arthur's wicket. The hero of the story, a schoolmaster named Tom Spedegue, is plucked from village cricket and makes an incredible Test debut against Australia, taking 7 for 31 with high full tosses.

In his autobiography, Sir Arthur is at pains to stress his love of rugby. At Edinburgh University he played as a prop forward, being noted for a good turn of speed despite his weight. He describes rugby as the finest team game known to man and bemoans his 'wretched training' in Stonyhurst's own field game. Holmes fans will recall that in 'The Sussex Vampire', Robert Ferguson enlists the help of the great detective by letter, adding as a postscript: 'I believe that your friend Watson played rugby for Blackheath when I was three-quarter for Richmond.' As a Blackheath player in the 1880s, Dr Watson must have been near to international standard and would have lined up alongside the England captain A.E. Stoddart at Rectory Field.

Sir Arthur's involvement with golf was intermittent and he often gave up the game in disgust at his perceived lack of competence which he blamed on 'a deformed stance and an underdeveloped swing'. He described himself as 'an enthusiastic, but a very inefficient player – a ten at best, and at my worst outside the pale of all decent handicaps'.

In September 1894 during a tour of North America, he visited fellow cricket enthusiast Rudyard Kipling at his retreat in Vermont. The pair spent an afternoon hitting golf balls around Kipling's estate to the amazement of neighbours and assembled journalists. In his dotage, Sir Arthur would flick a few mid-irons round Crowborough Beacon Golf Course, often leaving his chauffeur to collect the balls. While in Davos in 1895 during one of his first wife's many attempts to throw off tuberculosis, he laid out a primitive golf course, but he was dismayed when it was destroyed by alpine cattle.

As a boxer Conan Doyle describes himself as 'a fair average amateur'. He did much to promote boxing within the Jewish community of the East End and his various houses were littered with pictures of contemporary fighters. He attended the major fights of the day and had tremendous respect for Welsh flyweight Jimmy Wilde. Sir Arthur believed that the quickness of movement which comes from boxing tuition gave Allied troops an advantage during bayonet fighting.

In a letter to G.K. Chesterton he stated that he would have preferred to have made a living with his fists rather than through writing or any other form of sport. His enthusiasm for boxing was common knowledge; in the summer of 1910 he was asked by the promoter Tex Rickard to referee the fight between James Jeffries and the negro Jack Johnson in Reno, Nevada. Sir Arthur declined and never regretted his refusal. Johnson knocked out Jeffries in the fifteenth at the end of an extraordinarily savage bout with racial overtones that make Schmeling–Louis in 1936 and its own attendant bigotry look like a bit of gentle milling at the Oxford and Cambridge Club.

Sir Arthur also had a passion for billiards, and when he designed his own houses the architectural plan had to revolve around the billiards room. He was a competent player and in 1913 he was persuaded to enter the London qualifying competition for the Amateur Championship at Soho Square. Amid much media interest he reached the third round where in a game of 1,000 up he was beaten by Harold Evans, the winning margin being 376 points.

Michael Coren has noted: 'For the last ten years of his life Conan

Doyle effectively became the missionary-in-chief of world spiritualism.' In the spring of 1923 he embarked on another lecture tour of America, his prize exhibit being a picture taken by the spiritualist photographer Ada Deane during the Cenotaph ceremony of the previous year. The print showed ghostly images of dead servicemen floating through the air during the two minutes' silence. To Sir Arthur's chagrin the photo was exposed as a fraud a year later when the *Daily Sketch* revealed that the faces were those of well-known footballers who even wrote in to confirm the fact.

In 1926 he was asked by the Chief Constable of Surrey to assist in tracking down Agatha Christie, who had disappeared while suffering marital problems and may have attempted to commit suicide under a pseudonym in a Harrogate hotel. (A walk-on appearance by Sir Arthur might have added a touch of class to Michael Apted's *Agatha*, an appalling 1979 film treatment of the incident starring Dustin Hoffman.)

Sir Arthur kept much of his vitality into old age and only a year before his death he allowed himself to be driven round Brooklands motor-racing circuit at high speed. However, he began to overtax his strength while following a hectic itinerary of lectures and seances during a tour of Scandinavia in 1929. He returned to Sussex with heart problems but would not lighten his schedule. In July 1930 he became agitated while on a deputation to Parliament requesting a relaxation of laws that related to the activities of spiritualist mediums. After collapsing in London he was taken to Crowborough, where he died of a heart attack.

Sir Arthur simply could not resign himself to the fact that all our conjectures are arbitrary and fate is beyond knowledge. He wrote a dozen books on spiritualist issues, lectured all over the world and contributed a quarter of a million pounds to psychic causes. A spiritualist rally at the Albert Hall six days after his death was attended by 12,000 people. Predictably many of the mediums present claimed to have made contact with him on the other side. Sir Arthur had an unshakeable faith in the next world. He was far too good for this one and often lost his way.

10

Aubrey Faulkner

b: 17.12.1881, Port Elizabeth, South Africa.
d: 10.9.1930, Walham Green, London.

A shilling's worth of gas floats in the room.
Despair not being wordy gets things done.
All the paraphernalia of gloom
Belongs to death and must be left someone.

Peter Porter, 'Suicide Unmasked', 1961

At around seven o'clock on the morning of 10 September 1930, the managing director of the world's first permanent indoor cricket school placed his mouth over the jet of a gas radiator. The suicide note to his secretary is an odd mixture of the sublime and laconic: 'Dear Mackenzie, I am off to another sphere via the small bat-drying room. Better call in a policeman to do the investigating.' Back in 1909 Aubrey Faulkner had been indisputably the finest all-round cricketer in the world. As an artillery officer in the Great War he had been brave to the point of folly. He was enormously handsome, constitutionally decent, wonderfully open, fresh and touched with genius. Sadly, under a conventional surface there lay unfathomable depths of pessimism. As a player he had been distinguished for his sloppy dress, reaching his nadir in 1906 when he played a whole Test match with his trousers held up by a piece of string.

His parents were affluent members of the Port Elizabeth middle classes. Aubrey attended the leading preparatory school Trinity High, where he excelled at cricket and rugby. As a youth he was dutiful but hardly an altar-boy. Recollections of Aubrey stress that he was enormously attractive to the opposite sex throughout his life; as a youngster his gallivanting with older women got him into scrapes that would have sunk a worthier man without trace. His father, Frank, was a violent alcoholic and philanderer and the pair had a tortured relationship which clouded the rest of Aubrey's life. He was devoted to his mother, Anne, née de Berry, and once told Ian Peebles how as a 15-year-old he returned from cricket practice to find his father blind drunk and beating his mother. Aubrey set about his father and knocked him out of his shoes.

Early in 1900 Aubrey was only too pleased to swap his tortured home life for service in the Boer War. As a 19-year-old he enlisted in a unit that became part of the Imperial Light Horse. With the Boers relying on guerrilla tactics, sabotaging supply lines and derailing trains, the Light Horse formed flying relief columns which would later assist in liberating Ladysmith and Mafeking. In the following autumn he settled in Cape Town where he worked as a clerk at the Corner House Gold Mining Company. He attended net practice at the Newlands Cricket Ground and was coached by Walter Richards, the former Warwickshire batsman. Aubrey made his debut for Transvaal in the 1902–03 season but his form was patchy. He came to the fore in December 1905 when he scored an undefeated 63 against Pelham Warner's MCC tourists. The innings brought him a place in all five Tests of the season and after a poor start he made scores of 34 and 45 in the final two matches. He bowled competently throughout the series and in the fourth Test at Cape Town he took 4 for 49 from 25.5 overs in England's first innings.

He was an immediate choice for the South African team that toured England in 1907. With Albert Vogler, Reggie Schwarz and Gordon White, he found himself part of an extraordinary cricket sideshow, a quartet of wrist-spinners. Aubrey's colleagues warrant a moment's digression. Two of them were double internationals: Schwarz played rugby for England, and White played quasi-official soccer for South Africa. They were all eccentrics and they were all doomed. One of the greatest leg-spinners of all time and undoubtedly Aubrey's superior, Vogler degenerated into a hopeless drunk. White died of his wounds on the Western Front two weeks before the Armistice and Schwarz died a week after it of pneumonia contracted on active service.

Aubrey had been brought up on matting wickets and his form was not helped by a damp English summer. In the Headingley Test he bowled superbly to take 6 for 17 and dismiss the home side for 76. The *Manchester Guardian* reported: 'Faulkner confirmed the view that he is the best bowler in South Africa. He got a tremendous amount of work on the ball and came quickly off the pitch, while he varied his flight in a deceptive fashion, bowling the hanging ball with great skill.' His form in other matches was uneven but in the final Test at The Oval he played a faultless innings of 42 in failing light to ensure a draw for the tourists.

Playing for Transvaal against XVI of the Rest of Transvaal in January 1909, Aubrey took 17 for 139 and bludgeoned 100 not out in less than an hour. In the following year he made 78 and 123 in the first Test against England at Johannesburg and took 5 for 120 in the tourists' first innings. The *Rand Daily Mail* had an interesting correspondent in the England and Hampshire cricketer and FA Cup-winning footballer Teddy Wynyard. Wynyard reported: 'Faulkner is an extraordinary cricketer. A great player this, with a great future.' The performance at Johannesburg made Aubrey the first South African to score a century, a half century and take five wickets in an innings during the course of a Test match. It would be 89 years before Jacques Kallis emulated this feat against West Indies at Cape Town in January 1999.

In the second Test at Durban he took 6 for 87 in England's second innings. The *Natal Mercury* commented: 'He disguises his break wonderfully and the batsman cannot tell which way the sphere is coming.' The run of form continued in the third match at Johannesburg where he scored 76 and 44, while at Cape Town he contributed a useful 49 not out to the home side's second innings. His 99 in the final game at Cape Town was a rearguard action after South Africa found themselves at 31 for 3. Aubrey's aggregate of 545 runs at an average of 60.55 and haul of 29 wickets at 21.89 produced a glowing evaluation in *Cricket*: 'For Faulkner's performances it would be difficult to speak too highly. His figures are eloquent testimony to his skill, and stamp him as one of the best all-round players in the world.'

He proved a mainstay of the South African team which travelled to

Australia in the 1910–11 season and his batting in the Test series was outstanding. In Sydney his team-mates were unsettled by the fearsome pace of 'Tibby' Cotter but Aubrey's scores of 62 and 43 allowed several of his partners to play themselves into form. At Melbourne he revelled in his savage square cut but exercised restraint while making 204 in five hours. The *Melbourne Argus* noted: 'There was no absolute mastery of the bowling, nothing iconoclastic. It was the one bad ball in each over that suffered . . . a great innings on a great occasion.'

By now he could not fail and at Adelaide he made 56 and 115 on a difficult wicket. On the eve of the fourth Test at Melbourne, Aubrey and his team-mates visited an aboriginal township at Healesville on the river Yarra, where he excelled at boomerang and spear throwing. His outlook was occasionally saturnine but despite these black periods he proved a good mixer. His superb knowledge of the game and ability to illustrate his ideas made him something of a guru; his colleagues would approach him for technical advice as they might go to a priest.

Aubrey finished the series in triumph, scoring 20 and 80 at Melbourne followed by 52 and 92 at Sydney. The *Sydney Morning Herald* reported: 'Faulkner again showed his pre-eminence by a faultlessly compiled 52. But as usual, he had the weight of the team on his shoulders and dared not play the forceful cricket of which he is capable.' The paper's final evaluation of Aubrey's contribution was: 'The most consistent player who ever toured Australia. The arena rippled with applause from his entrance to his exit.'

He averaged 73.2 (with no not-outs) in the Test series and his aggregate of 732 runs stood as a record until 1924–25 when Herbert Sutcliffe scored 734 for England against Australia. Aubrey was also superb in state and up-country games, scoring 252 against Broken Hill and making over 2,000 runs on the tour. However, his bowling was erratic and he was frequently unable to deliver his googly. The series was by no means a happy one and there was much bad blood between players and management over the treatment of Albert Vogler. The popular and irrepressible Vogler had embarked on what would be a 40-year assault on his liver and his drinking bouts caused him to be dropped for three Tests.

In June 1911 Aubrey married Florence Millicent Thompson at the Gardens Presbyterian Church in Cape Town. The pair sailed for

England on the *Dover Castle* almost immediately after the ceremony. It was Aubrey's intention to play for Surrey or Middlesex as an amateur. His plans changed and the couple settled in Nottingham where he played high-class club cricket. In May of the following year he scored a brilliant 131 for MCC vs Nottinghamshire at Lord's. *The Times* concluded: 'Mr Faulkner scarcely made a mistake. He timed the ball splendidly and although he exercised restraint, he rarely failed to punish any loose ball.'

A few days later he scored 122 not out for South Africa against Australia at Old Trafford. Reuters reported: 'Faulkner alone saved his side from disaster. His defence is not graceful to watch but the soundness of method is unmistakable.' Aubrey offered a sitter to Bill Whitty when on 36 but the rest of the innings was faultless and he scored freely all round the wicket. The match was part of the Triangular Tournament between England, Australia and South Africa. Apart from a half-century at Lord's, Aubrey did little with the bat that summer. Despite damp, unresponsive wickets, his leg-breaks and googlies posed problems throughout the summer, and in the eighth match of the series at The Oval he ripped through the English line-up to take 7 for 84 from 27.1 overs. He bowled right through the innings and took out the heart of the England batting, dismissing Hobbs, C.B. Fry and Jack Hearne.

Aubrey played regularly for the Nottinghamshire Amateur XI and Sir Julien Cahn's Nottinghamshire Ramblers in 1913 and 1914. He took all 10 wickets on two occasions and scored 229 against Pallingswick. More rewarding was his discovery and coaching of Tom Richmond, a talented leg-spinner who would go on to play for Nottinghamshire.

Aubrey was in colours as soon as hostilities broke out and served briefly as an infantry subaltern with the Worcestershire Regiment. Using Francis Lacey, the MCC secretary, for a personal reference, he obtained a transfer to the Royal Field Artillery (RFA) as a temporary lieutenant. He spent February 1915 on an observation mission at the Western Front with the RFA's 13th (Western) Division and then served with 68th Brigade as a temporary captain. In June he left France for Thessaloniki via Alexandria. During the voyage he joined the RFA's 10th (Irish) Division under Lieutenant-General Sir Brian Mahon, his old commander from the Boer War. His division trekked north-westwards across the Belasitsa mountains to Macedonia, where he took charge of C Battery 54th Brigade. The unit was unprepared for constant skirmishing with Bulgar forces and many of his horses and mules were suffering from septic pneumonia. Men and animals encountered intense cold at Dudular while dragging themselves through treacherous ravines. Regimental diaries record that it was common for horses to freeze to death during the night and for men to die of exposure while in the saddle.

In August 1917 he was posted to 67th Brigade and sailed for Palestine in the same month. In early December his unit gave covering fire to the Royal Irish Fusiliers before clearing Turkish trenches and advancing towards Jeruit. Over Christmas 1917 Aubrey was promoted to temporary major and his unit supported 229 Infantry Brigade in its capture of Kereina Ridge. Retreating Turkish troops caused dire problems by poisoning wells. Many horses went mad through thirst and had to be shot, while troops were unable to wash for several weeks. In late December 67th Brigade played a key role in the capture and defence of Jerusalem, knocking out several Turkish machine-gun emplacements. Aubrey spent much of 1918 performing salvage work around Palestine before the Armistice with Turkey in October. During this period he suffered badly with malaria, which would trouble him for the rest of his life. His outstanding achievements were recognised and after being mentioned in despatches he was awarded the DSO and the Order of the Nile.

The war took its toll on Aubrey's health and he became irritable as a result of regular bouts of malaria and viral conditions. Florence tired of his vagaries and there may have been extra-marital affairs. The couple obtained a divorce in 1920. In August of that year he made one of his few serious cricket outings when he scored 112 out of 270 for MCC vs Minor Counties at Lord's. The *Morning Post* commented: 'The bowling was good – too good for the majority of the MCC side – but Mr Faulkner never looked to be anything but thoroughly at his ease. He scored at a good pace and kept the ball down excellently...his footwork was well up to the standard of his great years.'

A month later Aubrey was employed as games master at St Piran's, a prep school in Maidenhead, where he coached cricket and rugby. (In his youth he had played rugby for Eastern Provinces and had been a serious candidate for the South African side.) His pupils included a future England cricket captain, Freddie Brown. It was one of Brown's abiding regrets that Aubrey did not live to see him win Test honours. As a sporting mentor he proved resourceful and innovative, his more original training routines including a form of short cricket that was played in a fives court. He was popular with his pupils and Brown recalled in his autobiography: 'Nothing was too much trouble to him: he had unlimited patience and was always very kind.'

By 1923 Aubrey had transformed the standard of games at St Piran's and his curriculum had extended to the swimming pool. He made the whole school assemble at the poolside and placed an enormous tuck-box on the high diving board. After hurling himself off it with a good deal of grace he would clamber back up and reward boys who were intrepid enough to follow him with biscuits and chocolate. There were plans for him to go into partnership with the school's headmaster, Vernon Bryant, but these came to nothing when Bryant took to the bottle in 1924.

A few last flickers remained in Aubrey's cricketing lamp. In August 1921 he formed part of Archie MacLaren's bizarre 'England XI', a talented but unbalanced mixture of MacLaren's ageing cronies and promising undergraduates that defeated Warwick Armstrong's all-conquering Australian tourists. Aubrey's match-winning role is described elsewhere in this book in the chapter on MacLaren.

Three years later at the age of 42, Aubrey was persuaded to play for South Africa against England at Lord's after the tourists had been hit by injuries. He had not played regular first-class cricket since before the war and his inclusion excited much media interest. A *Morning Post* reporter wrote: 'When the scorecards were printed it was seen that the greatest of all South African cricketers, Mr Aubrey Faulkner, had responded to something like an SOS signal and consented to play. Those who had arrived at the ground early were not surprised at his inclusion, for, before play was begun, he could have been seen batting very nicely at the nets and sticking up his captain with some accurate and insidious googlies.' Aubrey came in at number eight and played a few exquisite leg glances before he misread Percy Fender's top-spinner and was bowled for a stylish 25. In the second innings he was run out for 12 when looking well set. He also bowled 17 expensive overs on a perfect wicket without any success, though he nearly had Jack Hobbs stumped early on in his innings of 211.

Aubrey's success as a cricket coach at St Piran's revealed his true vocation. In March 1925 he took on the lease of a large garage in Petersham Road, Richmond, and set up the Faulkner Cricket Academy, the first permanent indoor cricket school in the world. He had little money to spend on the project but augmented his income by working as a sports correspondent for the *Westminster Gazette*. For several months facilities at the school remained inadequate, with two cramped wickets and poor lighting. Pupils recalled that the netting hung so close to the brick walls that the ball could rebound and strike the batsman, while a fuse box in the roof directly above the bowler's head meant that extravagant flight could plunge the whole building into darkness.

Despite the rudimentary equipment, the school was flooded with pupils of all standards. In July the 17-year-old Ian Peebles visited it while on holiday from Scotland. He was already bowling something between a leg-break and a leg-cutter with proficiency, and soon became aware that the proprietor of the school was lurking in the background. Aubrey scuttled away to his office and dragged his assistant Arthur Downie into the nets: 'Come and see what I've found!' He observed the youngster closely for the next few days and Peebles recalled in *Spinner's Yarn*: 'Faulkner asked if I would like to stop and share his sandwich lunch. He said, "If you come to London you could be my secretary." This was an intoxicating prospect. "If I did," I asked, "do you think I would ever play for a county?" He looked at me thoughtfully for a moment. "If you come to me," he said, "you'll go a darn sight further than that."' Aubrey was rarely wrong in such matters; Peebles made his Test debut two years later.

In the following spring, after months of searching for more suitable premises, Aubrey inspected a larger garage at Farm Lane in Walham Green near Fulham. Like Brigham Young, he pronounced: 'This is the place!' He laid out six pitches with matting of varying speeds and the classes were packed with players of differing standards. His pupils recalled that he would take as much trouble with a duffer from the Ealing and Chiswick League as he would with an Oxbridge Blue. Having spotted a flaw, Aubrey could bowl the same ball over and over again until the batsman had eradicated his weakness.

With the increased overheads, funds remained scarce. Aubrey often bowled to his students for 12 hours at a stretch, occasionally having to use his left arm with which he delivered competent chinamen. He was still capable of mesmerising high-class batsmen, and when the Test player Jack MacBryan visited the school in 1927 he finally threw down his bat and stomped out of the net screaming: 'I can't play this bloody stuff!' Aubrey took the coaching extremely seriously and rarely relaxed. However, there were occasional moments of levity during visits from the Harker brothers, Joseph, Phil and Roland. They were all involved with the London stage as actors or scenic artists, and often brought the school to a standstill by performing riotous extracts from their shows at Wyndham's Theatre and organising impromptu table tennis tournaments.

In 1928 Aubrey married for the second time, his bride being Vera Alice Butcher. Ian Peebles recalls that she was pretty, sweet-natured and much younger than her husband. Vera acted as Aubrey's secretary and attempted to improve the school's finances. She had little success and as a widow she was left the pitifully small estate of £273 16s 6d. It is probable that Aubrey could have augmented the school's income by applying for a liquor licence and perhaps realised his plans to build badminton courts and a gymnasium. However, he was a lifelong teetotaller, having been deeply scarred by his father's alcoholism, and would not allow alcohol on the premises.

Superficially Aubrey often appeared convivial, but under a vivacious surface there lay manic depression. When he relaxed he could be riotously funny and he is remembered by many as an excellent mimic. Sir Home Gordon's summation includes the observation: 'He was always a moody man though pleasant to be with', while Mike Spurrier notes: 'To the uninitiated he often appeared gregarious and outgoing, whereas in reality he was repressed, introverted and unable to forge deep lasting relationships.' Aubrey had incurably high expectations of life and they proved his downfall. He was rarely free from worries over the finances of his cricket school and these frequently made him introspective. Like his contemporary Archie MacLaren, Aubrey was a mass of contradictions: tough yet vulnerable, affectionate and remote, austere and sensual. His central qualities, however, were his directness and dynamism, his understanding of youth and an overwhelming physical presence both social and sexual.

Aubrey hated the mediocre and proved a hard taskmaster to himself and others. The theme is picked up in a *Cricketer* obituary: 'He brought dignity to a game because he played it with his whole heart and mind – and they were big and manly both of them.' He was consummately modest about his cricket and war careers and endeared himself to many with his vitality. Neville Cardus's obituary tribute in the *Manchester Guardian* ended: 'I enjoyed his personal charm, frankness, downrightness, his genius for the game, his own quick cricket sense, his readiness to listen to points of view other than his own, his simple humour and his boyish love of a joke at the expense of the solemnity of the professional attitude.'

Aubrey was slightly over six feet in his socks and weighed 16 stone. He had a powerful frame, though the effect of this and his smouldering brown eyes were undercut by an incongruous toothbrush moustache. Before the war his stamina had been legendary and during the 1912 Triangular Tournament he often bowled mammoth spells. Despite his bulk he contrived to be graceful in everything he did and while much of his florid sex life remains a mystery, he is known to have been enormously attractive to women.

Ian Peebles's judgement may be devalued by personal contact, but writing as recently as 1977 he concluded: 'Faulkner has a strong claim to be numbered amongst the six greatest all-rounders the game has yet seen.' His 'two-eyed' stance made him strong on the on side and his leg glances were superb. Having been brought up on artificial wickets, he excelled at the pull and the cut and when driving he was adept at keeping the ball low. There is little doubt that in 1909 and 1910 he was the finest all-round cricketer in the world.

As a leg-spinner Aubrey could extract movement from almost any wicket and his googly often turned square. For such a natural athlete his run-up was surprisingly craggy and ungainly. It included several stutters and he would arrive at the wicket with elbows pumping madly, in the manner of Bob Willis. However, the final delivery was an easy, wheeling motion that disguised subtle variations in pace. He was a superb fielder in any position and his reflexes were electric. With the possible exception of Mike Procter, he remains the greatest all-round cricketer South Africa has produced.

By the late 1920s Aubrey was suffering from acute depression. His plans for the cricket school were frustrated at every turn and his constitution had been weakened by active service in two wars. He was also involved in several unsuccessful business ventures. One of these involved buying a large consignment of cricket bats from the prominent manufacturer Warsop and injecting them with latex in the hope that he would improve their driving qualities. This explains why his corpse was found in what the suicide note describes as 'the bat-drying room'.

He remained considerate and open-minded to the last, but in 1929 he told Alice that he might one day commit suicide by gas poisoning. In the summer of 1930 he attended the Oval Test which marked Jack Hobbs's retirement from international cricket. Aubrey interviewed Hobbs for the BBC after the match and a transcript in the *Listener* reveals much about his state of mind. Hobbs is cheery and optimistic about the future: 'I've had a good innings. I will have a fine time to look back upon.' By contrast, Aubrey seems disillusioned and dispirited: 'You're lucky. The majority of us are not so fortunate.'

> Returning to London, I called on his widow, who told me something which moved me deeply. In the latter days, when he seemed to tire of everything, he had but one unfailing interest. It was to look at the morning paper to see how many wickets, I, his discovery and protégé, had taken the previous day.
>
> Ian Peebles, *Talking of Cricket*, 1953

Amid the inane platitudes of Sir Home Gordon's autobiography there is a rare insight into Aubrey's mental state towards the end. Sir Home recalled the ill-advised swan song in the 1924 Lord's Test: 'He would not remain in the dressing room with the others and persuaded me to sit with him in the north turret. It was obvious then, not only that he would never play again, but that his own retrospect of cricket was mysteriously and unjustifiably gloomy. Already that cloud was overshadowing his mentality which drove him eventually to end his life. Earlier, in the era of his glory, he had confided that he felt an inward blackness that suggested the futility of his own magnificent prowess.'

On 10 September 1930 the blackness prompted him to seek relief through coal-gas poisoning at the age of 48. Few people have denied Aubrey's supreme talent and fewer still have ever said a mean thing about him.

11

Hesketh Vernon
Hesketh-Prichard

b: 17.11.1876, Jhansi, India.
d: 14.6.1922, Gorhambury, Hertfordshire.

Behold the keenest marksman!
The most accomplished shot!
Time's sublimest target
Is a soul 'forgot!'

Emily Dickinson, c. 1858

In March 1789 the Marquis of Loreto was presented with fragments of the megatherium, a supposedly prehistoric giant sloth whose remains had been found in a riverbank to the north of Buenos Aires. The bones were donated to the Royal Museum of Madrid by Charles IV of Spain and they prompted Goethe to write an essay in which many have seen the first rudimentary theory of evolution. King Charles's instructions to his ambassador in South America were succinct. He wanted a specimen of the megatherium dead or alive.

An extensive search proved fruitless and the narrative moves on 111 years to 1900 when Arthur Pearson, editor of the fledgling *Daily Express*, issued a similar edict. In January 1895 the surprisingly well preserved carcass of a large ground sloth had been discovered by a retired German sea captain, Herman Eberhardt, in a cave at Last Hope Sound, to the north of Puerto Natales in Patagonia. Professor Florentino Ameghino of the Buenos Aires Museum was immediately convinced that they were the fresh remains of an animal similar to the prehistoric mylodon, a relative of the megatherium. A lively debate raged for the next five years. In 1897 Dr Francesco Moreno excavated the cave and found several pieces of still-supple skin. Moreno was unsure as to whether the animal was extinct, knowing that the cave was extremely dry and salty and a carcass could have remained in good condition for many years.

Albert Gaudry, a prominent French palaeontologist, examined the remains and stated that the animal might well be found alive. He suggested that the mylodon was about the size of a rhinoceros and a close relative of the megatherium. Gaudry's findings suggested that the megatherium genus of sloths was by no means prehistoric, and he produced evidence to suggest that they were living in a semi-domesticated state alongside man into the first part of the Middle Ages. In January 1899 Moreno showed the skin fragments to the Zoological Society of London, and the eminent naturalist Sir Edwin Ray Lankester concluded publicly that the mylodon might well be alive. His statement caused worldwide interest and a posse of journalists descended on Patagonia with Klondike intensity. The *Daily Express* sent a wide-eyed but talented cub who was not only fired with his task but exceptionally loyal to his editorial team.

He was the son of Hesketh 'Paddy' Brodrick Prichard, an officer in the King's Own Scottish Borderers, and Kate Ryall, a daughter of General B.W. Ryall of the Bengal Cavalry. Paddy Prichard died of typhoid six weeks before his son, 'Hex', was born, after drinking from an infected stream in India. As a young, unaccompanied widow, Hex's mother sailed for England with her three-month-old son and initially took lodgings in London. By the age of three, Hex was showing an interest in guns and animals. His use of a toy pistol bordered on an obsession and he insisted on being taken daily to the Zoological Gardens in Regent's Park, where he had befriended a caribou.

Mother and son moved to Jersey in the early 1880s and as a seven-year-old Hex was launched on another lifelong interest. After watching a cricket match at Victoria College he spent a whole summer in his garden bowling at a single stump. At 12 he was hiring a variety of weapons and shooting curlew successfully while scarcely able to withstand the kick of the gun. In 1887 he entered Fettes, a prominent public school in Edinburgh, on a Foundation Scholarship. He could be intensely studious but was hardly an ideal student, and having smuggled a .410 weapon into his dormitory disguised as an umbrella, he was discovered shooting plover and had to bribe a policeman to avoid expulsion. In the classroom he showed interest in geography and spent hours drawing maps of South America. Few would have been surprised at his subsequent career. However, he was dreamy, had an unhealthy obsession with cricket and was delicate, having outgrown his strength. As a 14-year-old he was a shade under six feet tall and this premature growth held him back as an athlete.

Hex won a place in the Fettes cricket XI in 1893 and took 46 wickets at 10 runs apiece. The grudge match of the season was against Blair Lodge, whose opening batsman, Frank Townsend Jnr, would go on to play for Gloucestershire. On the night before the game a lower-school boy dreamt that Hex would dismiss Townsend with the first ball of the match. He followed the script and delivered a vicious yorker with his opening delivery. As Townsend struggled to put his bat in the blockhole he gave a simple return catch. Hex proved a mainstay of the school's attack in the following year and the *Fettesian* concluded: 'The best bowler we have had for a long time. Fast right hand, with a good break back...Unfortunately he is leaving, but he ought to do something in the future.'

Dennis Potter was fond of saying that any journey from adolescence to adulthood is a long one. For Hex it was abrupt. There was no family money and a university course was out of the question. He left Fettes while still in the fifth form, began studying law as an articled clerk to a solicitor in Horsham and played cricket for the town. Although he passed his initial exams with ease, his heart was never set on a legal career and he talked vaguely about working at the Natural History Museum.

He had been writing since he was seven and journalism was the obvious route forward. By 1896 he had resolved to become a writer but felt he needed to travel. He sailed for Spain and moved on to Portugal, Gibraltar and Tangiers, where he visited an opium den and interviewed a serial killer. He was blossoming as a stylist and was soon given a column in *Pearson's Magazine*. The pieces are sassy, open-minded and lucid; they show an infallible nose for the main action, a complete faith in his descriptive powers and a determination to ransack the truth from any situation. Hex seems to have been equipped early on with an immutable sense of who he was and a clear understanding that he would be required to prove it.

He returned to London in the autumn of 1896 and began writing short stories for *Cornhill Magazine* in collaboration with his mother. He was already prolific and thought nothing of churning out 2,500 words before breakfast. At a book launch he was introduced to Arthur Conan Doyle, who was then in his late thirties. With shared interests of cricket, spiritualism and prehistoric creatures, the pair took an immediate shine to each other and ignored the other guests. Having been thrown out of the party in the small hours they walked around London until dawn. Hex began moving in the same literary circles as Conan Doyle and at dinner parties they had to be separated as you do with twins larking in church.

In 1898 Hex was told that he was damaging his eyesight through excessive reading and he was encouraged to take another trip overseas. He was now a consummate stylist and needed little reminding of it: 'Panama...a crown of crumbling sandstone towers, sunridden in its hot corner of the ring of blue bay...like a very old man wheezing in the clean pure sunlight – on a hillside by the sea – that's it! and it's not my fault if you don't realise Panama.' Hex journeyed on to New York where he came down with malarial fever and a chill. The unexpected medical expenses left him penniless but he was saved by what he and his mother believed to be their telepathic powers of communication. A few days later while walking her dogs, Kate Hesketh-Prichard sensed that Hex was in dire need of funds and she immediately wired a cash transfer.

In October 1899 Arthur Pearson of the *Daily Express* decided that his readers wanted unusual travel reports. He settled on Haiti as a suitable destination for his ace reporter, being unaware that no white man had penetrated the country's interior since a native uprising in 1804. Hex was devoted to Pearson, who would later lose his sight and found St Dunstan's, a home for the blind in Sussex. He accepted the assignment and left for Haiti in November. In his *Where Black Rules White*, he sets an objective evaluation of Voodoo against a colourful backdrop of snake-worship, human sacrifice and cannibalism. He travelled from

Jacmel to Port-au-Prince, often sleeping on the roadside and on one occasion in a windowless room with six strangers. He was among the first Europeans to be allowed to visit La Ferrière, the citadel built by Emperor Christophe. Hex journeyed everywhere with a flask of rum and water, though he was obliged to padlock it after a native tried to poison him.

In June of the following year he made his county cricket debut for Hampshire against Somerset at Bath, where he clean-bowled the master stylist of the time, Lionel Palairet. He played occasional matches for the rest of the summer while recovering from the rigours of the trip to Haiti. His editors at the *Daily Express* had been impressed with the reports and when interest in Patagonia and its prehistoric sloths intensified, they asked him to travel to South America. Still only 23 years old, Hex leapt at the opportunity and by September 1900 he was on a boat for Buenos Aires. He knew that to travel successfully across the Andes he would need few men but plenty of horses. He insisted that his party should travel light and live off *guanacos* (a llama-like animal) which he shot for himself and his gauchos.

He spent the following month making a 700-mile trek from Trelew, a Welsh settlement on the Argentinian coast, to Lake Buenos Aires on the borders of Chile, which he considered to be a possible domicile of the megatherium or mylodon. He found no trace of the animal and spent the early weeks of 1901 travelling northwards to Santa Cruz in Bolivia. He soon became sceptical about Indian accounts of the animal and a letter to his mother ends with: 'A more hopeless task no man ever had.'

His loyalty to the *Daily Express* was unflagging and he struggled from Santa Cruz to Lake Argentino, skirting much of the Andes. By now he had only two European assistants. There was no sign of the mylodon at the southern side of the lake and he decided to renovate a steam launch some 80 miles away. The vessel had not been used for three years, but his assistants performed miracles in repairing it and the party proceeded along a treacherous stretch of the River Leona despite being battered by icebergs: 'Our life on the launch was one long history of daily peril.'

Hex returned to England in the spring of 1901, perhaps concluding that man is indeed the inventor of his own monsters. His friends were out in force to meet him at Victoria Station and the welcome party included Conan Doyle, J.M. Barrie, E.W. Hornung and Andrew Lang. They were all clamouring for information about the mylodon: Barrie wanted to sketch the animal while Lang wanted to write a poem about it. If Hex is remembered at all today it is through the discussion of the mylodon by the present-day travel writer Bruce Chatwin. While Chatwin's prose remains brilliant, even deathless, his writing teems with inaccuracies and shameful claims of primacy. In one of his few real insights, Chatwin notes that Hex's research into the mylodon provided Conan Doyle with much background material for *The Lost World*. Hex never had the luxury of carbon dating; definitive work on the mylodon has fixed its remains at an age of about 10,000 years.

Hex's first full season of county cricket came in 1902 and his haul of 38 wickets at 20.8 put him second in the Hampshire averages behind the South African spinner Charlie Llewellyn. A highlight of the season was his performance for Hampshire against the touring Australians, during which he took the prized wickets of Clem Hill and Syd Gregory. He spent the following autumn tracking caribou in Newfoundland. Hex always recoiled from slaughter for its own sake; he shot a few specimens when he felt the odds were fair but spent most of his time studying the animal's migration patterns.

In May 1904 he turned out for MCC and Ground against Kent, and on a fiery wicket he dismissed the first five batsmen for four runs, finishing with 6 for 23. Two months later he was still finding extraordinary lift from a good length and he shattered Albert Knight's hand in the Gentlemen vs Players fixture. The match was tense and at the death Hex strode to the wicket with the amateurs needing eight runs for victory. Ted Arnold was bowling at fearsome pace to a dense slip and gulley cordon, but Hex stood his ground and laboured to 4 not out until Arthur Jones hit a boundary. He spent part of the winter in the West Indies as a member of Lord Brackley's touring XI, his best performance being 6 for 17 against St Lucia. By now his writing had made him a wealthy man and in the spring he financed a hunting holiday in Norway for a group of his journalist friends.

A highlight of the 1905 season was his analysis of 8 for 32 from 17 overs for Hampshire against Derbyshire. In 1907 Hex toured Ireland with I Zingari and his social poise brought him the offer of a position

as aide-de-camp to Lord Aberdeen. In February of the following year
he became engaged to Lady Elizabeth Grimston, a daughter of the Earl
of Verulam. He had in his own words 'never looked at another
woman'. The couple married four months later and honeymooned in
Norway where they sailed round the Fröya Islands in a Viking long-
boat observing grey seals. For once Kate Prichard received few letters
from her son, but Hex still had an eye on his bank balance and wrote
up the trip for *Cornhill Magazine*.

Another major expedition came in 1910 when he explored remote
parts of Labrador. He and his companions were tormented by mosquitoes and were cut off from their supplies. With just one bullet left and
the whole party close to starvation, Hex managed to shoot a caribou.
The group struggled to New York where Hex was introduced to Teddy
Roosevelt, who had just been succeeded as President by William Taft.
Roosevelt had read Hex's *Hunting Camps in Wood and Wilderness* and
questioned him intently on the Patagonian puma. The pair wrote to
each other regularly and the correspondence covers a bizarre gamut,
from metaphysical poetry to pygmy elephants. In 1912 Hex gave
Roosevelt much encouragement when he failed to secure the
Republican nomination and ran unsuccessfully on his independent
'Bull Moose' ticket.

Hex could be a vigorous polemicist and in 1911 he was outraged by
the slaughter of rare birds for their plumage. He did much to formulate
the Plumage Bill of that year and exposed members in both Houses
who had financial interests in the trade. His article 'Slaughtered for
Fashion' in a 1914 edition of *Pearson's Magazine* is a devastatingly
eloquent tract that brought him the support of John Galsworthy.
Similarly, while he had no qualms about shooting an occasional elderly
bull seal, he was horrified by the extent of the grey seal cull in the Outer
Hebrides which he highlighted in *Cornhill* in 1913.

He was 37 years old when the Great War came and was refused
commissions in the Guards and the Black Watch because of his age.
His response was to strut around the War Office cursing. An obvious
role was that of war correspondent but initially the Allies were loath
to allow detailed reports in the press. Reluctantly Kitchener sent a
team of journalists to the front in March 1915, and as a *Daily News*
correspondent, Hex arrived at the Ypres GHQ in the spring. He filed

his first report only 200 yards from enemy lines. He was unimpressed by some of his colleagues and a letter to his mother dismissed a Reuters cub reporter with: 'Can't write, can't behave, and puffs his cigarettes in the faces of generals…I feel I could sing at his funeral.'

He spent the summer with the 10th Infantry Brigade of the 4th Division. By now open warfare had ceased and been replaced by static attrition in trenches. Much of Europe was becoming a fetid charnel house. Hex was horrified by the German use of gas and the devastation it was causing in Canadian units. His interest in marksmanship surfaced and he soon identified what would be his massive contribution to the Allied war effort. He had brought several telescopic-sighted rifles and sensed their possible application when observing the superiority of German sniping. Hex horrified fellow reporters when he crawled within 30 yards of a German trench to study its construction. There was, however, occasional light relief and in July 1915 he played a series of single-wicket cricket matches against the American correspondent Frederick Palmer using tennis balls and a broomstick. Palmer had played major league baseball for the Cincinnati Reds and won comfortably.

In the following month Hex was appalled when 15 infantrymen from 4th Division were killed by a single sniper in the space of a few hours. Within a few days he was instructing his mother to collect telescopic sights from his hunting friends in Britain and to despatch them immediately. (The Germans had already grasped the importance of sniping and produced 20,000 rifles with sophisticated optics.)

Initially Hex's ideas on sniping were regarded by GHQ as the caprice of an unbalanced if talented maverick. However, in September he was given the go-ahead to set up a sniping school on formal lines. 'I *am* glad, as really in all my life I have been more in it than the rest, and it doesn't do for me to hang back with the ruck.' Encouraging messages flooded in and Hex was deeply moved when he received an impassioned letter from Roosevelt, who was mortified by American neutrality under Woodrow Wilson. Teddy was now out of office and out of temper: 'If I had my way I and my four boys would be in an American Expeditionary Force beside you in the trenches. I have preached to my people as straight doctrine as I know how. I am sick at heart about Wilson.'

In late September Hex observed the beginning of the Battle of Loos and was devastated by the death of his friend Alfred Gathorne-Hardy in the first onslaught. His grief deepened a few days later when his county cricket colleague Arthur Jaques died in the second push. Using his favourite Jeffreys high-velocity .333, Hex was among the finest marksmen on the Western Front. He could hit a button on a German uniform at 180 yards and was widely known as 'The Professional Assassin'. He was often brought in to pick off troublesome snipers, which he did with alacrity but reluctance. 'My job is to kill Germans; I can do it best by teaching, by training, and I *shall* teach and train.'

By November he had acquired a superb knowledge of optics. His sniping school was fully operational at Steenbecque in the Forest of Nieppe and he often took his more gifted pupils on sallies to the front. There was still scepticism among senior officers but he received encouragement from Lieutenant-General Sir Richard Haking. Other influential helpers included John Buchan, who was acting as a war correspondent for *The Times*. (There are traces of Hex in Richard Hannay, hero of Buchan's *The Thirty-Nine Steps*.)

In the spring of 1916 Hex set up a permanent sniping school at Linghem near Montreuil. He was working himself towards an early death but his letters to Roosevelt indicated his tenacity: 'I won't be unlucky, I will succeed and get it acknowledged too. I have never lacked confidence, and I will take the biggest wad of it I ever did. You wrote me that I had a good opinion of myself! I have. If I hadn't I would have withdrawn from the battle long ago – of life, not the war.' Initially his academy was little more than a series of Armstrong huts but he was overwhelmed by bus-loads of aspiring snipers and by now GHQ was treating him with the respect he deserved. However, by the spring of 1916 he knew that his strength was giving way. His language was as figurative as ever and a letter to his mother included the observation: 'Machine guns are going off just like typewriters driven by lunatic children.'

With few competent subordinates, Hex found it impossible to delegate. In addition to running the academy he was writing papers on German sniping for the Intelligence Corps and extending his curriculum to include map-reading and jujitsu. A string of enthusiastic visitors to the school included Mrs Humphrey Ward, the novelist and suffragette. In October 1916 he was awarded the MC and the citation read: 'This officer has been responsible for more German casualties than any other officer in the Army.' Late in 1916 Hex was promoted to the rank of major amid mounting recognition of his technical ability. This had been illustrated in his increasingly sophisticated use of periscopes to identify enemy snipers, innovative experiments with camouflage and the application of telescopic sights to machine guns. His more gifted pupils at the time included Kingsley Conan Doyle, a son of Sir Arthur, who was proving a talented observation officer in the Hampshire Regiment. During a period of leave late in 1916, Hex wrote his superb *Sniping in France*. It was rightly greeted by all the superlatives going and Rudyard Kipling concluded: 'All I wanted was twice as many photos and twice as much letterpress.'

By October 1917 Hex was losing his thread in lectures and forgetting people's names. This decline coincided with the onset of heart tremors and the after-effects of blood poisoning from gas attacks in the trenches. In the following year he trained American snipers and was awarded the DSO in March. A few weeks later he was admitted to the Red Cross Hospital in Boulogne with heart problems complicated by abscesses. He was sent home as a semi-invalid with little zest for life. Fourteen operations did little to combat the effects of prolonged exposure to mustard gas.

Hex's physical characteristics made him an ideal subject for caricature. At 6 ft 4 in, with chiselled features, he looked like a young Basil Rathbone. His presence was always imposing and from early adulthood his orders were obeyed without question. His most consistent traits were observation, resourcefulness and initiative. Hex's relationship with his mother was intense; they were exceptionally close even to the point of writing fiction together, but few if any psychological conclusions should be drawn from this.

His bustling energy and high spirits were occasionally tempered by melancholy, which he described as his 'incubus'. Hex never saw cricket as anything other than a pastime. He was extremely good with children and his devotion to animals has already been illustrated. The family home in Gorhambury resembled a menagerie, his favourite pet being Sinbad, a large Labrador retriever who won him many prizes at shows. Hex's writing on wildlife is characterised by intensity, grace and wit. He was an expert on moose-calling and once brought Mayfair to a standstill when he rolled up a newspaper and performed a moose call for his friend C.B. Fry. Monologists of the highest order, the pair never tired of blasting each other with abstruse information; Hex would opine on the finer points of the caribou's migration patterns while Fry would respond with a lecture on the development of the iambic pentameter.

As a bowler, Hex had a sideways-on action that gave him a natural body-break from the off and lively bounce even from a full length. The final delivery came from near the left hip, with a slinging motion in the manner of Jeff Thomson. His main weapons were fine control of pace, unusual lift and a superbly disguised slower ball. An obituary in the *Fettesian* noted that he 'possessed the single priceless ability to go on bowling away at the same spot until the batsman played a careless or impatient shot.' For C.B. Fry he was 'a fast bowler with the action and delivery of a medium-paced bowler'. Hex often found a 'spot' when bowling from the Nursery End at Lord's and like Maurice Tate he gave the illusion of gaining pace from the pitch. On damp wickets he would reduce his pace and bowl brisk off-breaks.

As a batsman he was a 'nudger', his scoring strokes being limited to deflections that included a variety of leg glances and a hesitant late cut. As a tail-ender he often proved nerveless in a pinch, relying on a superb defence. Describing an innings against Joe Darling's 1905 Australians, *Today* noted: 'Hesketh-Prichard is a golden-haired giant, who can tell stories or bowl with something of the tempestuous delight of a fighter at a fair. He bats, however, more like a child scooping out sand with a wooden spade.' As a fielder Hex excelled at first slip. He had an excellent reach and despite his bulk he was surprisingly light on his feet.

Hex's best writing is the journalism of his youth and early adulthood. Shamefully, it has never been properly collected and republished as it should be. His fiction is long gone but his action novellas are sprightly and as good as the genre gets. The narratives draw heavily on his experiences in Portugal and centre around Don Q, a dwarfish and misshapen brigand who at turns can be brave, sardonic, revengeful, chivalrous, cruel and gentlemanly. The stories were extremely popular and, like Conan Doyle precipitating Sherlock

Holmes over the Reichenbach Falls, Hex was at one point obliged to kill off his hero. After a public outcry Don Q returned, more swashbuckling and picaresque than ever.

In 1921 a dramatised version of the Don Q stories was staged in London. The verdict in the *Pall Mall Gazette* was: 'The play is good of its kind, a frank and healthy melodrama with plenty of colour and life.' As equerry to the King of Spain, Don Q is falsely accused of killing a prince. He has to jump out of a window into a torrent and is presumed dead. He becomes a heroic outlaw who befriends the poor and preys on the rich. Many of Hex's characters have Zenda overtones and in 1925 a compound of his novels formed the script for Douglas Fairbanks Snr's blockbuster *Don Q, Son of Zorro*. There are many traces of Hex's narrative ideas in Martin Campbell's 1998 film *Mask of Zorro*, starring Sir Anthony Hopkins.

By early 1922 his health was declining rapidly. Several obituaries mentioned heart disease, but his major problem was an obscure form of blood poisoning contracted in the trenches. There were occasional remissions, and in his final weeks he talked of going to Ireland to shoot geese. As Hex lay dying at a nursing home in Dorset Square, his main interest was impending changes to the Newfoundland game laws, which he felt would harm the Eskimos. He was barely conscious in the final days and in June he was taken to his wife's family home at Gorhambury. He died there on 14 June at the age of 45.

As an idea conceived by an individual with little military standing, and implemented amid apathy if not opposition, Hex's sniping school was among the single greatest contributions to Allied efforts in the First World War. When his friends recovered from the trauma of his death, they began to celebrate his exemplary life. A tribute in the *Spectator* bears quotation. It was written by a young officer who had attended Hex's academy at Linghem and stayed on as a junior instructor. The author restricted his by-line to 'A.H.L.' 'This memoir is written as an act of justice to the memory of a great man who I will remember for sympathy, broad-mindedness, personal fascination of manner and indomitable courage.'

12

Leslie 'Chuck' Fleetwood-Smith

b: 30.03.1908, Stawell, Australia.
d: 16.3.1971, Melbourne, Australia.

A man with two cans,
One in each hand,
Sways on the street
Shouting nonsense.
But it's bitter
Claptrap, bombast,
Rough-bearded rant.

Douglas Dunn, 'Swigs', 1983

Under a 30-point front-page banner headline, the *Melbourne Argus* for Tuesday 25 March 1969 describes the theft of a handbag on the previous Sunday by two vagrants in the vicinity of Flinders Street Railway Station, Melbourne. The incident would normally have warranted half a column inch, were it not that one of the vagrants was a former Australian Test cricketer and probably the most gifted spin bowler the game has seen.

Chuck was brought up in Stawell, Victoria, to the north-west of Melbourne. The town had been the site of a goldrush in the 1850s and his maternal grandfather, Nathaniel Walter Swan, had gravitated there a decade later from County Monaghan after studying literature at

Glasgow University. A talented journalist and sadly forgotten novelist in the Jack London mould, his works include *Luke Miver's Harvest* and *Tales of Australian Life*.

On arrival at the goldfields Swan pegged a few unsuccessful claims before turning his attention to writing. His varied output included essays and short stories for the *Australasian* and the *Sydney Mail* based on gold digging in the Beechworth district. He settled in Stawell as editor of the *Pleasant Creek News* and was succeeded at the turn of the century by Chuck's mother, Frances. A spectacular snob with a caustic wit, Frances benefited from a team of quality sub-editors and maintained the journal's high standards. She had a keen interest in sport, having been a champion roller-skater and swimmer. Frances was also a competent pianist and a perceptive literary critic who did much to broaden the cultural scope of the paper. However, she lacked business acumen and recruited a financial manager, Fleetwood Smith, an accountant with a newspaper background in India. Smith had been born in the Punjab in 1874 and had dabbled with surveying before training as an accountant. Their relationship developed over a few late-night meetings and the pair married in 1901.

In 1913 Smith's brother (another newspaper editor) committed suicide by taking an overdose of strychnine amid business and domestic troubles. Needing to distance themselves from this perceived shame, Chuck's parents changed their name to the compound Fleetwood-Smith. In his intelligently sympathetic and superbly researched biography – to which this chapter owes much – Greg Growden describes how Frances introduced the infant Chuck to a Sydney columnist: 'Here's another little journalist!' She had not produced a writer but rather a prodigiously talented cricketer.

Chuck proved rebellious almost from the cradle and with his brother Walter he played truant from Stawell Primary School, enjoying nothing better than herding wild goats. He would bring 30 or more into the schoolyard just before the mid-morning recess and encourage them to rifle through the children's lunch bags. Initially he excelled at tennis and Australian Rules football, only turning his attention to cricket in his early teens. He soon became fascinated by spin bowling and like fellow cricket maverick, Bernard Bosanquet, he played 'twisti twosti' with his father on the family billiards table. This is a bizarre pastime in which the ball is flicked across the baize with the players attempting to deceive each other by combinations of spin. It seems to be an ideal way of nurturing slow bowlers. The nickname 'Chuck' was a convoluted family joke revolving around the polo term 'chukka'. It had nothing to do with the legality of his bowling action, which would have passed the most stringent inspection.

In 1917 Chuck was sent to the exclusive Xavier College in the Melbourne suburbs, where he was encouraged to concentrate on tennis. As a 12-year-old he attended the Melbourne Test in the 1920–21 Ashes series, and marvelled at Warwick Armstrong's control of the leg-break and Arthur Mailey's prodigious turn with it. He was precocious and obituary tributes in the school magazine recalled how he smoked a pipe from the age of 14, often carried a hip-flask and dated girls several years his senior. Chuck left Xavier in 1924. Records are hazy and the college is unhelpful to researchers. It is probable that he was expelled; the canker was in the rose. Chuck returned to Stawell and attended the local high school. He continued with tennis and began playing club cricket at Central Park. However, much of his time was spent chasing after (and usually catching up with) just about every presentable female in the area.

Greg Growden describes the professional integrity of Chuck's father. When his son was arrested in a Stawell hotel for under-age drinking with 20 or more youths, Fleetwood-Smith Snr had no hesitation in recording Chuck's name among the offenders in the *Stawell News*.

By his late teens Chuck was exceptionally good looking, dapper and poised. Generous pocket money allowed him to board trains bound for Melbourne or Adelaide armed with a bottle of whisky, and he frequently seduced female socialites in the sleeping cars. His parents were snobbish and anxious to submerge their middle-class Catholic roots by penetrating the upper echelons of provincial society. In 1930 they packed their problem son off to Melbourne but only after telling him to conceal the fact that he was a Catholic and take two years off his age. Chuck arrived in Melbourne with lively aspirations. He enjoyed a good drink, a shapely calf and the other fine things in life but there were no signs of the excesses and ultimate decline to follow. He was conscientious in his cricket practice and was offered trials in grade cricket with St Kilda CC by the Test player Bill Ponsford, who had spotted him at a coaching session in Stawell. At St Kilda Chuck covered for Bert Ironmonger when he was on state or Test duty and the veteran did much to encourage him.

As an orthodox slow left-armer, Ironmonger obtained prodigious spin from the stub of an index finger, having lost the top joint during a boyhood accident while using a mill on his parents' farm. He came close to death from loss of blood but was saved by his 11-year-old sister, who had the sense to put his hand in a bag of flour. (The glorious legend is that a decade later he lost another portion of the finger when demonstrating what had happened in the original incident.) Ironmonger produced several fine Test performances for Australia on home soil but never toured England, blaming his omission on the fact that he made a slurping noise when drinking soup.

Chuck ruffled a few feathers at St Kilda through his habit of imitating animals when he became bored in the field. Towards the end of the 1931–32 season he switched to Melbourne CC, who guaranteed him work in the close season. He attracted the state talent scouts and was pitched in to the Victoria side against the touring South Africans at the MCG. He took 6 for 80 from 23.2 overs and the *Melbourne Age* commented: 'He demonstrated methods entirely his own, turned the ball considerably and posed problems which many of the South African batsmen found difficult to solve.'

The *Melbourne Herald* front-paged with Chuck in his threadbare singlet, which he considered a talisman and wore in every important match for the rest of his life. This performance caught the attention of Arthur Mailey, who invited him on a private cricket tour of America. He proved a bad sailor but having recovered from the voyage, he proceeded to chase a good deal of skirt and was irrepressible when he spent a day in Hollywood on the set of Lionel Barrymore's *Rasputin and the Empress*.

The New York leg of the trip included a night at Florenz Ziegfeld's production of *Show Boat* at the Winter Garden Theatre and a baseball match between the New York Yankees and the Chicago White Sox, during which Chuck fell into deep conversation about ballistics with Yankees pitcher Vernon 'Lefty' Gomez. The American was an eccentric clown and womaniser himself and the pair were inseparable for the rest of the weekend. Chuck's performance with the ball was impressive and occasionally inspired, his haul being 238 wickets at 7.5 runs apiece.

He was unable to find regular work on his return to Australia and cricket expenses hardly covered an increasingly extravagant lifestyle. He proved little more than a remittance man and relied on cheques from his father. His form on the cricket field remained superb and in the run-up to the Bodyline series he took 6 for 22 against Queensland on his first visit to Brisbane. However, his bowling was badly mauled by Bradman in the game against New South Wales. Nobody in England had faced high-quality left-hand wrist-spin since the retirement of Charlie Llewellyn and the touring captain soon glimpsed a reality that eluded the English and Australian press. Douglas Jardine became convinced that with his prodigious and varied turn, Chuck might win the Ashes for Australia single-handed.

In an inspired move, he told Wally Hammond to risk everything with a calculated assault on Chuck during MCC's game against Victoria in the hope of knocking the 24-year-old out of Test contention. Hammond scored 203 while consistently thrashing Chuck's off-breaks through the covers and the *Melbourne Age* commented: 'The disappointment of the day was the bowling of Fleetwood-Smith, who appeared to be over-anxious and bowled faster than usual. There is no doubt of his abilities but he lacks judgement and experience.' Chuck returned the miserable analysis of 2 for 124 from 25 overs and his state colleague Bill Woodfull made the questionable decision to leave him out of the Test side. Alan Gibson recalled Hammond's reaction: 'Wally, who was capable of a generous gesture, went out of his way to locate the youngster and spent much time giving him words of encouragement and advice. Fleetwood-Smith never forgot this act of kindness.'

Chuck performed well in Sheffield Shield matches during the 1933–34 season, surviving several onslaughts from Bradman. There had been newspaper comment to the effect that Chuck had Bradman's number and The Don was more than usually belligerent on the youngster. Despite these maulings Chuck was picked as the third spinner alongside Bill O'Reilly and Clarrie Grimmett for the 1934 tour of England. The *Stawell News* noted that at a send-off party over 1,000 people crammed into the town hall, where Chuck's father accompanied the community singing on the piano. Several hundred residents were turned away while others were pleased simply to be in the building's corridors. Amid routines from a local tap-dance group Chuck made a gracious speech, in which he stressed his respect for Bill Woodfull and declared that a tour to England had been his ambition since boyhood.

Surprisingly, given their vastly different temperaments, Bradman and Chuck were close companions on the voyage out. As part of his middle-class upbringing Chuck had been taught to play bridge competently. Sir Donald has a passion for the game and the pair made up a four with a couple of passengers. The boat was also carrying the Australian Davis Cup team and Chuck acquitted himself well at deck tennis against Jack Crawford and Vivian McGrath. When the team stopped off in Egypt he proved fearless in camel races along the dunes outside Cairo.

Soon after their arrival in England the tourists attended the FA Cup Final and saw Manchester City beat Portsmouth 2–1. An early fixture was against MCC at Lord's. Chuck had already sent shock waves through the English counties and again he was singled out for special treatment. This time the assassin was Patsy Hendren, who crashed 135 with 22 boundaries. Woodfull might have realised that this was another desperate gamble, and it should also be noted that if he had possessed a ghost of an idea as to how to set a field for Chuck, Hendren might have been contained.

Chuck shrugged off the disappointment of not playing in the Tests and worked his way through a succession of hat-check girls and waitresses. He also proved a keen fisherman and spent a night fishing from Brighton's West Pier with Bill Ponsford and Arthur Mailey. In the morning everybody at the Metropole breakfasted on sole. His bowling improved steadily through the summer and he finished with 106 wickets at less than 20 apiece. One of the more impressive performances was 4 for 30 from 9.3 overs against Kent at Canterbury, where his victims included Frank Woolley. A tart evaluation in *Wisden* ends with: 'Of no great account either as batsman or fielder he was, as a bowler, one of the most interesting studies of the team.'

In February 1935 Chuck married Mollie Elliott in Melbourne. Her father, Henry, was a soft drinks magnate and Chuck began careering around the city in a Rolls Royce promoting the company's carbonates. There is an old adage: the cheaper the salesman the gaudier the patter. Chuck got on well with his potential clients but lacked the initiative to close any deals. His father-in-law was quite happy to bankroll him and rely on other salesmen, but this interlude did Chuck much damage. Recalling it in an interview just before his death, he smiled ruefully: 'Too many friends, too many social drinks.'

His form for Victoria brought him a berth on Australia's tour of South Africa and in late 1935 he bowled superbly against Western Province at Cape Town to take 7 for 71 and 5 for 32. The *Cape Argus* had employed Arthur Mailey as a guest correspondent. Under a sub-head of 'Man Who Must Be Watched', Mailey reported: 'While the fast men pounded fruitlessly over the turf, "Chuck" had the time of his life. Here potentially is the Australian bowler who will cause most concern to the cream of South Africa's batsmen…He is a nonchalant cricketer with the puckish mannerisms of Patsy Hendren.'

Chuck made his Test debut at Durban, where he took 4 for 64 from 28 overs in South Africa's first innings. He found acute turn but was occasionally erratic; Bill O'Reilly and Jack Fingleton showed courage by remaining in his leg-trap. Reporting for the *Natal Mercury*, the former South African player Herbie Taylor commented: 'The batting tactics gave the visitors too much of a moral ascendancy. Fleetwood-Smith alone commanded respect with devilish spin and lift.' Chuck did little in the second and third Tests and was sidelined for the rest of the tour by a damaged hand.

He returned to the international arena at Melbourne in January 1937. In their second innings Gubby Allen's English tourists made 323. Chuck was unable to find a consistent length, but he turned the ball prodigiously and was the only bowler to trouble Maurice Leyland as he breezed to 111 not out. Neville Cardus reported in the *Manchester Guardian*: 'Fleetwood-Smith spun abruptly with a length that fluctuated between long-hop, good occasional length, and poly-hop.' It was in this match, to his amusement and delight, that Chuck opened the batting for Australia. Bradman sent in Chuck and Bill O'Reilly as night watchmen while a damp wicket was drying, telling them: 'The only way you can get out on this pitch is to hit the ball. You can't hit it on a good wicket, so you have no chance on this one.' Chuck prodded about valiantly for a few overs but was caught by Hedley Verity off Bill Voce for 0 early on the following morning.

There was an odd and still unexplained incident straight after this game when four players (all Roman Catholics) were hauled in front of the Test selectors and accused of insubordination. The quartet was Chuck, Stan McCabe, Bill O'Reilly, and Chuck's state team-mate and Xavier College contemporary Leo O'Brien. Chuck had always been ill-disciplined, but to level this kind of accusation against players of the monumental integrity of O'Brien and O'Reilly was laughable. As captain, Bradman was proving unpopular, showing little control and still less charm. O'Reilly hardly had a good word to say for Bradman from this moment on and discussed the incident right up until his death 55 years later.

The fourth Test at Adelaide proved tense. England were set 392 to win and at the close of the fourth day they had scored 148 for 3. Wally Hammond had been rampant for much of the series, and on 39 not out he was poised to win the match for the tourists and give England a 3–1 series victory. Chuck had a quiet evening with Mollie at the Regent Theatre, where they saw the Clark Gable movie *Cain and Mabel*.

In the first over of the morning Chuck produced the ball of his career, a wickedly spun chinaman that drifted away in the air before biting sharply, finding a gate and knocking Hammond's leg stump out of the ground. Chuck went down on his knees before performing a jig. He then strolled over to his skipper, Don Bradman, and enquired: 'Was that what you wanted, Goldie?' With the possible exception of Shane Warne's dismissal of Mike Gatting at Old Trafford in 1993, it remains the ball of the century. For Neville Cardus, Chuck had been 'suddenly visited by genius'. Cardus continued: 'Natural genius; deadly unplayable revolutions, quick as a top off the ground, and exquisitely flighted, with the sinuous curve of temptation.' Chuck took 6 for 110 from 30 overs and kept Australia in the rubber.

In the winter of 1937–38 he attempted to lose weight by joining the Melbourne amateur wrestling circuit, where his natural ebullience was set off by a canary-yellow leotard. (Greg Growden notes that his flying tackle was original and fearsome.) At the time, Clarrie Grimmett had lost form having overindulged in his new invention, the flipper, and Chuck became second-choice spinner to support Bill

O'Reilly in England as part of Bradman's 1938 Ashes squad.

The tour opened at Worcester where Chuck took 8 for 98 in the home side's first innings. Here is an extract from *The Times* report: 'Fleetwood-Smith might during a quarter of an hour have sent back any batsman living and then in the next 10 minutes might have encouraged any normal cricketer...Gibbons was bowled by a ball which did all but burst.' In the first Test at Trent Bridge Stan McCabe scored 232, an innings which is widely regarded as among the finest of all time. Much of it was made with the tail-enders and Chuck proved canny in assisting his partner to farm the strike.

Two weeks later he enraged his captain and tour officials when, during the match against Derbyshire at Chesterfield, he spent a Sunday morning in a glider over the hills of Hathersage. Chuck's best Test bowling of the tour came at Headingley, where he took 4 for 34 from 16 overs in England's second innings. It should however be noted that several batsmen took liberties with him, having been tormented by Bill O'Reilly at the other end. In August he returned the worst Test analysis of all time: 1 for 298 from 87 overs as Len Hutton amassed a record-breaking 364. The figures tell little of the story and it is often forgotten that Chuck beat Hutton all ends up when he was on 40. With Hutton yards out of his crease and badly off balance, Chuck was dismayed to see Ben Barnett fumble an easy stumping chance. He hooted for joy when he eventually got a ball to turn, and later recalled that he woke up during the night and thought his arm was still going round.

Marriage to Mollie did not curtail his pursuit of women and there is a persistent rumour that he was found in bed with an English duchess. Chuck was reasonably discreet in his carousing and proved an excellent ambassador for the game. Early in the tour he received a letter from a terminally ill Welsh schoolboy. When the team reached Swansea he bought a bat, asked all of his team-mates to sign it and contracted a chill while seeking out the lad's cottage in a thunderstorm.

He was bowling well in state cricket when war broke out. He immediately enlisted with the Australian Infantry Forces and was posted to a training camp at Puckapunyal in central Victoria. A few months later Chuck transferred to the Army School of Physical Training at Frankston outside Melbourne, where he coached gymnastics.

Separation from Mollie did nothing for the marriage; his flings became more open and he had a much-publicised affair with Alice Power, a Melbourne caterer who was married and 11 years his senior.

He did not respond well to discipline within the PT corps and spent the final months of the war working as a longshoreman at the Melbourne docks, where he acted as an intelligence officer reporting on possible communist activists. In 1946 Alice Power's husband granted her a divorce citing Chuck as co-respondent, and a few months later Mollie filed for divorce, citing Alice. Chuck had an indifferent season for Melbourne CC in 1945–46 and many observers realised that the magic had deserted him. At an end-of-season dance the club wicketkeeper, Geoff Collins, introduced Chuck to his sister Beatrix, a former dancer. Chuck left Alice and set up home with Beatrix in 1947. They were married in the following year.

He could no longer rely on remittances from his own or Mollie's father and lapsed into a bout of the torpor experienced by so many first-class cricketers when they leave the game. His drinking increased and he was unable to hold down a regular job, but found occasional work as a labourer. He was declining physically and the matinée idol looks had gone for good. Chuck was devastated by the death of his mother in August 1948. His complexion became blowsy and it was not long before he joined the ranks of alcoholic Test cricketers. A depressingly large roster, it includes Albert Trott, Tom Richardson, Ernie Vogler, Bobby Peel, Gregor MacGregor and Percy Chapman.

By the end of 1948 Beatrix had left him and he was unwelcome in his home town where he often appeared drunk and incapable. There were many painful incidents in the local newspaper office. His brother Walter had grown tired of herding goats and had been editing the *Stawell News* for 20 years. Chuck proved a persistent embarrassment to other family members and there were unpleasant scenes in which friends of many years' standing refused to lend him money. In the 1950s he became a familiar figure in Melbourne's Skid Row, which is near Flinders Street Railway Station.

Greg Growden reports that Chuck never quite descended to meths and managed to avoid the horrors of battery acid. He could normally scrounge a meal from cricket fans and had enough loose change to buy cooking wine. A regular haunt was the Mornington racetrack. He was not a gambler, but the course provided a convenient base from which he could cadge drinks during the day. His nights were normally spent swigging from a bottle of sherry and hopping between suburban trains before collapsing in a goods yard.

Initially he associated with footloose bachelors but soon his cronies were out-and-out alcoholics. There was no shortage of help from old cricket colleagues and Leo O'Brien stood by him staunchly. Chuck managed to maintain a modicum of personal hygiene and was always allowed to take a shower at the Albert Cricket Ground. Here he used to observe the colts' practice sessions. He would get terribly excited if he saw a lad bowling wrist-spin and would offer to help. Coaches had to make the excruciating decision not to allow him near their pupils.

Chuck rallied slightly in 1962. For a while he held down a cleaning job at a publishing house but he was sacked in the following year for poor attendance. By the middle of the decade he was looking for food in litter bins and occasionally going barefoot. Even when turtle-up in the gutter he kept the vestiges of his former glamour intact, treating each new indignity with a smile. Greg Growden notes: 'There was an unwritten law among those stationed at Flinders Lane that Chuck should be left alone. He did not deserve the embarrassment of being carted in for being a vagrant. Under virtually no circumstances was he to be arrested.'

Local police officers could excuse vagrancy but their hands were forced in 1969. On Sunday 23 March, Chuck and the almost blind Frank Peacock stole the handbag of a Mrs Enid Mason outside Young and Jackson's Hotel on Swanston Street. Mrs Mason summoned a policeman and identified the pair, who were sitting only a few yards away. The officer recognised Chuck immediately but his only possible course of action was clear.

The arresting policeman was Brian Graham. Brian told me of his encounters with Chuck prior to the arrest: 'On many occasions when I was on patrol I would say to him: "Have you had a feed?" The answer was usually "No" and I would go and buy him a pie or a pasty. The shopkeepers knew who the food was for and rarely charged me.' Brian has pin-sharp memories of the incident stretching back over 30 years and he recalls how Chuck and Frank Peacock went quietly with him to Flinders Lane Police Station, where they were asked to empty their pockets. Mrs Mason identified various small items of property as belonging to her and the pair were charged with theft before being placed in the City Watch House.

Chuck and Frank Peacock appeared at the Melbourne City Courthouse on the following morning. Brian Graham had already contacted Leo O'Brien, who at the time was working for the Crown Law Department. O'Brien realised that the incident would make worldwide news but was shocked as he had to push his way through a thicket of cameras and jostling reporters. At the initial hearing Chuck was remanded on charges of vagrancy and petty theft and placed for two weeks in the infamous Pentridge Jail, whose former inmates had included Ned Kelly. In an impassioned piece for the *Melbourne Age*, Michael Ryan bemoaned the debacle of his boyhood hero and detailed Chuck's shabby attire of a green-toned shirt and gaberdine overcoat.

Greg Growden describes how Don Lawrence of the *Melbourne Age* arranged to see Chuck in jail and offered to pay his $50 bail on the condition that he did not talk to any other newspapers. Central to this offer was a promise that the *Age* piece would be compassionate, objective and lacking in sensationalism. Lawrence later recalled how Chuck still retained traces of his old wit. Pointing at a group of fellow inmates, Chuck smiled and said: 'It's amazing how the other half lives.' Pledges of support flooded in and the politicians Sir Robert Menzies and Sir Henry Bolte offered funds for his rehabilitation.

> So I met the Lord Mayor, I met his wife, but I didn't meet his daughter. Because as soon as Chuck went before me she put her arm through his and said: 'You're the one I've been waiting for' and away they went.
>
> Bill O'Reilly, March 1990

Chuck had an overwhelming sexual authority. Among Test cricketers his garish dress was only rivalled by that of C.B. Fry, and the dapper outfits were set off by his Clark Gable profile and a thick mane of sleek hair. Bill O'Reilly recollect: 'Chuck had a definite air about him. His very presence seemed to denote authority, breeding and cultivated capacities to handle any difficult situation which might arise.' His sexual appetite was prodigious and when on tour he flitted from one beauty to another like Candide in the harem. The ever- objective Ray Robinson regularly confirmed that he would bed up to four women a night. He seems to have relied on charisma alone; his chat-up routine was little more than saying 'hello' in the manner of Leslie Phillips when he meets an improbably buxom nurse in a *Carry On* film.

In the field Chuck could be entertaining for spectators but an annoyance to team-mates. When bored he would play imaginary golf shots or warble the hit songs of the day in a pleasant baritone, his favourite tune being Jimmy McHugh's 'I'm In The Mood For Love'. He used to enrage Clarrie Grimmett with magpie and whipbird calls, his show-stopper being a kookaburra. Bill O'Reilly had much affection for him but bemoaned the wasted talent: 'When the moon was high Chuck would go crazy, calling out various stupid chants...God had given him everything required of a bowler, except a brain-box. He was definitely a screw loose. He was the most devastating spinner I ever knew...He had more pronounced ability to spin the ball than any bowler I have seen or read about. In days when he was controlling the ball no team had a chance against him. He was generous to a degree when not in full control. When in form he was a killer...If you'd put my head on Chuck's shoulders he would have been the greatest bowler of all time.'

In minor games Chuck often stepped on to the field smoking a cigar the size of a vaulting pole and would only discard it when the ball came to him. Ray Robinson reflected: 'Sometimes he seemed to treat a critical match as nonchalantly as if it were Married vs Single at the grocers' annual picnic.' Robinson's reminiscences stress a lack of discipline and unwillingness to heed advice, though Chuck appears to have had abundant respect for Bill Woodfull. As a master and ultimately principal at Melbourne High School, Woodfull had an innate air of authority. However, Chuck suffered badly as a result of Woodfull's inability to understand spin bowling, and Arthur Mailey noted that the only captain who ever set an effective field for him was Vic Richardson.

Chuck had a beautiful, wheeling action that can still make old men see visions. Conjure up a mirror image of Shane Warne and you have an accurate picture of Chuck: the lazy approach, massive upper body and acute spin are common factors. Chuck was not particularly subtle in his bowling strategy since the prodigious turn meant that he rarely needed to rely on flight. However, he could be nerveless in toying with batsmen and once bowled Wally Hammond a whole over of top-spinners, having him stumped by Bertie Oldfield from the final delivery. Chuck's top-spinner was absolutely loaded; it had a slithering quality and nothing like it was seen until the advent of Bhagwat Chandrasekhar. His googly also had much over-spin, but usually turned enough to find the outside edge and was near impossible to detect.

The Australian captain Bill Brown once told me that Chuck's powers of spin were so pronounced that you could hear the ball buzz in flight, while Denis Compton used to maintain that Chuck spun the ball more than anybody in the history of cricket. He was certainly a nightmare for wicketkeepers. Initially Bertie Oldfield was unable to read him and arranged special practice sessions, while Ben Barnett relied on signals, something to which Oldfield would not condescend.

Chuck was one of the small band of cricketers who truly captured the imagination of Neville Cardus. In his *Australian Summer*, a diary of the 1936–37 Ashes series, Cardus concluded: 'Fleetwood-Smith, of course, has a licence for experiments. If I were his captain I should fine him for every maiden over he bowled.' Some 34 years later, in an obituary tribute, Cardus elevated Chuck to the status of a Thomas Hardy hero: 'Fleetwood-Smith became the sport of the ironic gods, for they lifted him up on expectation's toes only at the end to cast him out sardonically.'

Given his abilities at tennis and Australian Rules, Chuck's hand-to-eye co-ordination on the cricket field was surprisingly poor. He was an indifferent fielder (usually at mid-off) and was notoriously unsteady under a high ball. His batting was agricultural and relied mainly on what Denzil Batchelor described as 'mashie shots'.

> I like Chuck. He has a personality. He once gravely asked me, on hearing that I had been a war correspondent in Spain, why the police had not stopped the civil war.
> Denzil Batchelor, *The Game Goes On*, 1947

After the initial hearing Chuck appeared again at the Melbourne City Courthouse on 9 April 1969 and was defended by Frank Galbally, who would become one of Australia's leading criminal lawyers. The *Melbourne Age* noted that by now he was immaculately coiffured and resplendent in a lounge suit. Beatrix had reappeared, saying she would take responsibility for him, and the public gallery was packed with well-wishers. The charge of petty theft was adjourned for a year and Chuck was put on a good behaviour bond of $20 on condition that he attended the alcoholism clinic at St Vincent's Hospital. Beatrix asked to address the court, saying: 'I'm going to look after him and bring him back to his own self, the best way I can. Everybody's been marvellous. He can't help but come good.'

Chuck accompanied Beatrix to her trim little house in Williams Road, Windsor, an inner suburb of Melbourne. Here he gave a short interview to a correspondent from the *Age*, commenting: 'Beatrix saw I was in trouble and came to see what she could do. That's very good form after all that's happened...to come and settle up when things were crook.' Some months later Beatrix took over the management of a small hotel and Chuck was given responsibility for the garden, which he tended with care and skill. Later he worked part-time as caretaker at a neighbouring 12-storey block of flats. Chuck watched television highlights of the England vs West Indies series and, remembering his success against left-handers, he itched to have a go at Garfield Sobers. Scarred in every sense, he remained with Beatrix for over a year and appears to have been reasonably happy.

In August 1970 Melbourne was hit by an outbreak of Hong Kong flu. Chuck, who had been weakened by a prostate operation, contracted the virus and his condition was compounded by bronchitis, pneumonia and septicæmia. After keeping him alive on heart and kidney machines, doctors at St Vincent's Hospital dubbed him 'the miracle man' and his remarkable powers of recovery allowed him to spend Christmas at home with Beatrix. In March of the following year he was re-admitted to St Vincent's with chest ailments. He died on 16 March at the age of 62.

We can return to Neville Cardus for an epitaph: 'Genius is originality, and in cricket the man is a genius who does things superbly, masterfully, and entirely in a way of his own.' Chuck came as close to being unplayable as any bowler in the history of the game and he remains the principal and presiding genius of left-hand wrist-spin. It is heartening that he has two lineal descendants on the contemporary cricket stage in Paul Adams and Michael Bevan. Chuck's zenith and decline are a familiar tale of flawed genius and an old duality; he was possessed of great gifts and by terrible demons.

13

Basil Foster

b: 12.2.1882, Malvern, Worcestershire.
d: 28.9.1959, Uxbridge, Middlesex.

We tell ourselves stories in order to live.

Gabriel Garcia Marquez, *The Autumn of the Patriarch*, 1975

Basil came from a family of seven boys and three girls. His father, Henry Foster, was one of those impeccable English clerics of upper middle-class education and scant middle-class means. He had attended Winchester and Clare College, Cambridge, where he emerged as a strong cricketer who could not afford the substantial match fees, a detail which does Clare College little credit. He became a first-rate club cricketer and was a prominent member of the Worcestershire committee. After graduating in 1867, he attended theological school and took up a teaching appointment at Malvern College. His impact was immediate and his Arnoldian vision flourished in sympathetic surroundings.

Over a teaching career of 48 years, Henry Foster evolved into an amiable eccentric whose vitality and candour touched thousands of pupils. He took up golf and Malvern folklore describes how, when walking from his lodgings to evensong, he would amuse himself with a niblick and a couple of golf balls, scattering boys and masters who were obliged to take cover from a chronic slice. In August 1871 he married Sophia Harper, the daughter of an Essex cricket enthusiast. Sophia was the driving force in encouraging the children to play sport, and family legend narrates how she would fling lively underarm lobs to the boys before passing them on to their father for net practice. Her efforts were rewarded; R.E. 'Tip' Foster remains the only man to have captained England at cricket and soccer, while a sister, Ciceley, represented England at golf. The brothers also excelled at rackets, winning a total of 18 English amateur titles between them, and all seven played first-class cricket. The fourth son is our man.

Like his brothers, Basil attended Malvern. He was certainly no academic but soon excelled on the sports field. By 1899 he was a regular in the school cricket and football XIs. Given his demonstrable success, the evaluations of his performances in the *Malvernian* are harsh. The pieces have no by-line and it is probable that they were written by his father. His profile as a member of the 1899 cricket team reads: 'Has shown no improvement with the bat since last year, possibly the reverse. Lacks courage against fast or medium bowling, though thanks to a straight eye, he has made some useful runs. Excellent short slip.' A review of his soccer is similarly grudging: 'A reliable full back; his kicking and tackling being quite good. He does not go in hard enough and is very liable to get too far up when tackling.'

For a few terms Basil was taught by Reymond de Montmorency, father-in-law of E.W. Swanton. Basil was always able to turn something on for the big occasion and he was inspired in the annual grudge match against Repton in 1899, making 43 runs as his side won by an innings. However, de Montmorency seems to have done little for his technique and the end-of-season verdict is: 'His whole weakness lies in drawing away with his body, if not his feet, from every ball on the on-side or even on the wicket.'

At rackets he was simply brilliant and there were no question marks over his technique. In partnership with the future Hampshire cricketer William Evans he won the Public Schools Competition in 1899. The pair defended their title successfully in 1900 when they overwhelmed Rugby in the final, and the *Sportsman* commented: 'Foster has a brilliant service and is very clever in his returns.'

Two months later Basil's cricket again rose to the occasion when he scored 102 in an amazing 37 minutes against Repton. The innings was hardly chanceless; he was dropped four times and the *Malvernian* noted: 'Foster's innings was rapid and exciting, if somewhat unsound.

In the final overs he let out for home and glory... A cross bat shot to square leg was not infrequent while balloons were distributed galore... a curious mixture of judicious science and slashing abandon.'

In April 1902 the Old Malvernians played Bishop Auckland at Headingley in the FA Amateur Cup Final and ran out surprise 5–1 winners amid heavy fog. Basil was at inside-right and during the second half he troubled the opposition goalkeeper with several long-range shots. In the closing 10 minutes he set up Malvern's fourth and fifth goals with incisive passes to Paul Graeme and Sam Day. Basil played seven cricket matches for Worcestershire between 1902 and 1911. His appearances were normally the result of frantic telegrams from his brothers, who often struggled to get up a side. Basil's only innings of any note was a polished 36 against Middlesex at Lord's in 1911.

There had been more evidence of his versatility in 1903 when he won the English amateur rackets doubles championship with his brother Harry. Their opponents were Frank Browning and Basil's old schoolmaster Reymond de Montmorency. The *Morning Post* correspondent wrote: 'The honours of the match went to Mr B.S. Foster... all through the match he did the greater share of the work. He was very fast in the court, getting to nearly everything, and made several beautiful strokes just above the line.' Basil went on to win the doubles championship four more times before the outbreak of the First World War.

Sport at amateur level did little to support an already extravagant lifestyle and he soon found himself in urgent need of employment. After padding through a succession of menial jobs, Basil had a short spell as a junior master at Dulwich College. This proved disastrous and he decided to try his luck on the professional stage. There was no theatrical tradition in the family and, while his parents did not oppose his chosen career path, the decision met with a good deal of surprise.

He made his professional debut in April 1906 as Norman Popple in *Mr Popple of Ippleton* at the Marlborough Theatre. In the following year he appeared in the West End as Lieutenant de Coop in *Miss Hook of Holland*. A turgid musical comedy about the invention of a Dutch liqueur, the piece received a scathing review in *The Times*: 'There is a general disregard for the interest of the plot; chatter instead of dialogue; jingles and tunes instead of music.'

Basil combined drama with sport at this time and in March 1907 he was runner-up to E.B. Noel in the English Amateur Rackets Championships. A review of the final in the *Sportsman* included: 'In the first two games the pace which Mr Foster set was tremendous and his service was at times untakeable...Mr Noel looked hopelessly beaten but showed his best form at crucial moments...Mr Foster was always brilliant, Mr Noel was always cool.' Basil also won the doubles title in partnership with his brother W.L., 'Bill', and the report continued: 'Mr Basil Foster started badly...but when he got going, his style and swing in hitting the ball and his quickness were far in advance of the others.'

In the same year we find him playing cricket for MCC and making 78 against The Public Schools XI. His team-mates included the Anglo-Australian theatrical impresario Oscar Asche, who would do much to further Basil's theatrical career. Weighing 19 stone and with a devastating wit, Asche was a colourful character. He had already played minor counties cricket and a few years later he would send an immortal telegram to his casting agency: 'Send me a slow bowler to play Cassius.'

Other triumphs the same year included a dapper century in 70 minutes for Actors vs Authors at Lord's. Basil played flawlessly until he spooned an easy catch to A.A. Milne at cover point from the bowling of P.G. Wodehouse. Many of the runs were made in partnership with the ex-England captain and future Hollywood film star Aubrey Smith. The literary credentials of the Authors are quite stunning; in addition to the creators of Winnie the Pooh and Jeeves, the team included Sir Arthur Conan Doyle and E.W. Hornung, author of the Raffles stories. Basil revelled in the atmosphere of these matches and began playing for a team of cricketing actors, The Thespids, whose numbers included Gerald du Maurier, Basil Rathbone, Nigel Bruce and Arthur Pinero. From the world of music hall the team fielded Stanley Holloway and George Robey, both being cricket fanatics and members of the MCC.

These were undoubtedly the most eventful months of his life. In September he made a superb 86 for MCC and Ground against the exceptionally strong South African tourists. A Reuters correspondent wrote: 'Mr Foster hit well all round the wicket. By good and not wild hitting, he did what few batsmen have done against the visitors this season...' while the *Sportsman* described the innings with: 'Foster was quite brilliant on the off-side. He was only 95 minutes in making his runs, and although some of his shots through the slips were streaky, he gave no chance that went to hand.' The *Daily Telegraph* was equally impressed: 'He is, to judge from his form yesterday, a very good bat, playing in an attractive style and having plenty of hitting power, his cutting being especially good.' Basil hit a rich vein of form in June of the following year, on successive days scoring 100 for Hampstead vs Queen's Club and 159 not out for Free Foresters vs Woolwich Military Academy.

His theatrical career was blossoming and in the autumn he starred in *The Merry Widow* as Count Danilo, an aristocratic playboy attaché to the Ponderedrian Embassy in Paris. The song 'You'll Find Me At Maxim's' stretched his baritone register but he received rave reviews playing opposite Lily Elsie. The show had an enthusiast in the radio pioneer Marconi, who was almost a fixture in the audience. He was introduced to Basil backstage and they immediately took a shine to each other. Basil would spend many holidays on Marconi's yacht, the *Electra*, where he vamped his way through songs from the show to Marconi's stiff piano accompaniment.

In 1910 Basil played the Earl of Quorn in *The Dollar Princess* at Daly's. The cast included the 18-year-old Gwendoline Brogden. Gwendoline was born in Hull and came from a devout Catholic family with a passion for the stage. She was educated in Versailles and had made her first stage appearance as a 10-year-old at the Vaudeville Theatre in The Strand. Basil married her in June and after a short honeymoon they went on a nationwide tour with *The Merry Widow*. Gwendoline was pretty, vivacious and intensely musical, being a superb soprano and a fine pianist. The couple had a daughter, the future Lady Forwood. Basil and Gwendoline set up home near the Finchley Road, where a huge influx of guests made the house little more than a tennis club. Among their regular visitors was P.G. Wodehouse, with whom Basil would collaborate on many theatrical productions in the future.

Basil concentrated on sport in the first half of 1912. In April he won the English Amateur Rackets Championship when he defeated G.G. Kershaw. The *Athletic News* commented: 'In nearly every respect the winner is a great player. Eye, wrist, pace of foot, and a great power of hitting, especially back-hand, are his, and in grace of movement there is no one who is his equal.' In this year he also allowed himself an extended run in first-class cricket, playing 12 matches for Middlesex. Apart from an innings of 35 against Sussex he met with no success and he did not allow cricket to interfere with his stage career, which he consolidated by playing Vernon Blundell in *The Sunshine Girl*. A topical musical comedy with a superb score by Paul Rubens, the play is set in 'Port Sunshine' and is an extended skit on the pioneering model village, Port Sunlight, built by William Hesketh Lever to house the workers at his Wirral soap factory. Basil starred opposite Phyllis Dare and the supporting cast included George Grossmith Jnr, whose father and uncle are remembered for *The Diary of a Nobody*.

In the following year he defended his rackets title successfully. His opponent in the final was H.W. Leatham, who proved unable to deal with Basil's bewildering mixture of pace and spin. *The Times* noted: 'As a stylist, Mr Foster has no superior. Whether forehand or back-hand he hits the ball with perfect timing, enormous power, and above all a graceful flowing movement. Yesterday he combined his hitting with astonishing accuracy.'

Basil was appearing in *The Land of Promise* when war broke out. He was commissioned into the Royal Hampshire Regiment as a lieutenant and served with the 8th (Isle of Wight) Rifles. He was promoted to captain in July 1915 and was seconded to the military wing of the Royal Flying Corps in September 1916. Sadly, he was unable to fly because of damage sustained to his left eye in a collision on the rackets court. However, his sight was good enough for him to serve as a brevet major and he became a machine gun instructor and later a staff officer in the Training Directorate.

Gwendoline continued her theatrical career during the war and in 1915 she appeared opposite Basil Hallam in *The Passing Show* at the Palace Theatre. It became a hit, largely due to Hallam's showstopping number 'Gilbert The Filbert'. Basil was a great admirer of Hallam and would perform the song in laughably inappropriate contexts, occasionally producing a baldly smutty version that he reserved for male company. Both men were excellent lawn tennis players and they became intimate friends.

Hallam had a steel plate in his leg and in 1914 he had been rejected

◀ **Arthur Coningham** (1863-1939) Plaintiff in one of the most scandalous divorce cases of all time, Coningham spent six months in jail for fraud and died in a lunatic asylum.

▶ **Don Davies** (1892-1958) A victim of the Munich air disaster, Davies played cricket for Lancashire and amateur football for England. He remains the greatest football writer we have seen.

▶**Henry Hyndman** (1842-1921) War journalist, musician and an intimate friend of Karl Marx, Hyndman played cricket for Sussex and became the father of British socialism.

▼**Archie MacLaren** (1871-1944) Fierce critic of everything from fast bowlers to hotel staff, his 424 for Lancashire vs Somerset in 1895 was only overtaken by Brian Lara.

◄Albert Trott
(1873–1914) Alcoholic, gambler, simpleton and suicide. The only man to hit a ball over the Lord's pavilion.

▶ Cecil Parkin
(1886–1943) Clown prince, publican, lay preacher and magician. The Derek Randall of the 1920s and one of the great 'mystery' bowlers.

C. PARKIN
LANCASHIRE

◄ All five could have advertised the product and Lionel Tennyson is known to have chain smoked Balkan Sobranie. As professionals Parkin and Trott might have economised with Player's or Wills's.

(Roger Mann)

HON. L. H. TENNYSON.

A.C. MacLAREN.
LANCASHIRE

PLAYER'S CIGARETTES

Mr. A. C. MACLAREN.
LANCASHIRE

WILLS's Cigarettes.

A. TROTT.
MIDDLESEX

◀ **Richard Barlow** (1851-1919) Perhaps the most defensive batsman of all time, Barlow was a track athlete and concert singer, a goal keeper for Lancashire, and an appalling Test umpire.

▶**Julius Caesar** (1830-1878) Boxer, carpenter, alcoholic and pyrophobe, Caesar lost his reason after accidentally shooting dead a gamekeeper

▼ **'Chuck' Fleetwood-Smith** (1908-1971) One of the most talented spin-bowlers of all time, 'Chuck' fell from grace and after spending years as a tramp in the gutters of Melbourne he was arrested for petty theft.

(Roger Mann)

◀**Aubrey Faulkner** (1881-1930) Adulterer and teetotaller, war hero and suicide. Having played an entire Test match with his trousers held up by a piece of string, Faulkner became a superb coach.

(MCC)

◄ **Sir Arthur Conan Doyle** (1859-1930) As well as creating Sherlock Holmes, Conan Doyle found time to play against W.G. Grace at Lord's.

▼ Dr Grace bowls Dr Conan Doyle.

▲ **Hesketh Hesketh-Prichard** (1876-1922) A fast bowler for Hampshire, 'Hex' saved many lives through his direction of Allied sniping in WWI. He spent a year in Argentina looking for a prehistoric sloth. Remains of the animal can be seen at the Natural History Museum together with a life-size model. (Dominic O'Byrne)

◄ The greatest photographic hoax in history took in Sir Arthur Conan Doyle. The Cottingley fairies are now the subject of Charles Sturridge's superb film *Fairytale*.

▲ **Basil Foster** (1882–1959) One of the great cricketing actors, Foster played county matches while appearing on the West End stage. He was a brilliant theatrical manager and a close friend of Marconi and P.G. Wodehouse.

▲ **Hon. Lionel Tennyson** (1889–1951) Profoundly illiterate but a grandson of the poet. A dashing captain of England, gambler, percussionist and war hero. Made 63 in 80 minutes for England vs Australia batting with one hand.

◀ **Gerry Weigall** (1870-1944) Almost certainly the worst judge of a run in the history of cricket. In his mid-fifties he turned up at the Scarborough Festival with a full kit bag: 'I've come prepared in case somebody died during the night.'

◀▶ **Raymond Robertson-Glasgow** (1901-1965) Poet and schoolmaster, rhapsodist and columnist. For many the greatest cricket writer of them all.

(MCC)   (Gordon Hutton)

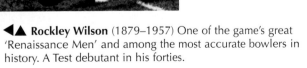

◀▲ **Rockley Wilson** (1879–1957) One of the game's great 'Renaissance Men' and among the most accurate bowlers in history. A Test debutant in his forties.

(MCC)

The *Indestructable Batsman*: or *The Skipper Coeur-de-Lion*. Cartoon by E. T. Reed, in the *Bystander*, July 13, 1921.

by the army when he volunteered for active service on the Western Front. Sadly, there were disgraceful scenes at the Palace when a pack of hysterical women pursued Hallam round the theatre and presented him with white feathers. A year later, after countless applications, Hallam was accepted by the Royal Flying Corps as an observation officer but was killed after a few weeks when his balloon failed. He had spent valuable seconds disposing of military papers and was unable to open his parachute in time.

In the immediate post-war years Basil and Gwendoline entertained lavishly at their London home and the company positively glittered. Guests included Aubrey Smith (who was besotted with Gwendoline), the future Edward VIII and Gilbert Frankau. A prominent novelist and librettist, Frankau had demonstrated exceptional gallantry at Loos and the Somme with the Royal Field Artillery. He is best remembered for his graphic descriptions of the Ypres battlefield.

Basil reappeared on the London stage in March 1920 in J.M. Barrie's *The Truth About Russian Dancers* at the Coliseum. In Barrie he had found yet another cricketing thespian. A review in the *Illustrated Sporting and Dramatic News* is enthusiastic: 'The whimsicality of Barrie is a thing easy to enjoy but difficult to analyse or explain...Mr Basil Foster's impression of Lord Vere is admirably restrained. It is one of the most difficult parts that he has yet undertaken, but his touch is sure and his work always carries conviction. His return to the stage is happily timed.'

In September 1922 Basil appeared as Frank Upton in *The Smith Family* at the Empire. *The Stage* was generally uncomplimentary: 'The piece wobbles irritatingly between musical comedy and revue, and its thoroughly good plot-idea has been allowed to run to seed.' However, Basil was singled out for attention: 'Mr Basil Foster acts gracefully and sings pleasantly as Edna's lover.' In April 1926 he played Major Sir Ronald Clive in a Miles Malleson play, *Conflict*, at the Queen's Theatre. The piece has a socialist message and focuses on the class struggle. While conceding that Basil was 'a convincing and very proper Tory politician', *The Times* dismissed the production with: 'The plot is conventional and the propaganda too insistent...the story is by no means original.'

Between 1928 and 1933 Basil collaborated with P.G. Wodehouse and

Ian Hay on many productions at the Shaftesbury and acquired a business interest in the theatre. In August 1929 he appeared as Captain Maitland in Hay's *The Middle Watch*. Set aboard ship, the piece was a risqué farce in which Ann Todd spent much of the action in pyjamas. The *Illustrated Sporting and Dramatic News* recommended it with: 'You may be assured that the whole riot is, of its kind, extremely good. Mr Basil Foster gives the captain's nonsense a courtly and official edge.' In September of the following year he took the title role in Wodehouse's *Leave it to Psmith* at the Shaftesbury. The *Stage* commented: 'Special appreciation was expressed of the suavity and aplomb displayed by Mr Foster as Psmith.'

Like any actor, Basil spent a certain amount of time 'resting' and in the late 1930s he had a succession of jobs at sports shops in the West End. He would give customers advice on choice of golf clubs and tennis rackets and Selfridges advertised him as their star attraction, putting a cardboard effigy of him outside the store. This depicted him in golf attire and a *Times* obituary tribute recalled: 'It showed him bareheaded, wearing a cardigan, seemingly in the act of reproving camera-men for the fuss they were making merely because he had won his match.'

Basil made his sole film appearance in 1935. *Radio Parade* concerns a troupe of amateur actors who have a nationwide success with a radio revue show. It is a pedestrian affair but benefits from the slick direction of Arthur Woods. Given a strong cast headed by Will Hay and Helen Chandler it is disappointing, but had modest success in America as *Radio Follies*. Basil would have been ideal for film work, but the damage to his eye showed up under studio lights and prevented him from taking his usual ladykilling roles.

In September 1937 he played Lord Peter Wimsey in *Busman's Honeymoon* at the Comedy Theatre. The *Stage* dismissed it with: 'Even in our fairly considerable experience of plays of this kind, we cannot remember one in which such a number of characters decorate their conversation with quotations from the classics, British and foreign. The play certainly towers above all the others we have seen as an anthology of famous verse and prose. Dramatically it is of less interest.' Two years later Basil stage-managed a repertory season at the Winter Gardens, New Brighton. His productions included *Number Six*, a detective story by Edgar Wallace, Guy du Maurier's *An Englishman's Home*, and an innovative version of Terence Rattigan's *French Without Tears*.

This experience landed him a lucrative position as resident manager and director at the Richmond Theatre in 1940 where he again appeared in *Busman's Honeymoon*. However, his fortunes declined in the late 1940s and early '50s and he was in financial difficulties for some time, until fellow Malvernian Sir Reginald Kennedy-Cox set him up as front-of-house manager at the Salisbury Theatre in 1952. He was a great success in the position and impressed both actors and stage crews. Basil administered the theatre with flair and astuteness; he would sit in the stalls during rehearsals in a bizarre Flanagan and Allen fur coat while offering useful advice. He was succeeded in 1958 by Reggie Salberg. In conversation with me, Reggie remembered Basil as impulsive, warm and totally unassuming, with superb knowledge of the technical aspects of stagecraft.

As a cricketer Basil might have been first-rate had he shown the necessary application. He ironed out the faults that marred his batting as a schoolboy but lacked the resolve to build a big innings. Like his brothers he was strong on the off side, with a savage cut and an elegant cover drive which he hit all along the ground. While he was graceful in his stroke-play, his pose at the wicket was marred by an ugly, crouching stance that reminded many observers of Gilbert Jessop. He was of no account as a bowler but his slip fielding was superb.

Despite being six feet tall Basil was extremely light on his feet and possessed a fine turn of speed. He cut a dashing figure on the golf course, playing in plus-fours and a Helen Wills eyeshade. He had a neat and slightly mechanical swing but could lace the ball 250 yards when the mood took him. For many years Basil was a stalwart of the Stage Golfing Society. He played golf intermittently but is known to have challenged the course record at Aberdovey, the retirement home of his parents. At football he started as a full-back but developed into a resourceful inside-right with admirable ball skills and exceptional tactical awareness. He was a commanding presence in the air and totally fearless, but was occasionally criticised for not doing enough work off the ball.

Basil prided himself on his dapper stage persona and there is no doubt that he was vain and inordinately concerned with his dress and physical appearance. He refused to wear glasses and had much Wodehouseian trouble with his monocle. Like many people with abundant creative energy, Basil found it hard to imagine what it was like to be without it. He was a highly gifted stage-manager who could make a good cast better and a bad one tolerable. On stage and as a director his enthusiasm and presence commanded attention. He had an overwhelming passion for dance, lighting, voice coaching, set design and any technical aspect of stagecraft. Basil longed to sustain the great British tradition of actor-managers in the manner of Herbert Beerbohm Tree and Frank Benson. He had wanted to set up an acting school since he was 16 and his experiences as a stage-manager at New Brighton and Richmond gave him enormous satisfaction.

Whenever appropriate the stage dominated his conversation. Throughout his life he was surrounded by adoring females and nobody would deny that he had a roving eye. He was irresistible to almost everybody whom he encountered and never had to cultivate friends. He remained consummately modest and considerate, being particularly attentive to servants and his social inferiors. He was natural at all times, although occasionally, when pursued by sycophants, he would lapse into a stage character which normally involved a Harry Lauder Scottish accent. Basil was appalling with money; he always over-tipped, and made large loans to his cronies and struggling actors that he could not afford.

Basil's marriage to Gwendoline was not a lasting success; in the mid 1940s he married Eileen Sleddon, an Anglo-Australian who ran the Galleyhill Nursing Home in Church Crookham, Hampshire. By the late 1950s he had become frail and in 1958 he received regular medical attention at the nursing home. In conversation with me, Basil's son-in-law, Sir Dudley Forwood, recalled that he retained the vestiges of his good looks and charm right until the end. Lady residents at the nursing home would wait until Eileen had gone out and push notes under his door.

In September 1959 Basil was taken ill with heart failure while visiting friends in Denham. After several emergency operations he died at a hospital in Hillingdon. He had been loving and widely loved. Early in his career he had come under the wing but never the spell, of Henry Irving. Basil would have hated the pretentiousness surrounding method acting and was an early subscriber to the Olivier dictum: 'Laddie, you've just got to go on, and do it, and *act*.' He adored the good things of life: cricket, golf, conversation, waywardness, ease; above all literature, the English language and the theatre. If he had not existed, his friend P.G. Wodehouse would have had to invent him.

14

Hon. Lionel Hallam Tennyson

b: 7.11.1889, Westminster, London.
d: 6.6.1951, Bexhill-on-Sea, Sussex.

Much have I seen and known; cities of men
And manners, climates, councils, governments,
Myself not least, but honoured of them all;
And drunk delight of battle with my peers...

Alfred, Lord Tennyson, 'Ulysses', 1842

Among the prized possessions of the National Sound Archive is an 1892 wax cylinder recording of Alfred, Lord Tennyson reading from 'Maud' and 'The Charge of the Light Brigade'. Amid the sonorous cadences and alarming static a keen ear can make out the gurglings of the poet's two-year-old grandson, a future Test cricketer. Twenty-nine years later the infant would arrive at Headingley as the England captain in a silver Rolls Royce, said to have been won after a £7,000 bet on which of two flies would defecate first.

The Poet Laureate died shortly after the recording session and Lionel once told Raymond Robertson-Glasgow that his only recollection of his grandfather was of 'a beard at the foot of the bed'. Lionel's father was christened Hallam after the poet's intimate friend at Cambridge. Lionel's mother, Audrey, née Boyle, was a sister of Cecil William Boyle, who won a cricket blue for Oxford in 1873 and played rugby for England.

Many anecdotes recalling Lionel mention his speech impediments; he had a severe lisp and a Malmesbury bray being unable to pronounce his 'r's, which meant that his favourite curse always came out as 'wuddy'. He spent his early childhood in the imposing surroundings of the poet's vast mansion, Farringford, on the Isle of Wight. The house appears to have been a shrine and Lionel would later note: 'My father was intensely loyal to everything connected with the memory of my grandfather...It was an atmosphere of veneration that was almost religious.' As a young boy Lionel showed interest in wildlife and country pursuits, charging around Freshwater Bay on a Shetland pony and creating havoc among farmers in the lambing and sheep-dipping seasons.

In 1899 Joseph Chamberlain offered Hallam Tennyson the Governorship of South Australia, and as a nine-year-old Lionel emigrated to Adelaide with his parents and younger brothers, Harold and Aubrey. Three years later he was enraptured by Tom Hayward's innings of 90 in the Adelaide Test match and resolved to play cricket for England. The family later moved to Melbourne when Hallam became Governor-General of Australia. By now Lionel's love of horses had surfaced, and a lifetime's gambling began when he persuaded a footman to put his weekly pocket money on an outsider in the Melbourne Cup which duly trotted up at long odds. Lionel's parents socialised with Dame Nellie Melba, who made a deep impression on the adolescent Lionel.

Early in 1904 Hallam resigned from his post since he wanted his children to be educated in England. Lionel was sent to a prep school in Cheam before starting at Eton in the summer term of 1904. In later life he professed to be unacademic, but he was by no means a dunce and won form prizes for French. It is also interesting to note that while he appeared cut out for a sporting and military career, his school friends were not limited to athletes. Lionel's social circle included the Hon. John Manners, who was a mainspring of the college drama society. In 1908 Manners directed and played the lead in an outstanding production of *Hamlet*. Manners appeared certain to make his mark on the British stage. Six years later he would lie dead on the Western Front, the victim of murderous crossfire outside Soissons.

Lionel was also close to Alfred Duff Cooper, who would write the

definitive biography of Talleyrand, the French diplomat and states-
man. Other friends at Eton were Billy and Julian Grenfell, whose
father, Lord Desborough, was one of the most versatile sportsmen of
the Victorian era and the moving force behind the 1908 London
Olympics. Lionel was particularly fond of Julian, a promising poet,
who was killed by shrapnel at Flanders in 1915.

As a schoolboy cricketer Lionel was of no great consequence. He
played for Eton against Harrow at Lord's in 1907 and 1908 as a fast
bowler but achieved little. As a batsman he found difficulty in adapt-
ing to damp wickets. He had been coached on concrete pitches in
Australia and was often dismissed while driving on the up. From his
mid-teens he was extremely attractive to the opposite sex and was a
heart-throb among the barmaids of Slough. In his final year at Eton he
caused a minor scandal by courting a schoolmistress from Windsor
several years his senior.

The family decided that he should try for Trinity, Cambridge, the
college of his father and grandfather. He was given extra tuition at
crammers but passed the entrance examination with flying colours. As
an undergraduate he remained a raw fast bowler. He performed well
in the Freshmen's match and made scores of 38 and 51 going in at
number nine. Reviewing the second innings, *The Times* commented:
'Tennyson showed that he can bat with power and played an excellent
innings, hitting all round the wicket.' Lionel also took 3 for 57 from 14
overs and the same report stated: 'The batsmen appeared uncomfortable facing his fast deliveries which occasionally bumped rather high.
Had Tennyson been bowling with any luck he would undoubtedly
have taken more wickets...' Cambridge's Anglo-South African
captain, J.N. Buchanan, was unimpressed. Lionel was not offered any
more trials and did not play in any first-class fixtures.

> His earliest days were lived under two awe-inspiring
> shadows: of Government House, Melbourne...and of the
> ghost of the old Poet Laureate, deep-voiced, shaggily
> bearded, stumping in cloak and sombrero along the corri-
> dors of Farringford. This sort of upbringing might have
> been complex fodder for the more regrettable type of

modern novelist. But Lionel survived. If he had ever known what a complex was, he would have hit it over the Southampton pavilion for six.

A.A. Thomson, *Cricket My Pleasure*, 1953

Lionel failed his first-year examinations in some style and in August 1909 he joined the Coldstream Guards as a subaltern. A letter of recommendation to the regiment from Canon the Hon. Edward Lyttelton, his headmaster at Eton, praised him highly: 'At school Lionel showed himself to be a boy of unusual energy and exceptionally fine physique. He is absolutely trustworthy, has good organising power and plenty of common sense.' Two years later he was living well beyond his means, spending a fortune on fox hunting and escorting a bevy of debutantes to fashionable venues in Mayfair. He was lucky not to be cashiered when he invited half the chorus girls from the Gaiety Theatre to enliven an evening's guard duty at the Tower of London. Lionel and his companions were discovered by a senior officer who simply retired to his room in amazement.

Ever since his boyhood success in the Melbourne Cup Lionel had fancied himself a shrewd judge of horseflesh, and he decided to augment his modest pay on the turf. He began betting heavily at Alexandra Park and for 12 months he could do no wrong, noting: 'At the zenith of my success, money was coming into my hands in an apparently inexhaustible supply in the manner that oil gushes from the earth in a newly bored well in America.'

There is an old racing adage that sometimes the sharp money gets a little too sharp for its own good. In the spring of 1912 Lionel lost £1,000 in a day at Hurst Park. He proceeded to Newbury, where he promptly blew another £6,000. Undaunted, he headed east to Windsor and lost £1,000. He was now in dire need of funds; he had three days before a series of cheques he had written to bookmakers would bounce as far as anything he had delivered as a pace bowler. Lionel gathered up his courage, returned to the Isle of Wight, and made a clean breast of things to his parents. Over two days the atmosphere at Farringford was as fraught as a Tennessee Williams play. At the eleventh hour his father decided to keep the family honour intact and Lionel's debts were settled in full. However, the payments were made on the condition that he should immediately leave the Coldstream Guards and join the less glamorous Rifle Brigade, where he would have fewer chances to indulge in expensive hobbies and might well be posted to India.

At the beginning of the 1913 season Lionel was prolific in army cricket and in July he made 110 on his debut for MCC vs Oxford University at Lord's. He opened MCC's second innings with Meyrick Payne and the pair put on 175 in 90 minutes. Lionel was dropped three times but attracted the attention of the Hampshire selection committee. He made his debut for Hampshire two weeks later against Worcestershire at Dudley where he scored 28.

In his second match, against Essex at Leyton, he blasted 116 in 105 minutes and *Cricket* commented: 'The poet's grand-son is a fine forcing bat...He gave no chances and hit seventeen 4s.' The *Morning Post* was similarly impressed: 'The Essex bowlers were powerless to stop his fierce hitting.' At Trent Bridge in late July he was imperious while making 111. His run of form continued and in the following week he clubbed 96 runs against Yorkshire. *Wisden* selected him as one of the Cricketers of the Year but its profile sounded a note of caution: 'He is essentially a brilliant bat, hitting well all round the wicket...He may or may not have the qualities that make for permanent success.'

The performances brought him a berth on Johnny Douglas's tour of South Africa in the following winter. Lionel played his first Test match at Durban. He was dropped by Gerald Hartigan before scoring but went on to make a robust 52 before falling lbw to 'Dave' Nourse. The *Natal Mercury* report mentioned that Lionel's running with Jack Hobbs was uncertain, but the correspondent complimented him on his savage square drives and precise placement. Lionel did little else during the Test series and was unhappy on matting wickets, but he endeared himself to his captain and team-mates with his vitality and hard work in the field. His only other performance of note was 105 against XV of Northern Natal at Ladysmith.

As a career soldier he went to France shortly after hostilities broke out. He served as a staff captain in the British Expeditionary Force with the 60th Infantry Brigade and spent three years at the front, where he displayed extraordinary gallantry, proved nerveless under fire and was wounded three times. Given that the life expectancy of a young officer was two weeks this is quite extraordinary. He seems to have been an outstanding candidate for the DSO and was disappointed not to have been honoured in this way. It is probable that he annoyed somebody in a senior position at the War Office. Lionel's military experiences are described in the first volume of his autobiography, *From Verse to Worse*, and in his mud-spattered manuscript diary which is kept at the Imperial War Museum. At times it represents the Western Front as a grim but gentlemanly shooting party.

In the spring of 1918 Lionel married the Hon. Clarissa Tennant. Always known as 'Clare', she was a member of the Tennant brewing dynasty and the daughter of Lord Glenconner. Clare's uncles and aunts included Margot and Herbert Asquith. Lionel and Clare were shrewd operators at the bridge table, played the Asquiths for considerable stakes and regularly fleeced them. In his memoirs Lionel confesses that he continued gambling despite his experience in the Coldstream Guards and lost £7,000 at roulette in a single evening. Lionel was devastated by the death of his mother in December 1918. She had been running the Afton Down Hospital for injured servicemen on the Isle of Wight, and after over-taxing her strength she succumbed to pneumonia.

Lionel left the army in 1919 when it became known that his regiment was going to be posted to Baghdad. Hampshire were in need of a cricket captain; the prominent amateur Arthur Jaques had been killed in 1915 during the second push at the Battle of Loos and the pre-war captain Edward Sprot had retired. Lionel took over, but neither Hampshire nor its new leader produced performances of any note in 1919 and 1920.

In the winter of 1920–21 Johnny Douglas's England tourists were whitewashed 5–0 by an Australian team led by Warwick Armstrong which is still regarded as among the strongest of all time. Douglas retained the captaincy for the first two Tests in England in the summer of 1921 but losses by 10 and 8 wickets prompted the selectors to look elsewhere for a leader. The team at Lord's remains one of the weakest England has ever fielded. Lionel was selected for this match, arriving at the ground a few minutes before start of play having played cards at White's until the small hours. In his first innings he was made to look elephantine when he was stumped off the bowling of Arthur

Mailey for 5 having charged down the track. Early in the second innings he had a stroke of luck when Hanson Carter shelled a simple catch behind the wicket. Lionel went on to make 74 not out, which the *Cricketer* described as 'a thoroughly useful and courageous perform-ance... it put new heart into some of the most pessimistic of England's followers.'

In the aftermath of yet another defeat, the 39-year-old C.B. Fry was touted as a replacement for Johnny Douglas. Fry was unhappy with his form against pace bowling and stood down after injuring a finger. Still a maverick and hardly part of the game's administrative hierar-chy, Fry was respected for his technical knowledge. Immediately prior to the Headingley Test he travelled to Lord's, where he recommended Lionel as having the leadership qualities needed in such a grave situ-ation and possessing enough courage to frustrate the all-conquering Australian pace attack of Gregory and McDonald. Fry would have agreed with Alan Gibson's evaluation of Lionel: 'He was never really a sound enough player to get into the England side, but his warm, sometimes explosive character was good for a demoralised team.'

The selectors concurred. Lionel went into mild shock when he received a telegram inviting him to captain his country. He rolled it into a ball, threw it at the ceiling, snatched the rebound and exclaimed: 'Good heavens, they've asked me to captain England.' Armstrong won the toss at Leeds and the tourists eased their way to a total of 407. Early in the innings Lionel split the flesh between the thumb and fore-finger of his left hand while trying to stop a rocket of a drive from Charlie Macartney. He struggled on but was disturbed to see Jack Hobbs leave the field in obvious pain; it was soon discovered that the Surrey opener had appendicitis. By a bizarre coincidence both Hobbs and Lionel's wife Clare were suffering from appendicitis at this time and were operated on by the same physician, Sir Berkeley Moynihan, at the Leeds Infirmary. On the morning of the second day Lionel woke early with his mind in turmoil. He checked on the progress of Clare and Hobbs before walking down Westgate, where he bought a junior size cricket bat. He was unsure whether he would be able to go to the wicket and held himself back to number nine. With his side struggling at 165 for 7 and needing 92 to avoid the follow-on he had no option.

Lionel swallowed enough painkillers to put out a mule, before entering the fray and the record books. Nobody was expecting him to bat and he noted in his memoirs: 'When I was seen coming out of the pavilion there was such a tempest of applause that it was enough to nerve any man to glorious deeds.' He had strong forearms and holding the bat in his right hand like a tennis racket, he swatted at Gregory and McDonald's thunderbolts. With adrenalin acting as an anaesthetic he somehow raced to 63 in 80 minutes, hitting 10 fours. Many of the runs were made in partnership with Johnny Douglas who had lost the captaincy but not his place in the team. Hardly lacking in spunk himself, Douglas could only look on in awe. For *The Times* it was 'an innings which will be remembered as one of the greatest exhibitions of determination and opportunism ever seen in a Test match'.

In the second innings Lionel again batted one-handed, and scored a breezy 36 including a straight six. Towards the end of the game he also took a brilliant one-handed catch to dismiss Johnny Taylor but he could not prevent an Australian victory by 219 runs. In his first year covering Test cricket for the *Manchester Guardian*, Neville Cardus quoted from *Ulysses*: 'We are not now that strength which in old time / Moved earth and heaven...' On the following morning Lionel thanked Cardus for the write-up, ending with the enquiry: 'That bit of poetry. Jolly good – whose was it?' Cardus enlightened him and Lionel trotted off saying: 'Great stuff – I must read some of it.'

There was controversy in the next Test at Old Trafford when Lionel declared the England innings closed at 5.50 on the Monday evening. The game had become a two-day fixture since there had been no play on Saturday. During the interval the Australian wicketkeeper, Hanson Carter, fished out a *Wisden* from his trunk. Wizened of feature, Yorkshire-born and an undertaker by profession, Carter had a superb technical knowledge of the game. He explained to Warwick Armstrong that the declaration should have come when the players were taking tea, so allowing the Australians at least 100 minutes' batting. Lionel was obliged to send his not-out batsmen back to the crease.

The spectators had little understanding of what was going on and suspected the unpopular and charmless Armstrong of gamesmanship. There was a tumult of abuse, whereupon Armstrong sat down on the wicket and refused to continue until the noise abated. (The atmosphere was lightened considerably when a quick-witted Lancashire mill-hand suggested that the 22-stone Australian might employ his time by acting as the heavy roller.) Matters were only resolved when Lionel walked over to a particularly unruly section of the crowd, explained exactly what was happening and confessed that it was his fault. The barracking turned to cheering. Lionel was never one to bear grudges. When some 16 years later he found himself in Sydney as part of a world cruise, he immediately looked up Armstrong and the pair spent a weekend golfing.

By the final match England had fielded 30 different players during the series. Ronald Mason described it as 'a creditable shot at the possible maximum of 55'. The Oval Test degenerated into a meaningless draw, during which Lionel played a fine innings of 51 before being clean bowled by McDonald. It was also a good season on the county circuit and against Leicestershire at Portsmouth he scored 152, putting on 259 in under two hours with Philip Mead.

In June 1922 Hampshire played Warwickshire at Edgbaston. The home side scored 223, whereupon Harry Howell skittled out Hampshire for 15 in half an hour. There were eight ducks; Mead top scored with 6 not out and Lionel was the second highest scorer with 4. The Warwickshire skipper was a future England captain, the Hon. Frederick Calthorpe. He was fond of golf and suggested to Lionel that since the match was bound to finish early, they should play a round of golf at Stourbridge on the final day. Lionel's response was: 'You won't be playing wuddy golf on Fwiday, Fweddie, you'll wuddy well still be here!' Lionel and his army of travelling cronies immediately placed bets at odds of up to 100 to 1 that Hampshire would win the game. Calthorpe imposed the follow-on. Alex Bowell (45), George Brown (172), Walter Livsey (110 not out), and Lionel (45) combined to produce a total of 521. Alec Kennedy and Jack Newman then bowled superbly and dismissed Warwickshire for 158, giving Hampshire victory by 155 runs. Lionel ensured that the train back to Southampton was awash with champagne and the victory remains among the most improbable recoveries in the history of cricket.

A revealing aspect of Lionel's captaincy style can be seen in the Middlesex vs Hampshire fixture at Lord's in July 1923. *Wisden* gives a dry description of Philip Mead's innings of 145: 'Mead played a masterly innings – largely of a defensive kind – and received consistent support. He took three and a half hours to complete his hundred, but hit so hard afterwards that he added 45 runs in another hour.' Not for the first time the almanack leaves out the human detail. As soon as the batsman reached three figures, a Post Office boy rushed to the wicket carrying a telegram. It read: 'Mead – get on or get out – signed Tennyson.' Mead and Lionel were good friends; when the Hampshire left-hander lost his sight in later life, Lionel would often shepherd him around the Southampton pavilion and spent hours describing the course of play to him.

On his first trip to South Africa Lionel had befriended Solly Joel, a financier and sportsman who had made millions from the Kimberley diamond mines. His vast fortune allowed him to become one of the most successful racehorse owners of the day and Lionel had benefited from inside knowledge of his stable. In the winter of 1924–25 Joel sponsored a cricket tour to South Africa, selecting Lionel as captain and Archie MacLaren as manager.

Lionel had recently taken up playing the drums and began sitting in with the ship's band on the voyage out. He was joined by Harold Gilligan, who was superb on water whistle and tenor saxophone. In his autobiography Lionel congratulated himself on having added some zest to the jazz performances. This is far from the truth. Peter Sellers used to say that he was the worst percussionist of all time. Lionel had the drop on him and there were complaints from the instrumentalists and audience that he was incapable of following even the simplest tempo. A cabin boy was instructed to filch Lionel's equipment and, egged on by the mercurial Charlie Parker (the Gloucestershire spinner not the American saxophonist), MacLaren ceremoniously threw Lionel's drum-kit overboard.

Lionel's highest score was 57 and in all matches his average was 16.1 from 31 innings. Perhaps remembering the incident with the drums, he was scathing about MacLaren's contribution to the tour, describing him as 'indolent and lugubrious'. Lionel's golfing partner was Charlie Parker, who played off scratch and was said to have been capable of winning an Open Championship had he not concentrated on cricket. Lionel invited him for a round at the Royal Durban Golf Club; there Parker tried to improve Lionel's swing, which resembled an octopus falling out of a tree. However, he refused to help Lionel look for his ball in the rough for fear of the black mamba snakes that still infest the course. Lionel was close to the professionals and went fishing on the Zambezi with his Hampshire colleague Alec Kennedy.

The summer of 1925 was Lionel's best period with the bat. In first-class matches he hit 1,335 runs at an average of 30.34. A highlight was 184 in 165 minutes against Middlesex. Jack Durston and Gubby Allen were making the ball spit from a good length on a lively Southampton track, and Lionel was lucky to be dropped in the slips when his score was 4. He was playing with new-found composure and the *Daily Telegraph* congratulated him with: 'He is a vastly improved batsman who now possesses a defence, having lost the recklessness of his early days.'

In his superb biography of Percy Fender, Richard Streeton notes that during this period Lionel's finances were more than usually stretched. Fender was proving successful in the family wine business and invited Lionel to become a partner. Lionel knew nothing about wine other than how to drink it in bulk but Fender's shrewd intellect had sensed that as a PR man the Hampshire captain would be ideal. His recollections to Streeton included: 'Lionel knew everybody and had the knack of bringing in business. He was an extrovert and some people thought him irresponsible. But he never let me or the business down.' The firm soon added to its range of own brands, and a whisky liqueur bearing a blue coronet label and the initials 'LT' became a best seller.

In the winter of 1926–27 Lionel organised his own tour to Jamaica. It was sadly marred by a motor accident in which Ernest Tyldesley, Jack O'Connor, Dennis Sullivan and Herbert Lock all sustained injuries. The side was short of bowling and on true wickets, six of the seven matches were drawn. The captain's only real success came in the final game against Jamaica at Sabina Park, where he scored 90. The *Daily Gleaner* correspondent was impressed, noting: 'His back play is among the finest I have ever seen.'

Playing for Lords and Commons vs MCC in the following summer, Lionel found himself facing the leg-breaks of a youthful Jim Swanton. In conversation with me, Jim recalled that he had not yet mastered the googly but could produce a slithering top-spinner which occasionally nipped in from the off. It proved good enough to clean bowl Lionel, who was highly indignant during the tea interval: 'Nobody told me you had a wuddy wong'un!'

Lionel organised another tour to Jamaica in the winter. The batting revolved around Philip Mead, who made four centuries in five matches. Lionel hit form at Montego Bay against XV of Cornwall County with a score of 125. Within a few seconds of Lionel reaching three figures the donkey that pulled the heavy roller gave birth to a foal, which was promptly christened 'Lionella'. Lionel had been on 90 overnight and the *Daily Gleaner* reported: 'Major Tennyson gave a display of forceful batting combined with sound defence that would be hard to beat. If he is successful today it will be the most popular century ever scored on the island.'

Immediately after the tour of Jamaica Lionel travelled to New York. Prohibition was at its height but he appears to have found adequate supplies of bathtub gin. He mixed widely in American sporting circles and visited Madison Square Garden. Lionel was ringside at elimination bouts to decide the American boxing team for the forthcoming Amsterdam Olympics and he befriended the legendary promoter Tex Rickard, who was a keen observer of amateur prospects. On the same evening, Rickard introduced Lionel to Jimmy Walker, the Mayor of New York. The pair took an immediate shine to each other, played draw poker into the small hours and spent several days golfing on Long Island. Walker also took his new friend to Harlem where Lionel insisted on studying the great jazz drummer Arthur 'Monk' Hazel from close quarters and no doubt proffered occasional advice. In 1932 Lionel was distressed when it became known that Walker's administration was undoubtedly the most corrupt that the city had ever seen.

Later in 1928 Lionel succeeded as the third Baron Tennyson on the death of his father. Lionel and Clare had divorced a few months earlier and life on his own appears to have done his cricket no harm. He had a fine year on the county circuit and against the touring West Indians he scored the only double century of his career, 217 at Southampton. He treated Learie Constantine with disdain and *Wisden* commented: 'The Hampshire captain hit with glorious vigour.'

In the Australian season of 1928–29 Percy Chapman's England tourists retained the Ashes against a strong Australian side under the captaincy of Jack Ryder. An enterprising reporter on the *Morning Post* asked Lionel if he might like to write a poem celebrating Chapman's victory. As usual Lionel was in need of cash and he gladly knocked out four verses. They include the lines: 'Larwood's swift and terrible ball/The fasts of Tate with their lift and fire/The courage of Jardine cool and tall/The craft of White which cannot tire.' In his autobiography Lionel recalled how he trotted along to the *Morning Post* offices, where he was asked how much he wanted for the manuscript: '"For poetry," said I, "I couldn't think of asking less than a hundred pounds, cash on delivery."' An urbane sub-editor informed him that this was more than his respected grandfather had ever received and 20 times as much as Milton had been paid for *Paradise Lost*. Lionel pointed out that as a poem by one English cricket captain to another, the work was of particular interest: 'My dear fellow, these verses are unique in English literature.' Some sharp rejoinders were followed by an offer of £50. This met with an indignant refusal, whereupon Lionel took his hat and his leave. He would later present the poem to readers of his autobiography 'free, *gratis* and for nothing'.

At the age of 39, Lionel was still capable of scoring 125 not out to win a match against Glamorgan at Southampton in 1929. Another sparkling century came in the 1932 Gentlemen vs Players fixture. Lionel had been deeply offended by speculation that he was no longer worth a place in the side, and bet one of his critics a bottle of champagne that he would score a century. On a damp Oval wicket he gave several slip chances early in his innings but soon got his eye in and proceeded to cane the professionals, making 112 in a shade over two hours. The bottle of Moët was waiting for him at the boundary rope. Lionel grabbed it, drank the lot and disappeared into the pavilion in search of a game of bridge. Early in 1933 he wrote inaccurately about the Bodyline series from a London base for the *Illustrated Sporting and Dramatic News*. He never allowed a little ignorance to stand in his way, and with only limited knowledge of the circumstances and playing conditions he supported Jardine to the hilt.

In April 1934 Lionel married Carroll Elting, the daughter of Howard Elting of Buffalo, Ohio. Carroll was trim, graceful and as American as divinity fudge. She is still occasionally celebrated for her prowess on the dance floor, a darting wit and earrings the size of chandeliers.

Lionel organised a tour of India in the winter of 1937–38. His squad included Bill Edrich, James Langridge and George Pope and it was close to Test standard. Lionel was accompanied by Carroll and a

French maid. Carroll would have no truck with English class distinctions and mixed freely with the professionals. She adored dancing but despaired of her husband, whose footwork on the dance floor was as leaden as his movements at the wicket. By contrast, Bill Edrich could glide around like Victor Sylvester and enjoyed nothing better than an extravagant tango. Early in the voyage Lionel came down with dysentery. He was confined to his bunk, where he was restricted to a diet of mashed potatoes and ginger ale. Carroll was reasonably attentive but often slipped away to cut a step with Edrich. Bill's recollections of the voyage included this: 'Dancing one night with Lady Tennyson, I said: "How's his Lordship?" "Oh, he's lost about three stone but it won't do him any harm."'

By the end of the tour everybody was suffering from dysentery and Lionel became unusually acerbic. He had told his players to accept all decisions with good grace. However, when Peter Smith was given out lbw after playing a perfectly good leg glance, Lionel asked the local umpire if, having started the day blind, he was now bereft of his hearing.

The tourists were also guests of the Maharajah of Porbander, who laid on hunting of various kinds. As a special treat for Lionel, the Maharajah organised a panther shoot, tying a goat to a post as bait and leaving Lionel and the other amateurs in a hut to await the arrival of the panther. Alf Gover was fascinated by the scenario and had shinned up a nearby tree. After a tense 30 minutes the panther appeared; Lionel levelled his Purdey shotgun and fired. As he turned to his companions, elation was transformed into rage and despair when Gover's resonant baritone sounded through the darkness: 'My Lord, you've shot the goat!' Lionel was now 48 years old but he managed to score a century at Karachi, hitting two sixes and 13 fours in temperatures exceeding 100 degrees.

Ian [Peebles] being a son of the manse, and me a Catholic, each time over our final one-for-the-stroll back to the office, I demanded to hear the classic *faux pas* of Lord Lionel Tennyson with whom Ian had toured India in 1937. On board ship, his Lordship had made a great friend of the then Prime Minister of Australia, Joe Lyons, a devout

Catholic and proud father of a large family. 'They got along splendidly,' recalled Ian, 'and whenever there was a pause in the conversation, Lionel was ready to fill it.'

'You've a lot of Catholics in Austwalia,' he said. 'Yes, indeed,' replied Mr Lyons with pardonable pride, 'about a third of the population.' 'You want to watch 'em,' cautioned Lionel. 'You can't twust 'em – and what's more, the buggers bweed like wabbits!'

Frank Keating, *Passing Shots*, 1988

Lionel remains a striking contradiction of the adage that no man is a hero to his valet. For much of the 1920s he employed the Hampshire wicketkeeper Walter Livsey as his manservant. Given the irregular nature of Lionel's finances, it is hardly surprising to find that Livsey was paid sporadically. On the few occasions that Lionel was flush he would enquire of his batman what wages were owing. The answer could be as much as 'Three months', my Lord', whereupon Lionel would lay a large amount of cash across the dining-room table. Sadly, by the end of the day he had normally borrowed it all back.

Livsey appears to have been as much of an eccentric as his master and there is a legend that he occasionally kept wicket in his motorcycle gauntlets. He also served as chauffeur and drove Lionel around in a Rolls Royce. In a county match, Lionel once made an unsuccessful appeal against the light. A wicket fell immediately and Livsey was next man in. He stumbled to the crease and called out: 'Where are you, my Lord? I can hear you but I cannot see you.'

Lionel could be maladroit to the point of genius. At a fancy-dress ball in the 1920s, having won the booby prize of a pumpkin for his representation of Judge Jeffrys of 'The Bloody Assizes', he threw his trophy at Sir Home Gordon, missed, and knocked the Mayoress of Folkestone out cold. The clumsiness was not limited to physical matters; at the height of the Spanish Civil War he nearly caused a riot in Gibraltar by wearing an MCC tie, its colour scheme being an exact match of the Spanish Royalist flag. Lionel's London base was a flat in Jermyn Street and he always insisted that Livsey drive him to White's Club, a distance of 80 yards. His humour could be delightful and he dedicated the first volume of his autobiography to his grandfather, 'still the greatest author in the family'.

Lionel's playing colleagues included Charles Knott. At 85 years of age, Charles is warm, informed and full of anecdotes. He gave me the following story. As a Hampshire amateur in his mid-twenties he was involved in a flourishing antiques business. During a chat at George Brown's pub in Winchester, Lionel invited him to visit Farringford and to make an offer for some furniture that he said he no longer wanted. Charles selected some pieces and a price was agreed. A week later he was surprised to receive a stiff letter from a firm of solicitors saying that the furniture was not Lionel's to sell. It is sad to record that Lionel borrowed significant amounts of money from the young amateurs and was often slow to pay it back, if at all. John Arlott's summation is: 'He did not always behave with a dignity befitting a peer of the realm. On the other hand, he was never mean or little; and his humour, like most of his capacities, was large.'

While Lionel was undoubtedly hard-up for most of his life, he was always honourable in the matter of expenses and never descended to 'shamateurism'. However, he was happy to joke about the subject. Alf Gover once described how Lionel and C.B. Fry discussed the matter at a sports forum during the Second World War: 'Lord Tennyson stood up and thrusting his right-hand palm uppermost out in front of him, said, "The pro takes it *this* way." Then, putting his arm behind his back with the palm of the hand still uppermost, he turned to Fry and, with a huge grin on his face, said: "And we took it *this* way, didn't we, Charlie?"'

Lionel was proud of his poetical heritage. The story is possibly apocryphal but it is said that he became indignant when a wager was struck at White's that he would not be able to name ten of his grandfather's poems. He gave the titles of seven confidently and, after some hesitation, another two. He then jotted down 'If', whereupon there was a protest: 'Why, that's by Rudyard Kipling.' Lionel's riposte is alleged to have been: *'What An Absent-Minded Beggar* I am.' The story is narrated by Alan Gibson, who suggests that Lionel was not up to this kind of erudition. This may be uncharitable; *The Absent-Minded Beggar* had been written by Kipling at the height of the Boer War as a fundraising exercise for widows and orphans. It was successful and raised a quarter of a million pounds in a matter of weeks. Lionel certainly didn't study the Poet Laureate's work closely and there is a legend that during a Gentlemen vs Players match he once laid all-comers 10 to 1 that his grandfather had written *Hiawatha*.

Facially Lionel resembled a young Orson Welles. Without a hint of self-aggrandisement he says in his autobiography: 'I was born with great physical strength, a robust constitution almost insensible to fatigue, high spirits and a superabundance of energy.' He spent much of his life overweight at around 17 stone, but in military uniform and evening dress he could look superb. As a cricketer he dressed like an unmade bed, turning out in shabby flannels with his shirt open almost to the navel. He would occasionally add to the effect by batting in a huge, shapeless brown trilby that appeared to have been run over by a truck. Lionel occasionally puffed at a briar but usually chain-smoked Balkan Sobranie through a holder the size of a billiards cue. While his hand-to-eye co-ordination was superb, he was clumsy in his footwork at the batting crease, in his bowling run-up and during his occasional sorties on to the dance floor. He frequently had to perform something resembling a Scottish sword dance in order to avoid stepping on his wicket.

Lionel's batting was undoubtedly swashbuckling. He had a good eye and was able to hit across the line with confidence but was also noted for powerful straight drives. Another of Lionel's team-mates, Gerry Hill, once told me that the county ground at Southampton came alive when Lionel stepped out to the crease. Gerry also recalled that Lionel's limited foot movement meant that he hated batting against high-class leg-spin. He lived in fear of 'Tich' Freeman and 'Father' Marriott, but was marginally happier against finger-spin and always fancied he could hit Jack 'Farmer' White out of the Taunton ground. He was often caught in the attempt.

By contrast, against pace bowling Lionel was fearless, even magnif-icent, and never minded being hit. However, he often lacked the patience to graft out a long innings, and C.B. Fry's evaluation was: 'Had he chosen to devote himself to mastering the formal technique of batting instead of amusing himself with hitting a long ball at least once an over, he would have been a great player.' Lionel normally fielded in the gully. He was hardly electric in his movements, but Johnny Douglas once said he was worth his place in any county side for his catching alone. As a bowler Lionel had few attributes other than a healthy burst of pace in his opening overs.

As a captain Lionel's authority on the field was unquestioned but he had little ability to read the game. John Arlott dismissed his leadership with: 'He was idiosyncratic, erratic, hasty, at times simply and wildly reckless.' Ronald Mason's evaluation of Lionel is: 'He had panache but lacked subtlety. There is no convincing evidence that he was an especially intelligent tactician; but he was a perversely optimistic personality and there can be no doubt that he carried with him an invigorating dynamism.' As an opponent Lionel was always generous. In 1930 he kept his players on the field amid torrential rain at Southampton so that Bradman could reach 1,000 runs before the end of May. Similarly, when the Yorkshire player Edgar Oldroyd was left stranded on 99, Lionel contrived to bowl an extra delivery to allow the batsman to reach three figures.

Lionel spent the last years of his life at Bexhill-on-Sea. He became a stalwart of the Cooden Beach Golf Club and pottered round the course as part of a regular morning foursome. His short game was appalling and when out of temper his putting could resemble a hockey dribble. Lionel wrote the second volume of his autobiography, *Sticky Wickets*, in 1950. He confessed that he found writing more difficult than batting and might well have echoed the quip of his cousin Margot Asquith: 'A well-written life is almost as rare as a well-spent one.' The book received some polishing from Raymond Robertson-Glasgow and is a sustained joy.

Lionel ended his memoirs with: 'I am still a somewhat impoverished Baron of the United Kingdom with the right to sit and vote in the House of Lords which I have never done since this wretched Labour Government got into power.' His finances had in fact stabilised and he lived comfortably in a suite at the Cooden Beach Hotel. On the morning of 6 June 1951 he had a heart attack. A chambermaid found him dead in bed with *The Times* open at the racing page. The big race of the previous day had been the Zetland Stakes at York, won by the hot favourite, Dornoch Lad, at 5–2 on (distance a head, carrying 8 st 12 lb). We will never know if Lionel was on Dornoch Lad, but Jim Swanton once speculated as to his final words: 'Another wuddy loser.'

15

Gerry Weigall

b: 19.10.1870, Wimbledon, Surrey.
d: 17.5.1944, Dublin, Ireland.

I should not talk so much about myself if there were anybody else whom I knew so well.

Henry Thoreau, *Journal*, 1857

Clive James once said that the aphorism is a revealing form to the point that anyone who cultivates it deliberately is certain to be no good at it. Gerry Weigall is a glorious exception and is still widely celebrated for his terse sayings. Here are just a few: 'Never run on a misfield'; 'Never cut in May'; 'Never hook until you have made 84'; 'Never play off the back foot from the bottom end at Canterbury'.

He was born into a family of artists, his grandfather Henry being an innovative sculptor and a close friend of Coleridge. Gerry's father, Henry Jnr, was a painter, best known for his full-length portrait of the Duke of Wellington. In 1866 he married Lady Rose Fane, a daughter of the Earl of Westmorland and a great-niece of the Duke of Wellington. As a debutante she had charmed Napoleon III. Rose was a talented essayist and a regular contributor to the *Quarterly Review*. She and her husband were tireless charity workers and gave much support to the London Boys' Brigade.

Gerry had five brothers: Fitzroy, Julian, Louis, William and Evelyn, and a sister, Rachel. The family estate, Southwood House in Ramsgate, included a cricket ground of near county standard. With assistance from a few local youngsters, the brothers put up a fine schoolboy team that was capable of beating senior club sides including the Royal Marines from nearby Deal. There was a strong theatrical tradition in the family and Gerry's parents entertained touring stage companies, who were occasionally capable of forming a cricket team.

Gerry was never unduly concerned about the dense foliage of his family tree and steered his own course from boyhood. He showed no ability as a graphic artist but became stage-struck as an adolescent. His early education was at Aberdeen House, a prep school in Ramsgate, where he excelled at cricket. Gerry went on to Wellington College in the autumn of 1884. His cricket at Wellington was mediocre, his only innings of note being 40 not out against Charterhouse in 1888. His main contributions to school life were as a stalwart of the debating and dramatic societies. In 1887 he appeared as Moses in *The School for Scandal* and in the following year he played the title role in *Henry V* to much acclaim. His views on the debating floor were already reactionary. He supported Lord Randolph Churchill vigorously while denouncing Home Rule for the Irish and proposals to expand the franchise. His reflections on the monarchy included: 'The glitter of Royalty impresses the Indians and makes them respect us.' Gerry once approached a liberal stance when saying that he was opposed to conscription but ended his speech with: 'The best way of improving the army would be to create individual schools to train destitute boys as soldiers.'

In September 1889 he entered Emmanuel College, Cambridge, to study for an ordinary degree. With his striking good looks and quirky opinions he had an immediate impact on university life. In his youth Gerry might have stepped straight out of an early Evelyn Waugh novel, being an amalgam of Boy Mulcaster and Basil Seal. As he matured he began to resemble the retired colonels who populate Saki stories.

Gerry was prominent at the Emmanuel athletics day in the Easter term of 1890. He won the 100 yards with the respectable time of 11 seconds and in the quarter-mile he came second in 54 seconds. Gerry had been showing eccentricity since his earliest days at Wellington. One of his more unusual habits when fielding was to walk around the incoming batsman, inspecting him from every angle like a farmer assessing cattle at an agricultural show. His behaviour produced constant joshing from opponents and team-mates to which he remained sunnily indifferent.

He played poorly at trial matches in the summer of 1890 and was nowhere near winning a blue, but he was successful in college games and averaged 35.1 from 14 innings. A profile in the Emmanuel magazine summarised him thus: 'Our best bat, he scores freely and in good style. Fields well at point and was successful as a medium-paced bowler, breaking both ways.' Gerry seems to have been active in college life, being on the committee of the debating society and playing a bit part in a production of *The Pirates of Penzance*.

In May 1891 he made 265 for Emmanuel against Peterhouse. He was a failure in that year's Varsity match with scores of 11 and 2 and did little in first-class cricket for the university. By now he was well known to the Kent selectors and he made his debut against Warwickshire at Edgbaston, where he played an assured innings of 73. *Wisden* described him as 'a young batsman of great promise' and *Cricket* concluded: 'This was an impressive display of cricket only marred by one chance when he had got 45.' Perhaps the best performance was 61 against MCC and Ground, whose bowling attack included W.G. Grace at the top of his bent. The Doctor took 7 for 38 in Kent's first innings and *Wisden* reflected: 'Mr. Grace probably bowled as well as ever he had done in his life.' As an opener Gerry appeared to relish the challenge and he repeatedly drove Grace with the spin through the off side.

Gerry would play 127 matches for Kent over the next 13 seasons without ever holding down a regular place. He was later praised by one of his captains, J.R. Mason, for being 'always ready and willing to turn out, even when invited at the last minute'. In his early seasons Gerry annoyed his team-mates by chattering constantly in the field to Manley Kemp, an equally eccentric character. As captain of Oxford in 1884, Kemp was late when going out to bat against Cambridge and was found lying on his back in the dressing room reading Molière. Gerry won another blue in April 1892 when he played rackets against Oxford. At Queen's Club he and W.S. Burns were defeated 4–0 by A.D. Erskine and F.S. Cokayne. Gerry and Burns were a scratch combination while Erskine and Cokayne had been playing together since they were schoolboys at Charterhouse. Gerry managed to sustain the rallies in the third game but he and his partner were overwhelmed by their opponents' power and court coverage.

By now many of his cricket team-mates had noticed that running successfully between the wickets with Gerry called for what the Fat Man in *The Maltese Falcon* describes as 'the most delicate judgement, Sir'. Recalling the 1892 Varsity match, C.B. Fry noted: 'This was the game in which the Cambridge player Gerry Weigall did more to win the match for Oxford than anyone on our side.' In Cambridge's first innings Gerry came in at number three after the early loss of a wicket. He was soon joined by his captain, Stanley Jackson, who had already played Test cricket and was among the best batsmen in the world. Jackson was beginning to tap the bowling around confidently when Gerry played a gentle cut to point. The ball was misfielded and deflected towards the covers. In a moment of madness Gerry called Jackson for an impossible single, hesitated and remained rooted in his crease. Jackson arrived at Gerry's end to be greeted with the immortal words: 'Get back, Jacker – *I'm* set!'

Gerry went on to top-score with 63 not out but was implicated in two more run-outs involving C.M. Wells and A.J.L. Hill. Views as to who was the culprit varied but *Wisden* absolved Gerry of blame: 'Wells and Hill seemed to the ordinary observer to have quite lost their heads.' However, the legend grew that Gerry had run out three of his colleagues. It is often said that before the game the Oxford captain, Lionel Palairet, had ordered his bowlers not to dismiss Gerry on any account: 'Leave him alone and he'll run enough people out for us to win.' E.H.D. Sewell later reflected that with his charisma and air of authority, Gerry could prompt team-mates into a doomed single against their better judgement. Academically Gerry had been on a knife-edge, his interests at Cambridge being limited to cricket and horse racing. In April 1893 he performed disastrously in a history paper and his tutors indicated that it would be best if he left the university.

In July 1897 Gerry made his highest first-class score, 138 not out for Kent against the touring Philadelphians at Mote Park, Maidstone. It was hardly a flawless performance and he struggled against the world-class swing bowling of Bart King. Three months later he married Josephine 'Effie' Harrison, the daughter of William Harrison, a captain in the Royal Artillery. The couple took a flat in the King's Road. They had a son, Jack, who served in the First World War as a private, being wounded on the Western Front. He emigrated to Rhodesia and worked as a shunter for the Rhodesian Railway Board before becoming a policeman. Gerry was never unfaithful, but he was hardly attentive and 'Effie' was unable to cope with his manifold vagaries. The marriage was annulled after a few years.

Gerry never had a bean and was only too pleased to avail himself of free bed and board on cricket tours. In 1903 he visited the United States with the Kent side. He proved an ideal tourist, being perpetually cheerful and a tireless organiser of deck games. Despite his social success he could not buy a run and scored an aggregate of 2 in three matches. The cricketers travelled to Canada and perhaps for the only time in his life, Gerry was lost for words as he stared for several hours in childlike awe at the Niagara Falls.

Broke as usual, Gerry reluctantly accepted a job on the Stock Exchange in 1903. He worked as a small-time jobber in the volatile South African mining market, known at the time as the 'Kaffir Circus'. *Rialto* magazine soon nominated him the best-dressed man on the Exchange. The prize was 300 La Corona cigars and his nearest rival was over 500 votes behind him. Gerry was not particularly numerate and was never going to make a killing. In 1907, after the death of Charles Alcock, he applied for the post of secretary at Surrey CCC. He was treated as a serious candidate but lost out to William Findlay, the Oxford and Lancashire cricketer.

A year later he was discovered conducting business for a clerk at another jobbing firm. Gerry's friend was a member of the Exchange but not a partner in his firm. This was a major transgression of contemporary rules and Gerry was suspended for two years. He protested in a letter that ended: 'The few small transactions that Mr Johnstone did through me were not of a character, considering his position and length of membership, to have raised any suspicion and put me on enquiry.' Gerry's usual hauteur cut little ice and he never returned to the City. He had no private means and was obliged to try his hand at journalism. A series of peppery articles in the *Field* for 1910 included: 'I am dead against the pooling of gates. If a county cannot stand on its own legs, neighbours should not be obliged to buy it crutches.'

In August 1914 Gerry captained a strong Kent Club and Ground side against the touring Merion CC of Philadelphia. Chasing a target of 153 against the clock, the Americans had all but won the match when they stood at 151 for 3 with two deliveries left. To his eternal shame, Gerry instructed one of his bowlers to finish the over with underarm grubbers. Given all his ideas on cricket ethics, it is incredible that he should have stooped so low. Europe was already at war and the incident did not cause anything like the furore that occurred 67 years later when Greg and Trevor Chappell employed similar tactics for Australia in a one-day international against New Zealand.

At the age of 44 Gerry was unlikely to see active service but he happily volunteered as a private with the Territorial Infantry Force. Fiercely proud of his physical condition, he was delighted to be passed as medical category 'A'. In December 1914 he was promoted to temporary captain and posted to the 9th Kent Cyclists' Battalion at Canterbury. He prided himself on his eyesight and supervised lookout operations on the coastline between Dover and Folkestone Warren. Not surprisingly, he had many run-ins with his colleagues. Gerry's habit of dogmatising in a robust Johnsonian manner could be laughed off at a cricket match but it struck many as inappropriate when he began pontificating about matters touching on national security.

The battalion received bad publicity in October 1915 when a patrol on Romney Marsh shot and killed a poacher who had unwisely run away when challenged. Later in the war Gerry observed and logged Zeppelin activity. In March 1917 his unit relocated to Ramsgate. Gerry lodged with his sister Rachel, who had converted the family home into a hospital for Belgian servicemen. The estate had a barrack-type building in its grounds which Gerry's mother had built in order to provide summer holidays for underprivileged children from London. Rachel was continuing this work for war orphans and Gerry gave the boys cricket coaching. Gerry spent much of his life in search of employment and the war gave him an occupation and modest wages. By June 1919 he was at a loose end and he applied for a post at the Army School of Physical Training in Aldershot, citing Lord Hawke as a referee. He had no suitable qualifications and received a brusque rejection letter.

Gerry had an abiding love for what Larkin called 'the miniature gaiety of seasides' and the happiest week of his year was the

Eastbourne cricket festival. In 1920 he covered the festival for the *Field* and became particularly animated after a post-match dinner at the Grand Hotel. Amid much Bertie Woosterish braying from his cronies, Gerry was giving a lengthy discourse on the correct way to play a late cut: 'Thrust your head into first slip's navel, sir!' He was being observed with a mixture of fear and astonishment by several old ladies who had assembled in the hope of listening to a string quartet. Sadly an extravagant flourish of his walking stick knocked a glass of Benedictine over them. By midnight the party was making a racket like the whole of London Zoo in rut and the management of the Grand called a halt. This did not stop Gerry from continuing his lecture in a corridor, clad in pyjamas.

Gerry's outstanding contribution to the game came in 1922. He had been hovering around the Canterbury nets when he saw a youthful Les Ames have an unsuccessful trial as a batsman. Gerry observed his athleticism in fielding practice and gently inquired if he had ever considered becoming a wicketkeeper. In the same year Gerry brought out his instructional manual *Cricket: The Art of Playing the Game*. It is a deceptively substantial little book, in which he advocated ballroom dancing as a way of improving footwork. Like C.B. Fry he believed dancing to be a crucial ingredient in the development of co-ordination and posture.

In the following year, at the age of 53, Gerry resolved to demonstrate his stamina by entering the Amateur Squash Championship. His decision amazed the squash world and there was an additional touch of opera when he was drawn against Roger Wethered. Wethered was 24 years old and at the peak of his varied sporting prowess. Two years earlier he had tied for first place in the British Open at St Andrews and lost in a play-off. He was also among the best amateur squash players in the world. The match had all the ingredients for drama and Gerry's friends packed the viewing area at the Bath Club. There was a tumult of applause and good-natured abuse when Gerry made his entry. Gerry appeared sanguine and pottered over to Freddy Wilson of *The Times*: 'Never know, sir. He might sprain an ankle.' The response was measured and sceptical: 'He might. But it's extremely unlikely that he'll sprain both.' Gerry acquitted himself surprisingly well, going down 15–6, 17–18, 15–9. He showed his usual tactical awareness but was unable to retrieve Wethered's forehand smash. Freddy Wilson reported: 'Mr Weigall watched it almost motionless and quite hopelessly.'

Kent appointed Gerry as captain and manager of the second XI in October 1923. He immediately sought to establish himself as a guru, telling his young charges that they were a bunch of graceless Philistines who were about to be licked into shape. Gerry's training methods included a programme of physical jerks with Indian clubs. He gave advice to his young players on all matters; when one of his pupils complained of a hangover on the day of a match he recommended an iced shampoo at the barber's and a pint of Pimms.

Gerry was unimpressed with many aspects of second XI and Minor Counties cricket. After winning the toss at a rural venue in Buckinghamshire he sauntered out to the middle and inspected a very lush wicket. On being asked what he was going to do, he pronounced: 'I think we'll bat, sir, before the flowers begin to grow.' At a similar fixture he arrived to find that the pavilion had no clock: 'No clock, sir? The clock is more important than a lavatory.'

In the winter of 1926–27 Gerry was a member of Pelham Warner's MCC touring party to South America. At the age of 56 he performed surprisingly well and made 73 against Concordia, an innings which *Wisden* described as 'a bright display taking plenty of risks'. In a tour diary Pelham Warner recalled Gerry's jovial, avuncular presence. He was extremely hairy but showed no qualms about displaying his unattractive, lily-white torso. At a hotel in Montevideo his appearance in bathing trunks for a pre-breakfast dip sent a bevy of ambassadors' wives scurrying from the pool. Invective was Gerry's strong suit but he had some self-deprecating humour too. He observed the departing women, scrubbed his chest (which resembled a matting wicket) and exclaimed: 'Virility!'

At a ball given by the Buenos Aires Jockey Club he became enchanted by a fragrant young thing whose figure-hugging cocktail dress was set off by a dazzling rope of pearls. Gerry stepped straight up to her and with an extravagant bow, pronounced: 'Always wear black with pearls, ma'am, you look magnificent.' It transpired that the object of his attentions was the wife of a prominent gangster and he was lucky to leave the party alive.

Gerry's one and only god was the Kent batsman Frank Woolley. In 1928 Woolley started the season badly but went on to find a rich vein of form. The Ashes squad was selected early in the summer and Woolley was overlooked for Percy Chapman's England touring party to Australia. Gerry denounced this decision as 'the worst crime since the Crucifixion'. The full force of his spleen was directed at Woolley's replacement, the modest and consummately stylish Maurice Leyland, who was dismissed as 'a cross-batted village-greener, sir!'

The Kent committee persuaded Gerry to resign as coach in 1929 since his methods and dogmatic opinions were not being received well by a new breed of increasingly sophisticated professionals. He proved something of an embarrassment in the following season when he lurked around the nets and barked abuse at his successor Edward 'Punter' Humphreys. In 1933 the club advertised for a commercial manager. Gerry was in the vanguard of applicants but was rejected out of hand on the grounds of his lack of business acumen.

Gerry wrote extensively for the *Cricketer* in the 1930s. As a journalist he was vigorous but rarely subtle. His pieces are pugnacious, prone to slogans, over-simplified and – in the main – absolutely right. Pelham Warner was appalled by his grammar and once suggested that Gerry should have a look at Macaulay. Gerry's response took Warner's breath away: 'What, George Macaulay, the Yorkshire bowler? Surely I see enough of him in the summer?' He refused to heed any of Warner's advice, ending one argument with: 'My words are golden and you're jolly lucky to have them.'

Naturally Gerry pontificated during the Bodyline Tests to all who would listen. With the series at its height he was hovering around Piccadilly when he was spotted by Archie MacLaren, who was in a taxi. MacLaren ordered his cabbie to stop and the pair proceeded to illustrate how they would deal with Larwood's short-pitched deliveries. MacLaren played imaginary hooks and Gerry performed elaborate contortions while executing a series of square cuts. Michael Down recalls that only a mass of blaring motor horns from stationary traffic brought the pair to their senses. Down continues by describing how Gerry and Archie were often spotted having dinner at prominent restaurants. Since they were both usually penniless there was considerable interest as to who, if either of them, was paying the bill.

Gerry's iconoclasm was the rather gaudy mask of a conservatism that embarrassed him. Like most people who organise their lives badly, he loved giving advice. When the Australian tourists of 1938 played Kent at Canterbury, Jack Fingleton was dismissed lbw by Alan Watt for 23. As he trudged towards the pavilion he was greeted on the boundary rope by Gerry in full Wodehouseian splendour. Gerry reached for his umbrella and played a defensive stroke showing Fingo his error: 'What I like most about you, Fingleton, is that you know your limitations.' (Fingo later confessed that he was sorely tempted to wrap the umbrella around Gerry's neck.)

The umbrella went just about everywhere with him although he was not above snatching one from bemused spectators. Arthur Mailey describes it in his autobiography: 'The Weigall parasol was mainly used to give instructions on cricket, but for good measure he also used it for fencing, angling, showing us how Lindrum played his cushion cannons and how King Edward VII put the gun to his shoulder for partridge.'

Right up until the outbreak of the Second World War Gerry was holding his own in good club cricket, fielding at point with the vigour of a man half his age. He always maintained that he had eyes like a cat. In the early months of the war he was pottering around his London flat during a blackout without the aid of a torch. He fell heavily and never really recovered. He moved to Dublin shortly afterwards but visited London regularly to cover school matches for the *Cricketer*, using the Athenaeum as a base. Sadly, his vitality had disappeared for good. Gerry died in the Royal City of Dublin Hospital in May 1944 at the age of 73.

At a lithe 5 ft 8 in, Gerry weighed a shade over 11 stone throughout his adult life. He remained erect and active even in late middle age. His contemporaries recalled that he was wiry and had a slightly angular quality. His movements were staccato but graceful, and even balletic when he became agitated. Gerry was undoubtedly vain and when he went prematurely grey he applied colouring to his Terry Thomas moustache. His face was set off by shaggy eyebrows, piercing blue eyes and a nose like a lobster claw. In a letter to me, Margaret Maxwell (née Weigall) summed up her cousin: 'He reminded me of a military-style terrier. He spoke rapidly and with much economy, always wearing a bowler hat and a rather tired-looking dark suit.'

Gerry prided himself on his physical condition into middle age, attributing his fitness to a series of physical jerks which he performed daily. In his mid-fifties he travelled to the Scarborough cricket festival with a full kitbag, telling Henry Leveson Gower: 'I've come prepared just in case somebody dies in the night.'

Gerry was unselfconscious and hopelessly anachronistic. The majority of MCC members treated him with a mixture of bewilderment and suspicion. By contrast he had a small fan club among the Middlesex professionals. His arrival at Lord's for county games could descend into pure vaudeville. As he approached the pavilion, players would hang over their balcony and scream at him. Jim Sims normally led proceedings, greeting him in an impossibly patrician voice: 'Jerreh!' Gerry enjoyed the attention and would stop to orchestrate the applause and catcalling until he was told to sit down by indignant spectators.

In an age still recovering from the ravages of the First World War, Gerry's cheerfulness and impish irascibility were a gale of fresh air. He called everybody 'sir', not out of deference but in order to add cadence to his sentences. When he was unable to reinforce his points with an umbrella or walking stick he would take off his straw hat and thump it with his fist. Gerry saw himself as an autocrat of taste and cricket wisdom. He had an unrivalled repertoire of abuse, once describing Ian Peebles's decision to bat first on a damp wicket at Canterbury as 'criminal', 'lunatic' and 'pusillanimous'. He later dismissed an agricultural last-wicket stand between Peebles and Jim Smith as 'a prostitution of the art of batting'.

> One night there was a metaphysical debate between Charles Fry and Dennison Ross. This was soaring stuff. I could dimly apprehend only a few of the simpler arguments flashing far above me like the fiery tails of comets. At midnight, when the talkers were looking down on the peaks of the moon, Gerry Weigall woke up: 'That's right, Charles,' he summed up approvingly, 'it all boils down to playing with a straight bat.'
>
> Denzil Batchelor, *Days Without Sunset*, 1949

Gerry once remarked: 'The best day one can have is to make a large score in a big match at Lord's and thence to a play.' He had a deep passion for the stage, with a particular love of Shakespeare. It made him supportable and saved him from being a buffoon. Theatre was a minor obsession and he could quote at length from Restoration comedies. The stage was never far from his conversation. Gerry's quirky but firm convictions covered an extraordinary gamut; almost in the same breath he could be cheerfully dogmatic about subjects ranging from the desirability of uncovered pitches to Ellen Terry's interpretation of Ophelia. Gerry's family was saturated in the theatre and his cousin, Arthur Weigall, married a sister of the famous actress Beatrice Lillie. Arthur was a prominent archaeological journalist. He was an expert on the Temple of Luxor and gained a scoop in 1922, when he happened to be in Egypt at the time of the discovery of the tomb of Tutankhamun by the Earl of Caernarvon and Howard Carter. He mixed impeccable archaeological writing with a series of blockbusting historical novels, including gems such as *Bedouin Love*, *The Young Lady From Hell* and *Laura Was My Camel*.

Gerry was knowledgeable and enthusiastic about ballet, being a fan and friend of Adeline Genée, whose portrait his father had painted. Genée was one of the foremost ballerinas of her generation. In 1903 she took London by storm with her portrayal of a coquette in Katti Lanner's production of *The Milliner Duchess* at the Empire Theatre. Gerry attended regularly and was fiercely proud of having access to Adeline's dressing room, occasionally taking some of his better-behaved cronies to see her.

Gerry was a middle-order right-hand batsman. Despite the extravagant praise in the Emmanuel College magazine, it appears that his style at the wicket was cramped and rather ugly. C.W. Alcock's verdict was: 'If his style fails to reach the ideal, he watches the ball well.' Gerry's limited repertoire of shots featured an off drive that he often skewed through an arc from cover to third man. He is known to have had a superb square cut and he occasionally played a hesitant leg glance. He refused to hook or pull, considering the strokes to be abominations. Gerry believed that all cricket shots should be played from a sideways position and even objected to the introduction of the box since it encouraged chest-on play.

He was convinced that the best method of dealing with slow bowling was to charge down the wicket, and whenever he saw a batsman struggling against spin he would bellow: 'Jump to him, sir!' The fiascos in the 1892 Varsity match may well have been exaggerated over the years, but there is little doubt that his judgement of a run was appalling. A list of all-time bad runners would have to include Denis Compton, Geoffrey Boycott and Inzamam-ul-Haq. Gerry's shade sits comfortably (and no doubt cheerfully) at the top of the pile.

Gerry switched his allegiance from rackets to squash in later life. He was a driving force in making the British Open a truly international tournament and did more than anybody to promote squash in the United Kingdom when the game was in its infancy. He was regarded as an authority on technical matters, working effectively to standardise court dimensions and equipment. The Squash Rackets Association recognised him as an ideal publicity agent and sent him on several trips to Europe.

One of Gerry's favourite maxims was: 'Never eat pie at a cricket lunch.' In a game between MCC and Bradfield, the menu was steak and kidney pie followed by apple pie. All eyes turned towards Gerry, who nibbled at some cheese and biscuits and was in high dudgeon for the rest of the day. His advice was not limited to cricket matters; the Weigall canon included 'Never hunt south of the Thames' and 'Never drink port after champagne'.

Gerry could be wayward, quickly bored and moved by whims. For all his dogmatic manner of expression, he often lacked an inner confidence. The aphorisms were a veneer over a complex and sensitive character. Gerry became a confirmed bachelor after the failure of his marriage and his cousin Margaret recalls: 'He seemed a bit lonely and was very pleased to be asked to share a meal.' Similarly, his great-nephew, David Weigall, described to me how on the country house cricket circuit Gerry once overstayed his welcome. His hostess was obliged to point out, quite bluntly, that she had a large party arriving, only for Gerry to say that he would be happy sleeping in the greenhouse.

Whatever his self-doubt, superficially he always appeared pleased with his personal enigma. As a cricketing monologist his only rivals were C.B. Fry and Raymond Robertson-Glasgow. Gerry's maxims went down well with some, while others reflected that free advice is worth exactly what it costs. He was richly imitable and is still occasionally imitated. Many recollections portray him as an anachronism; he was polemically anti-modernist, his prejudices ranging from rubber-soled cricket shoes to the reverse sweep.

He could talk the Sphinx off its plinth and seemed capable of resuming an argument in the middle of a sentence. Having struck an attitude he usually plugged away at it. Gerry sometimes talked a good deal of nonsense, either out of pure self-indulgence or in order to see how far he could get without arousing opposition. He was of course fair game for burlesque, his most consistent mimic being C.B. Fry who adored him. Gerry once opined: 'There are only three people who know anything about cricket: Archie MacLaren, Charles Fry and myself. I know more than the other two.'

At least one lesson seems to have been absorbed after the run-out incident with Stanley Jackson, and the linchpin of the Weigall philosophy was: 'Never take a single to cover on a hard wicket.' It was a maxim that he drilled into his charges when captaining the Kent second XI. In 1927 he often opened the batting with the future England table-tennis player Leslie Todd. On a blazing July afternoon Leslie trotted out to the wicket with Gerry. He saw his skipper play the ball gently to cover and heard a scream of 'Come on, sir!' Ian Peebles takes up the story: 'Todd found himself run out by a handsome margin and started the long journey home. A lesser mortal might have apologised for what seemed almost a betrayal. Gerry turned to the young man with a triumphant air. "Just shows you, sir, just shows you!"'

16

Raymond Robertson-Glasgow

b: 15.7.1901, Murrayfield, Edinburgh.
d: 4.3.1965, Buckhold, Berkshire.

Life is an ever-rolling wheel
And every day is the right one.
He who recites poems at his death
Adds frost to snow.

Mumon Gensen, 1322–90

The first days of March 1965 saw 60,000 square miles of Great Britain cut off by blizzards, with army units struggling to clear snowdrifts of up to 20 feet. At Pangbourne in Berkshire, a 63-year-old ex-schoolmaster and journalist was suffering from melancholia. Early in the morning of 4 March he took an overdose of sleeping pills. The ambulance, delayed by snow, was slow to arrive. The patient died on the way to hospital and a coroner at Reading recorded a verdict of suicide, attributing death to poison by barbiturates. On the following day a litany of impassioned obituaries stressed the persistent idealism, wit and integrity of the greatest cricket writer we have seen.

In his autobiography Raymond narrates his upbringing at Craigmyle on Deeside, and the evocation of Edwardian childhood is unrivalled. He describes his father, Major Robert Robertson-Glasgow, as 'an intellectual and athletic Tory democrat who cursed the substitutes of modernity and was lonely in the crowd'. His mother, Muriel, née Holt-Wilson, was the daughter of a Suffolk clergyman. She never enjoyed good health and spent much time abroad. Naturally Raymond dwells on his early cricket instruction, which took place in a stable and was conducted by Henry Plumb, the family chauffeur. Plumb was orthodox in his views on the ideal bowling action but dismissive of Raymond's Swiss governess and her interminable algebra lessons: 'It's all my eye and Fanny Adams, and where is the sense in mucking about the alphabet without coming to any words at all?'

In 1908 Raymond was sent to St Edmund's, a prep school in Hindhead, Surrey, where he proved confident, gregarious and popular. At the time he was devouring the Sherlock Holmes stories. He was intrigued to discover that Conan Doyle was living half a mile away and spent many hours lurking in the author's garden. His childhood holidays were nomadic jaunts along the south coast and he stayed in a succession of boarding houses, with Brighton as the focal point.

Headquarters were Miss Hemmings's establishment in Preston Street, where fellow guest Mr Roberts 'spent much time and energy in suppressing what might have been the belches of the century'. Raymond's landladies are larger than life and one of the many merits of his autobiography is a Betjemanic ability to capture the idiom of a variety of social classes. Raymond spent much time on the Palace Pier, where he excelled at automatic single-wicket cricket, and he began a lifetime's addiction to nicotine on his frequent walks to Peacehaven. By this time his literary enthusiasms were wide ranging and he hung around The Elms at Rottingdean in the hope of obtaining Rudyard Kipling's autograph.

In September 1914 Raymond went to Charterhouse with an open scholarship. He describes himself as 'old enough to feel the war but too young to take part in it'. There are sections of his memoirs that could be lifted straight out of *Goodbye Mr Chips*: 'A genial lad was William Bunnett. At sixteen he enlisted in Canada and was killed in Flanders before his seventeenth birthday.' During the next five years Raymond idolised many of his tutors, notably the brilliant classicist and athlete Frank Dames-Longworth: 'Once when a young and timid scholar, seeking to render from Greek the lamentations of Medea, said: "Woe is me for the children I begat!" Dames-Longworth shouted: "Sit down, boy, for Heaven's sake, till you can get your sexes right. Women don't beget; they bear; a fact of which you may one day become cognisant to your cost."' Raymond's closest friend at Charterhouse and for the rest of his life was Edward Holroyd Pearce, the future Lord Pearce. In their third year, the pair were occasionally invited to supper and informal Schubert recitals given by a 28-year-old English teacher in the middle school. Ten years later the master would die on or near the summit of Everest. His name was George Mallory.

By 1918 Raymond was a mainstay of the Charterhouse cricket XI and he opened both batting and bowling against Winchester, making 23 and dismissing Douglas Jardine. In 1919 he again clean bowled Jardine while taking 6 for 90. It was also a successful season with the bat and he made 537 runs at an average of 38. In August of that year Pelham Warner raised a strong team to play a combined Public Schools XI. Over two innings Raymond took 5 for 73, his victims including the former England opener Reggie Spooner and the South African wicketkeeper Percy Sherwell.

In the following month Raymond went up to Corpus Christi, Oxford, with an open scholarship to read Classical Moderations. His university contemporaries included Anthony Eden, T.E. Lawrence and Robert Graves. Raymond was immediately enchanted by the university and always saw it in aquatints: 'To me Oxford is the Walled City, with a door of which in fancy I alone have the secret and the key, and I can go there when I want to touch the hem of eternity.' He contributed to many aspects of college life and at football he proved a competent goalkeeper. Raymond also represented the college at hockey, rugby and tennis. He socialised widely but was almost inseparable from Edward Holroyd Pearce, who had also gone to Corpus from Charterhouse with a scholarship.

> Nature endowed Raymond with a good mind, a deep sense of beauty, a gargantuan appetite for the ridiculous and a vast, wide ranging, affectionate interest in his fellow-men. He detested coldness, cynicism, or pretentiousness. Generally he managed to melt it, like a blowlamp, by his own warmth.
>
> Lord Pearce, *The Pelican Record*, June 1965

Raymond won cricket blues in all four years but his bowling performances were disappointing. He sent down a total of 90 overs in the Varsity games but took only two wickets. A highlight came in the 1923 fixture when he scored a spirited if agricultural 53 as part of Oxford's total of 422. As a freshman Raymond played against Somerset at the Parks. The visiting captain, John Daniell, was impressed with his cricket and general vitality. Having been brought up in Scotland, Raymond had no residential ties with a first-class county. The wily Daniell discovered that Charlie Foxcroft, the Bath MP, and Prebendary Archdale Palmer Wickham, an eccentric Somerset wicketkeeper at the turn of the century, were both distant cousins. The result was that he was invited to play for the county in his vacations. (John Arlott quipped that Raymond's only residential qualification for Somerset was that he had once changed trains at Yeovil Junction.)

In his first season of county cricket Raymond took 5 for 33 from 10 overs against Leicestershire at Weston-super-Mare, where he would occasionally amuse the crowd by disappearing into the beer tent after the fall of a wicket. He was popular at Taunton and socialised with Sammy Woods, who partnered him at whist and skittles. The pair would also murder Woods's favourite Gus Ellen music-hall numbers, during which Raymond would drown Sammy with his strangulated tenor. During the match against Essex, Raymond clean bowled Charlie McGahey with a full toss. McGahey stormed off muttering 'I've just been bowled by a chap called Robinson Crusoe.' In cricket circles Raymond was known as 'Crusoe' for the rest of his life.

The match against Essex also marked the start of a friendship with the England captain, Johnny Douglas, who invited him to stay at his Hampstead flat. Raymond could be absent-minded and on the first night he left a bathroom tap running. An ex-Olympic boxer, Douglas was hard pushed to fight off a battered dowager from the ground floor who rushed in to complain that the flood had caused her lounge ceiling to disintegrate. It was a successful if short cricket season during which Raymond took 55 wickets for Somerset at 20.9. John Daniell was pleased with his choice and invited the youngster to return in the summer of 1921, though with the caveat: 'For heaven's sake, don't bring that bloody straw hat.'

Raymond (and the hat) returned in the following season but his haul of 16 wickets from 150 overs was unimpressive. During the Christmas term of 1921 he began suffering from the depression that would impose enormous restraints on the rest of his life. He suffered a severe breakdown at Easter and began to indulge in what he highlights as 'that most abject and clinging of drugs, self-pity'. His GP advised him to convalesce in Jersey: 'Here I met a man with the only perfectly purple nose I have ever seen. Perhaps he had taken Beachcomber's advice: "How to cure a red nose – carry on drinking till it's purple."' Raymond recovered well and played badminton at the Jersey Racquets Club, where he fancied himself in love with his mixed doubles partner.

He spent the summer of 1922 with his books and played only one match for Somerset. Raymond gained a first in the classical part of his tripos, but a further mental breakdown in the run-up to finals meant that he left Oxford with second-class honours. His cricket blossomed in 1923 and a haul of 58 wickets at 17.11 apiece put him second in the Somerset bowling averages behind Jack 'Farmer' White. One of his finest performances came in June 1924 when he took 9 for 38 against Middlesex at Lord's. Raymond was chosen for Gentlemen vs Players a few weeks later. On a lively wicket he produced fearsome lift, dismissing Herbert Sutcliffe and Jack Hearne. A few berths were still available on Arthur Gilligan's Ashes tour to Australia and he nursed hopes of being selected.

The invitation was not forthcoming. Raymond returned to his old prep school as an assistant master, teaching English literature and classics alongside his elder brother Bobs. Sadly his fits of depression meant that he was often absent. Many of his pupils from St Edmund's are alive. I have corresponded with or met several dozen of them and to a man they remember Raymond with gratitude and proud delight. John Willett's summation is: 'He was intelligent, witty, and accessible to all ... one of the most blithe and delightful human beings I have met.' At this stage in his memoirs, Raymond notes: 'I was still aware that something was far wrong in my health.' In the winter of 1931–32, he made a suicide attempt. His sense of humour remained a lifeline to sanity, but he was occasionally obliged to attend a residential clinic at St Andrew's Hospital in Northampton and these absences puzzled the many pupils who doted on him.

Raymond's best cricket was now behind him. However, he co-founded the Arabs with Jim Swanton and occasionally played for the team. He also turned out for Grayshott CC at Hindhead; crowds of boys would follow him as he chugged to the ground on his motorbike before opening the bowling in tandem with a Mr Messenger. Raymond recalls his partner's reaction after unsuccessful lbw appeals: 'When the umpire failed to accept the bait, Mr Messenger would shake his head sadly, as a sick child refusing a cream bun.' His experience of village cricket prompted him to make some inspired though tongue-in-cheek generalisations. He was dogmatic in his assertions that professional gardeners make the best medium-pace bowlers and house painters the most reliable long-stops.

Raymond's stock delivery was an inswinger produced from a high but chest-on action. In his prime he could make the ball straighten off the pitch and combined with the in-swing, this often proved a match for the best batsmen in the country. Like Maurice Tate, he insisted that his wicketkeeper should stand up. Ronald Hope-Jones recalls his bowling as being 'beautifully fluent, easy and controlled'. Raymond once described himself as 'good enough to have played for England without being laughed at'. He used to have a recurrent dream in which he was picked for his country and came in with a few runs needed for victory. In the dream he would play a drive through the covers and set off for a single, but find himself running in a bog, making no progress despite encouragement from the square leg umpire, who turned out to be the Emperor of Abyssinia. Raymond could extract life from any wicket in the country though after a pasting from Jack Hobbs and Andy Sandham at The Oval he once clambered up the pavilion steps and confided to Ben Travers: 'It's like trying to bowl to God on concrete.'

As a batsman he had an excellent eye but a primitive technique. At Charterhouse he often opened the innings. However, in first-class cricket his batting was negligible and he would toss a coin with Jim Bridges for the right to go in last, occasionally emerging from behind a sightscreen with his bat and an ice cream. Raymond wrote fluently about golf but his own technique was crude. As Henry Longhurst once said of Bobby Jones, he was 'an uncomplicated man who simply stood up and gave it one'. He played much golf while at St Edmund's, but his massive drives and errant short game were unsuited to the tight fairways and alpine contours of the course at Hindhead.

> I remember, many years ago, before I had mastered the short approach, I played a chip-shot that caused the ball to alight on the head of a Lanarkshire sheep. In the afternoon, at the same hole the same sheep was there. It ambled up to me, as if to resume what it meant to show me was an undisturbed acquaintance. Men have turned vegetarian on less provocation.
>
> > R.C. Robertson-Glasgow, *All In the Game*, 1952

Raymond had an uncomplicated relationship with his pupils, who respected him not only for his sporting abilities but his charisma, his social skills and a remarkable ability to generate enthusiasm for English literature. Major Michael Edwards remembers that while Raymond's charges never dreamt of misbehaving in class, they were comfortable with him at all times. Raymond was careful not to have any obvious favourites but would discreetly present books to his more gifted pupils.

At no time was he concerned with merely imparting information; his abiding concern was to stimulate enthusiasm for English literature. He would write out extracts from Victorian novels and discuss them in class. Favourite pieces included the drowning of Steerforth in *David Copperfield* and the decline of Captain Newcome in Thackeray's *The Newcomes*. Raymond's spontaneous, free and witty translations of classical texts are still remembered by many. He was omnipresent during games sessions; in addition to coaching cricket he would play scrum-half during rugby practice, coach older boys on the school's nine-hole golf course and organise billiards competitions. His voice had mellowed since Oxford and he was a mainstay of the Christmas pantomimes.

By the early 1930s Raymond was honing his prose style by contributing occasional sports pieces to the *News Chronicle*. In March 1933 he was asked to cover the Varsity golf match as a last-minute replacement for the *Morning Post*'s regular correspondent. His sub-editors were impressed and in the following month he succeeded Pelham Warner as cricket writer. He immediately moved to London. Raymond's vitality burst upon contemporary cricket writing like a clap of thunder on a placid summer's day. He himself noted: 'Cricket reporting used to be a solemn affair, and the press-box at Lord's recalled the Silence Room of a Carnegie Library in Scotland.' When not at cricket grounds, Raymond spent much time with Winnie Morgan-Brown, the eldest daughter of Cyril Morgan-Brown, who had founded St Edmund's. Having missed his last tube Raymond would often stay with Winnie at her flat in Regent's Park Terrace. Occasionally he would return from an alumni dinner a little the worse for wear and she would make a good fist of writing his column for the *Morning Post*.

Crusoe remained with the *Morning Post* until 1937 when it was acquired by the *Daily Telegraph*. Even amid the grind of the county circuit, his prose remained supple and clear. He had an instinct for detail that can still emit pulsations in the reader's memory, and a style that is spare, exact and subtly musical in its phrasing. Shamefully, his work from this period has never been properly collected and republished, though his monographs have been carefully edited by Alan Ross. His writing is always subtle and urbane and has abundant reserves of grace, but it remains accessible. He expressed himself with a rippling elegance and wit which none of his would-be imitators has captured. His own literary enthusiasms included Charles Lamb, to whom his prose style owes much. Raymond brought a bracingly airy and lyrical playfulness to sports journalism. We are all in his debt.

Relief from county cricket came in the form of visits to Oxford for net sessions where he was greeted as a sainted guru by undergraduates whom he would regale with his (often obscene) nonsense verse. Raymond moved to the *Observer* in 1938 but suffered a further mental breakdown in the spring. When his condition became severe he returned to the St Andrew's Hospital in Northampton. Here he met and fell in love with one of the nursing staff, Elizabeth Hutton, née Powrie, the widow of Peter Hutton. Elizabeth was 40 years old and had also been brought up in Scotland. She had trained at the Victoria Infirmary in Glasgow and her first husband had played cricket and hockey for Stirlingshire.

By now Raymond's brother Bobs had broken away from St Edmund's. In partnership with Ivor Sant and Bill Ward-Clarke of St Edmund's, he had founded another prep school, St Andrew's, at Pangbourne. Raymond lodged at St Andrew's and made a good recovery. In August he travelled to The Oval for the fifth Test against Bradman's tourists and saw Len Hutton make his record-breaking 364: 'There I sit while Hutton produces strokes fit to make a cat leave its fish.'

Raymond continued to cover cricket for the *Observer* in 1939 and in the winter he reported on rugby. He had now entered a phase of almost complete remission from his depression that would last for 15 years. However, at 38 and with a long history of mental ill-health, he was hardly likely to be called up. He contented himself by serving with the Home Guard at Pangbourne, where he performed night patrols with a bellicose 70-year-old gamekeeper: '"Shoot 'em," he said, "whether they put their hands up or not. Someone else can do the talking afterwards."' In the spring of 1943 Raymond attacked 'shamateurism' in *Wisden*, advocating the abolition of the amateur and professional distinction. In the following August he married Elizabeth Hutton and the couple set up home at a cottage within the grounds of St Andrew's.

Having recovered nearly all of his old vitality, Raymond worked more or less continuously for the *Observer* from 1946 to 1953. His activity widened and he contributed to *Tatler*, *Golf Monthly* and *Men Only*. In the winter of 1950–51 Raymond and Elizabeth followed England's Ashes tour of Australia under the captaincy of Freddie Brown. It was a busy time; Beau Vincent drank himself into a stupor on the voyage out and Raymond began filing copy for *The Times*. Initially he was shocked by the raucous behaviour of Australian crowds, but he was welcomed everywhere and soon warmed to his hosts. He travelled everywhere with John Woodcock, who recalls: 'Raymond had the background of a classical scholar, combined with a riotous imagination and a sense of humour which lit bonfires of goodwill.' He was certainly the busiest member of the press corps and the need to bring a different perspective to the play for both his readerships was a challenge.

He remained active in the early 1950s and would turn out for Authors vs Publishers at Westminster School, where he could still make the ball kick from a good length. He had brief stints at both radio and television commentary but was not suited to either. However, during the visit of the Australians to England in 1948 he had given five-minute broadcasts after the BBC nine o'clock news in which he summarised the day's play during the Test series. These talks were witty, apposite and much acclaimed. In August 1953 he tired of cricket reporting. Alan Ross recalled: 'He simply got up in the press-box one afternoon, put on his old battered trilby and raincoat, and announced he was calling it a day. He went back to his home in Berkshire and never reported on a first-class cricket match again.' Raymond took on a column in the *Sunday Times* entitled 'Country Talk' in which he discussed aspects of country life and its characters. He was an avid letter-writer and began corresponding with the many readers from all walks of life who contacted him.

The abiding impressions of Raymond are of extraordinary high spirits masking mental fragility, an incredible intellect and a steady contempt for ostentation. For Cardus he was 'tall and handsome and agile, domed of forehead and as charged with brain and wit as anybody'. If Raymond had a kindred spirit among his press colleagues it was fellow poet Alan Ross. Here is Ross again: 'Crusoe was as difficult to stop in full flow as either Cardus or Fry, and he was noisier than either. Underneath the raconteur and joker there was, nevertheless, a man of consideration and charm, also of a gravity that seldom got into his writing.'

He had little business acumen and was generally disorganised, though he had an excellent memory for birthdays and anniversaries and would regularly send telegrams to his friends and associates. His electric wit was only disrupted by compulsive giggling. He rarely stopped talking, and looking back on his time at Charterhouse he reflected: 'I was underweight on tact; over-fond of society, yet a slave to monologue; convinced that if silence was golden, it was a bare nine-carat.'

Raymond was 6 ft 2 in tall with piercing blue eyes. His body was angular and he was staccato in his movements. He also had a disconcerting habit of shoving his face very close to his companion before weaving away. He dressed appallingly, his standard garb being a shabby sports jacket and ill-fitting grey flannel trousers. Sandy Singleton, an Oxford contemporary, recalled: 'I cannot remember seeing him really well dressed, even in formal evening attire; somehow he always looked as if he had just arrived from a previous party, and a pretty rough one at that.'

Countless occasional essayists quote from *Cricket Prints*, recognising Raymond as a reliable barometer of the era. In 1995, over 30 years after Raymond's death, the eulogies at Harold Larwood's funeral included extracts from his pen portrait. Compared with his essays and journalism, Raymond's poetry is disappointing though his occasional nonsense verse rivals that of Edward Lear and Lewis Carroll. The cricket poems are freely available in many anthologies. The strongest is 'First Slip', in which Raymond berates a fielder who has spilled a chance from his bowling: 'As if it wasn't just the sort of catch/A child would hold, at midnight, with no moon.' Sadly many of the poems are mannered: they are saturated by routine alliteration, though an occasionally innovative use of metre (often showing the influence of Siegfried Sassoon) saves them from being mediocre.

Raymond was a popular figure at St Andrew's from 1939 until his death. He never performed any kind of regular teaching role but would host literary evenings for senior boys, during which he would read extracts from P.G. Wodehouse and A.P. Herbert. He was of course a regular visitor to the cricket nets and was supportive of the school chapel. By now he was widely respected as a journalist, but he showed no interest in anything other than writing and refused to sit on editorial boards.

In the mid 1950s Raymond again began suffering from bouts of depression that became increasingly regular. E.W. Swanton noted the wild swings in mood: 'The tragic key to Crusoe's life was the acute mental depression that plagued him in black, inevitable cycles, alternating with the exultation and mental brilliance when all his best work was done and he was the most scintillating company in the world.' Raymond is an outstanding example of what Alistair Cooke has described as 'the pedestrian old-school virtues; loyalty to friends, respect for the old, a distaste for conspicuous wealth, for gossip and for boasting'. In his final years he was disturbed by what he saw as a decline in the values on which he had been reared and he became polemically anti-modernist: 'Tradition knows how to die bravely. Theories will not fill the empty chair.' He is occasionally remembered now for a pure, running wit, a striking resemblance to Alastair Sim and a prose style which can make Arlott and Cardus seem like tired agency hacks. His throne is empty.

17

Rockley Wilson

b: 25.3.1879, Bolsterstone, Yorkshire.
d: 21.7.1957, Winchester, Hampshire.

Echo on echo, pupils make a world
which is their bronze and yours, and they will join
link on bright link to make the legions shine
with ethics and with elegance. The absurd
becomes a simple weather, clear and fine.

Iain Crichton Smith, 'Hamlet In Autumn', 1972

The subject is a polymath of high intelligence and devastating wit. He saw himself as a Renaissance Man and came close to being one. Electric repartee and perfect aplomb make for a heady compound; at the top of his bent Rockley Wilson could make everybody else in the room sound retarded.

His parents were Canon William Wilson and Martha, née Thorp. Rockley began playing cricket on the vicarage lawn at Bolsterstone with his brother, Clement, who would also become a Test cricketer. After attending the prep school Bilton Grange at Dunchurch he went to Rugby in 1892 with a scholarship. His cricket coaches there included players of the calibre of Tom Emmett and Alex Watson. In 1897 Rockley captained the Rugby cricket team and topped both the batting and bowling averages. He made 460 runs at an average of 51.11 and took 31 wickets at 14.93.

A highlight with the bat was an innings of 206 not out against New

College, Oxford, which the college magazine described thus: 'Innumerable changes were made to the bowling but none had the slightest effect... Wilson scored at a great pace off all the bowlers, his cutting, leg-hitting and driving being all equally good.' In its end-of-year review the magazine summarised Rockley thus: 'A thoroughly keen and good captain, under whom a modest team developed into a good one... Slow right-hand bowler, with considerable command of the ball and knowledge of the game.'

Cricket seems to have got in the way of other activities and one of his school reports reads: 'Has two thoughts for cricket to every one for his work. Chapel attendance very irregular.' Rockley was also the best long-distance runner at Rugby and won the mile competition three years running, his best time being 4 minutes 26 seconds. He was regarded as a certainty for a blue at Cambridge but injury put an end to his career as an athlete. Rockley was active in the school debating society and took several agreeably progressive positions. He once proposed: 'It is right and reasonable that women should be able to vote in Parliamentary elections.' He observed that it was indefensible that women should be prevented from voting in the same way as lunatics, and that there was no evidence to suppose that they were intellectually inferior to men. His motion was defeated by 36 votes to 12.

Rockley was competent at rackets and fives. As a rugby player he hovered on the fringe of the school XV, being a competent place-kicker. At a concert in 1896 he sang a solo from Charles Villiers Stanford's *Songs of the Fleet*. His athletic and academic prowess led to his being made head of school. In his final year at Rugby, Rockley was entered for a Latin competition without his knowledge. In a fit of panic he obtained a copy of a previous entry and submitted it. He was astounded when he was awarded the prize and immediately confessed everything. Many of the masters respected his honesty after the initial lack of judgement but Frank Fletcher, a future headmaster of Charterhouse, pursued the matter. Rockley was asked to leave in the summer of 1898 and spent a term lodging with his brother Clement at Cambridge.

Rockley went up to Trinity, Cambridge, in September 1898 to study classics. In the following spring he scored 60 and 9 not out as well as taking eight wickets in the freshmen's match but this did not tempt the

Cambridge captain, Gilbert Jessop, to select him for the opening first-class fixture against A.J. Webbe's XI. To his surprise he still took part in the game. As a last-minute replacement for the visitors Rockley made 117 not out and 70 against his university, the second score coming on a badly worn wicket. A century on a first-class debut is a rarity, and the first innings was all the more remarkable because he had been up till five in the morning playing poker on the eve of the game. These performances secured him a regular place in the Cambridge side but he had an abysmal season. He did however manage to make 39 in the second innings of the Varsity match.

By now he was showing a resolute defence when the odds were against him. Against Surrey on a damp Oval wicket he spent 45 minutes at the crease without making a run. His county debut for Yorkshire came in June against Somerset at Hull. *The Times* reported: 'Mr. Wilson showed most skilful cricket for his 55, in getting which he did not make a mistake.'

In his second game against Warwickshire at Edgbaston he made 79 and the *Morning Post* described how he 'showed patient defence combined with stylish and correct hitting'. At the time, Yorkshire were putting out one of the strongest sides ever fielded by a county in the history of the game. Later in life Rockley took pride in having played for the club in its heyday and he once remarked: 'One doesn't neces-sarily know cricket just because one has played for Leicestershire.'

In 1900 Rockley performed well for Cambridge against Oxford, scor-ing 45 and 23 not out. His finest hour as a university cricketer came in the Varsity match of the following year when he made 118 and took 5 for 71 in Oxford's first innings. His batting was dogged rather than dramatic but *Wisden* noted: 'Wilson was quite the hero of the match, playing an admirable innings . . . and bowling with rare steadiness.' As Cambridge captain in 1902 he would have loved to lead from the front but he was dismissed for 13 and 26. However, he bowled well and over two innings he took 8 for 119, his accuracy keeping a fine Oxford batting side under restraint. In his one match for Yorkshire in this season, Rockley made a cultured 63 against Worcestershire at New Road.

Lord Hawke was fond of Rockley and had a high opinion of his bowling. In 1903 Hawke invited him to play a full season of county cricket prior to his taking a teaching position at Winchester College. In the spring, Teddy Buckland, the cricket master at Winchester, fell ill and Rockley was asked to start immediately. He threw himself into his duties, which were to teach cricket and French. (Hubert Doggart once told me that even in the classroom his lessons were 30 per cent French and 70 per cent cricket.)

Hawke still expected much from Rockley and early in 1912 he persuaded him to tour Argentina with MCC. Most of the games were played in Buenos Aires. Against South Argentina Rockley made 105 runs and took 5 for 45. At Palermo he bowled superbly to take 6 for 36 against the Argentine Republic. Rockley played intermittently for Yorkshire in 1913, making 104 not out in 110 minutes against Essex at Bradford. He hit two sixes, a five and 13 fours and *Wisden* commented: 'He was a little uncertain with some of his strokes, but drove in great form.'

Soon after the Great War broke out Rockley was commissioned into the Rifle Brigade. He upset military decorum by calling his subordinates 'sir', and his commander once told him: 'Rockley, you might be the best slow bowler in England but you're the worst bloody subaltern I've ever had in my battalion.' It was a trying time but he maintained his sense of humour and in a letter to his brother Clement he noted: 'Man tried to cut his throat this morning. Doctor gave him "Medicine and duty".' Man's comment, "Them army razors."'

Rockley spent a few months in France before being transferred to a Cyclists' Battalion on the Isle of Sheppey. A significant problem arose; he was unable and unwilling to ride a bike. As hostilities continued Rockley realised that there was an equally important theatre of war in the Middle East. After a good deal of study he became proficient in Turkish and he was sent to Palestine in 1918.

The war brought out some of his best witticisms. Rockley found himself crossing the Lake of Galilee with a party of high-ranking officers and he was left by General Allenby to pay the boatman, who made impossible demands. The pair haggled for 10 minutes. Rockley then scuttled back to his party, mopped his brow and confided to Allenby: 'No wonder Jesus walked!' Later he was lucky to survive when an incompetent doctor gave him a massive overdose of calomel. He spent most of 1918 at Army HQ outside Jerusalem, analysing captured enemy material. Rockley took every opportunity to visit biblical sites, enjoying trips to the Garden of Gethsemane and the Mount of Olives.

He was able to play a little coarse cricket near Jerusalem and described these matches in letters to his brother. The correspondence has an elegiac quality. Talking about the former Surrey captain Lord Dalmeny, Rockley concluded: 'Fat and clumsy now alas – he was such a beautiful field 1904–6.' Rockley was distressed at being separated from his set of *Wisden* and the letters include requests for recondite cricket statistics: 'How many overs did James Horlick bowl for Eton against Harrow in 1904?'

The cricket games remained a lifeline to sanity for many, and Rockley was incensed when Bedouins stole a matting cricket pitch. He consoled himself by adding to his stamp collection but felt aggrieved when he realised that both his clerks had better collections than he did. Rockley threw himself into his duties but had no military ambitions: 'I'm not a captain yet but they've promised to make me one. I don't care a blow. What I should like is the end of the war.' Rockley remained in the Middle East well after the Armistice and spent the early months of 1919 acting as an intelligence officer at Aleppo. He was impressed by the town's citadel, which he describes as 'a sort of glorified Scarborough Castle', but did not take kindly to primitive latrines: 'There is a distinct opportunity here for Mr Doulton.'

Rockley returned to Winchester in the summer of 1919. Douglas Jardine, a future England captain, was waiting for him as a pupil. In the classroom Rockley penetrated Jardine's harsh exterior and Jardine later paid many extravagant tributes to him. However, on the field Rockley found him extremely headstrong. Thirteen years later, on being told that his former pupil had been chosen as captain for what would prove to be the Bodyline tour, Rockley made one of his best-known quips: 'We shall win the Ashes – but we may lose a Dominion.'

Soon after his return to Winchester it became known that Rockley had bought some Arabic clothes in the Middle East. He was putty in the hands of the older boys, who asked him to bring them into class. Persuading him to put the clothes on was easy and he was challenged to impersonate a Muslim praying. Rockley was soon on all fours and intoning to Mecca when his colleague the Rev. A.T. Williams stepped into the room. Williams simply retired in astonishment.

Rockley was always somewhat delicate and had not enjoyed the rigours of army service, but he soon recovered his vitality and began bowling well. A highlight in 1919 was a hat-trick for Gentlemen vs Players at Scarborough, where his victims were George Hirst, Alec Kennedy and Arthur Dolphin. Rockley ended the season with 36 wickets at an average of 16.58. For Raymond Robertson-Glasgow he had 'shown an ignorant and negligent age the meaning of length'. In the following season he was again inspired, taking 6 for 29 for Yorkshire against MCC and 5 for 20 against Hampshire. He finished fourth in the national averages with 64 wickets at an average of 13.84. Rockley simply tugged at his necktie and observed that he was 'the discovery of the season'.

Towards the end of the summer Reggie Spooner decided that he was not fit enough to captain the England touring party to Australia. The selectors nominated Johnny Douglas, but realised that they would need another amateur with good social skills if Douglas's brusque mannerisms were not to upset the Australians. They settled on Rockley, who accepted immediately. He soon found himself racing through the Bay of Biscay on the SS *Osterley*. Rockley could not have been more surprised had Aladdin turned up with his lamp and put him on a magic carpet to Baghdad. It appears that the headmaster of Winchester at the time, Dr Montague Rendall, was not a cricket fan. When Rockley put in a written request for leave, the response was: 'Who are the MCC and what are they doing in Australia?'

At 42 years of age Rockley was an oddity as a debutant Ashes tourist. He had to put up with much joshing from the professionals, all of whom adored him. On the voyage out a passenger died of typhus at Colombo. When the cricketers arrived at Fremantle they were obliged to stay on board for several days before being moved to a quarantine camp at Woodman's Point. Their mood was not improved by the antics of Ernie Jones, the ex-Australian pace bowler. Jones had been harbourmaster at Fremantle for many years, and would row out to the quarantine area each morning in a dinghy and scream abuse at Douglas and his team. The tourists amused themselves with fishing, football and bridge, even managing to organise a dance when they borrowed a gramophone player from the ship.

They were pitted against one of the strongest cricket teams of all time, a remorselessly competitive unit under the leadership of Warwick Armstrong. At Sydney in the first Test, Armstrong and Herbie Collins were particularly belligerent in taking the home side to victory by 377 runs. The series curled up its toes there and then. Armstrong was soon shooting fish in a barrel and there were four more heavy defeats. It was never envisaged that Rockley would feature prominently in the arduous Test matches. He did not play until the final game at Sydney, where he bowled brilliantly when taking 3 for 36 from 22.3 economical overs. Most importantly, he managed to put a break on Charlie Macartney and Jack Gregory, both of whom were in full cry. In his tour diary Percy Fender noted: 'Wilson had so few chances that one can hardly gauge anything from what he did do. He finished with a superb performance at Sydney, and many people wondered why he had not played more.' In all matches on the tour he took 30 wickets at an average of 14.5.

Rockley was unimpressed with the captaincy of Johnny Douglas. During one of the early games he wrote to his sister, Phyllis: 'God help England if Douglas is captain throughout.' Douglas had caused much bad feeling by electing to bring his wife and mother-in-law to Australia, and Rockley continued: 'Douglas's womenfolk disgrace us everywhere ... we have been a failure socially.'

The team managers were Frederick Toone and Pelham Warner, and at dinners Rockley was often invited to get on his feet and leaven the unflagging mediocrity of Warner's Empire-binding speeches. Rockley undoubtedly had the common touch, and even when his abstruse classical and biblical references went over the heads of his audience, he always held their attention and made a good impression. Deep in the goldfield territory, the tourists were entertained at a ball by the combined townships of Kalgoorlie and Boulder. Rockley likened the two mayors to the kings of Judah and Israel, Jehoshaphat and Ahab. He was making obscure allusions to drought and an uneasy but profitable relationship between neighbouring rulers. One wonders how many of his audience appreciated the references.

While sailing to Australia Rockley had written a consummately witty and urbane article for *The Times* describing life on board ship. This was well received and, perhaps unwisely, he agreed to write a regular column for the *Daily Express*. He was unable to make the transition to popular reporting and received a brusque telegram from his editor: 'Reuters record play adequately, we want *comment*.' Attempting to enliven his copy, he criticised a run-out decision given against his team-mate Abe Waddington during the first Test at Sydney. In a match against New South Wales, Jack Hobbs was obliged to field while in intense pain from a hamstring injury. He could hardly move and was jeered repeatedly by spectators. Both Rockley and Percy Fender were understandably incensed by this behaviour and roundly condemned it in their newspaper columns. They should have realised that the reports would be cabled back to Australia within a few hours. Rockley and Percy Fender soon found themselves about as popular as lepers.

Later in the match Rockley batted competently while making 30 in extreme heat. As he returned to the pavilion he was greeted with a torrent of jeering and shouts of 'Get home, you squeaker!' The barracking distressed him immensely. He stopped at the boundary and began remonstrating with the mob, until the former Australian all-rounder Monty Noble took one of his arms and shepherded him away to the dressing room. Jack Hobbs recalled in his autobiography: 'Even members in the pavilion – usually calm, reserved critics of the game – rose and hooted Mr Wilson, a truly astonishing display.' Tension reached another high point during the match against Victoria at Melbourne and Johnny Douglas had to ask for policemen to be stationed around the boundary. Cecil Parkin once recalled: 'The crowd rose against Mr Wilson like animals.' Parkin was devoted to Rockley and stood between him and a mob of howling spectators.

Of course, Rockley's hosts on the social circuit recognised him as gallant, modest and full of an indulgent and rueful humour. Sadly, the trouble at matches continued and he was made to feel older than Noah. He was hardly electric over the ground and was often advised to 'take a cab for it'. Rockley had a safe pair of hands together with good anticipation and even in his forty-second year he was by no means a liability in the field. However, a long-standing shoulder injury meant that he had to flick the ball in underarm. The spectators attacked this weakness and screamed: 'Shall we throw it up for you, Miss Wilson?'

Rockley even offended Johnny Douglas's martinet values by his friendship with the Warwickshire professional Harry Howell. As self-elected postmaster, Howell would greet Rockley in a familiar manner when distributing letters. This infuriated Douglas, and Howell was given a formal caution. Rockley had been a keen card player since his days at Trinity and liked nothing better than a game of draw poker with Cecil Parkin, Jack Hobbs and Howell. Whatever the weather, he always travelled with a large overcoat. When he was playing cards on a train he would spread this over his knees as a makeshift table. While the team was travelling from Melbourne to Bendigo, a carriage door accidentally opened and Rockley's coat flew out into the night. Somebody foolishly pulled the communication cord and the train came to a halt. Rockley regarded this as irresponsible but had no hesitation in strolling down the track to retrieve his coat. Of course a journalist observed the incident and there were newspaper stories under the heading: 'The Man Who Stopped Our Train.' The incident gave rise to more bad feeling but Rockley was amused when he received a parcel containing a length of lavatory chain.

With Douglas busy showing his wife and mother-in-law the sights, Rockley often acted as captain during up-country games. Here he proved successful as a tactician and motivator. While he would allow plenty of levity from the professionals off the field, he had no time for practical jokes on it. When Patsy Hendren performed his familiar trick of throwing in an apple rather than the ball, he received a scalding rebuke. At the same time, Rockley was a fan of Hendren's mock-drunk act and often invited him to perform it at dinner parties.

In the following summer he topped the English first-class bowling averages. His 51 wickets from 370 overs at 11.19 put him ahead of Wilfred Rhodes and Frank Woolley. In 1922 the Yorkshire captain, Geoffrey Wilson (no relation), fell ill towards the end of the season and Rockley took pride in leading the side to victory in the county championship. He regarded this return to form as an unexpected bonus and retired from county cricket in 1923 after playing a few matches in August.

The little that Rockley wrote is incisive, urbane but never precious. His style has a jaunty assurance but is devoid of eccentricity or jargon, and he could be quietly dogmatic about subjects ranging from the lbw law to the demise of underarm bowling. One of the finest pieces is an article in the *Cricketer* for 1943 entitled 'Frederick Lillywhite and His

Guides'. Rockley had great fondness for Lillywhite and recognised the importance of his contribution to cricket literature. Rockley's work on Lillywhite's almanacks has since been extended by David Smith.

Rockley's prose has a Johnsonian conciseness and resonance. He once wrote to *The Times* complaining that appropriate caps were not being worn in the Varsity match, and closed the letter with: 'It is no time for motley.' He was a world expert on early cricket prints and in 1940 he organised an exhibition of Francis Hayman's work at Burlington House as part of a British Empire Exhibition. Hayman (1708–76) was a significant influence on Gainsborough. He produced several cricket scenes but is best known for his engravings in *Tatler* and a depiction of the wrestling scene from *As You Like It*.

Rockley's bowling was on the slow side of medium and he concentrated on a rolled leg-break. He could also make the ball move the other way with little variation in his action. As a bowler he was not a genius, not an innovator and not a landmark talent. He was simply very competent. On the contemporary cricket stage his closest counterpart is Chris Harris of New Zealand. Rockley could often snaffle a wicket through sheer persistence on a good length. When trying to enliven the footwork of a young Winchester batsman, he once announced that he was going to hit him on the toe with the next delivery and did exactly that.

A.A. Thomson's summary was 'urbane, cultured, almost apologetic and, at the bowling crease, deceptive and deadly'. Rockley was often encouraged to experiment with his bowling and broaden his repertoire but he took the Jane Austen approach: 'Stick with what you know.' He had a low arm action and applied minimal spin to the ball. With his keen cricket intelligence he realised that a leg-break which turns a foot normally produces no more than appreciation from close fielders. A leg-break which turns two inches often takes the outside edge of the bat.

As a batting coach Rockley was a firm believer in getting behind the line of the ball, a principle which he drilled into his pupils: 'When I play back and miss the ball, I like to see it hit Wilson.' In his later years Rockley's batting became defensive but he was strong on the on side and his driving could be joyous. Rockley had a keen interest in soccer and a thorough understanding of the game, which allowed him to referee serious wartime matches in the Middle East. He was also fond of billiards and played the game to a good standard. Rockley's height was 5 ft 9 in and he weighed 11 stone in his prime. He gave the impression of being somewhat delicate; for Cardus he had 'a look of Aryan innocence'. Rockley was popular with boys and fellow masters at Winchester who appreciated his unaffected enthusiasm and modestly worn learning. He once sent shock-waves through the genteel quadrangles of the college when he invited a local working men's club to attend the debating society.

Rockley never married. As an undergraduate he was devastated when a girl he had been courting was killed in a railway accident. After returning to Winchester at the end of the Great War, he lived near the school in James's Lane with his sister Phyllis. She would not allow cricket prints in the drawing room and her brother was delighted when she made an exception for a particularly fine Henry Roberts engraving. The rest of the house was crammed with cricket lithographs, and a picture of Fuller Pilch at the wicket dominated the dining-room. After retiring as cricket coach at Eton, George Hirst used to make an annual visit to see the Winchester vs Eton match. Rockley was only too pleased to give his old county team-mate lunch. Old George inspected the picture of Pilch, who is depicted playing forward and leaving a slight gate between bat and pad. Hirst mused: 'Thi knows, ah think ah could have got wun through there.'

The emphasis of Rockley's cricket coaching was on encouragement, though he occasionally became frustrated with his less gifted charges. When asked to give extra tuition to a hopeless young batsman, he tossed up several overs of half-volleys, finally exclaiming: 'My dear boy, you must hit *one* in the middle of the bat before you meet your maker!' Similarly, Rockley once despaired of a young wicketkeeper and commented: 'Reminds me of the Ancient Mariner. Stoppeth one of three.' He had keenly felt views on 'shamateurism' and delighted in echoing the quip of a gateman at the Saffrons, Eastbourne: 'Ten ruddy schoolmasters and only one amateur.'

Cricket analogies permeated every aspect of Rockley's life. When hosting dinner parties he would make elaborate table plans and place his guests as though he were setting a field: 'Would you mind going to cover? I think we'll have you at square leg.' He would end by instructing his manservant to stand behind his chair: 'Raymond, I wonder if you could keep wicket?' Rockley's impromptu asides could be creasingly funny though many of the better ones relied on knowledge of Latin or Winchester traditions. In a game at Shrewsbury, Rockley was asked by an enthusiastic games master for an evaluation of the school's left-arm opening bowler, Bobby Armitstead: 'What do you think of Armitstead? Isn't he rather like Bill Voce?' Rockley muttered to his brother Clement: 'A little *sotto voce* I think.'

Unless he was riled, his humour was gentle and self-deprecating. He could occasionally be scalding but was aware of the no-man's-land between wit and lapses of taste. The abiding impression is one of sophistication but he could be surprisingly earthy. Rockley once described himself as 'not a fool, but no scholar'. He had a hesitant, insistently courteous manner of speech which made the epigrammatic flashes all the more startling. In conversation he would lean close to his companion, finger his necktie and repeat the punchline from his anecdotes. Rockley was open-minded, lucid and sweetly intelligent with the amused, slightly unworldly air of one of Trollope's clerics.

As a wit he had energy, verbal invention, natural timing and a fastidious ear. He constantly sought to uphold what he regarded as decent modes of behaviour. Rockley once opened a door for an American tourist at Harrod's. He received no acknowledgement and followed her around three floors, tugging at his collar and saying: 'Madam, it would have been an even greater pleasure had you said thank you.' Like many, he recognised Sir Home Gordon as a Philistine. Seated near him at a dinner during the Scarborough Festival, Rockley greeted him with: 'Very nice to see you, Sir Home. I saw your father's grave this morning.' After reading descriptions of the Rillington Place murders he quipped: 'They'll have to rename it Corpus Christie.'

In the mid-1950s Rockley began suffering from heart problems and stopped taking an active part in life at Winchester. One of his last outings was to Lord's in 1957 when he perched high in the pavilion and saw his old university win the Varsity match. He died of cardiac failure shortly afterwards. A *Times* tribute ended: 'Not only was he a superb exponent, coach and scholar of the game, but he also made it for his pupils a school of civilised values.'

We can send Rockley out with the mother of all anecdotes. There are many variants: I had this one, complete with mimicry, from Jim Swanton. We know that Rockley had a high-pitched voice with a whispering quality. He often repeated phrases that pleased him and fiddled with his clothes constantly. During a game at Lord's in 1921 Rockley was in the Long Room with some of his cronies. From his earliest days in major cricket Rockley had recognised Lord Harris as a bore. Rockley observed his Lordship beating a majestic path down the room and told his companions that he was confident he could make Harris shake hands. As Harris passed by, Rockley leapt out of his seat with 'Morning, my Lord,' and proffered his palm. Harris frowned and allowed Rockley to brush the very tips of his fingers. Obviously delighted, Rockley sat down, tugged at his tie and turned to his pals: 'Lucky to get a touch, really, lucky to get a touch!'